Pilgrimages/Peregrinajes

feminist
constructions

Series Editors: Hilde Lindemann Nelson
and Sara Ruddick

Feminist Constructions publishes accessible books that send feminist ethics in promising new directions. Feminist ethics has excelled at critique, identifying masculinist bias in social practice and in the moral theory that is used to justify that practice. The series continues the work of critique, but its emphasis falls on construction. Moving beyond critique, the series aims to build a positive body of theory that extends feminist moral understandings.

Feminists Doing Ethics
 edited by Peggy DesAutels and Joanne Waugh
Gender Struggles: Practical Approaches to Contemporary Feminism
 edited by Constance L. Mui and Julien S. Murphy
"Sympathy and Solidarity" and Other Essays
 by Sandra Lee Bartky
The Subject of Violence: Arendtean Exercises in Understanding
 by Bat-Ami Bar On
How Can I Be Trusted? A Virtue Theory of Trustworthiness
 by Nancy Nyquist Potter
Moral Contexts
 by Margaret Urban Walker
Recognition, Responsibility, and Rights: Feminist Ethics & Social Theory
 edited by Robin N. Fiore and Hilde Lindemann Nelson
The Philosopher Queen: Feminist Essays on War, Love, and Knowledge
 by Chris Cuomo
The Subject of Care: Feminist Perspectives on Dependency
 edited by Eva Feder Kittay and Ellen K. Feder
Pilgrimages/Peregrinajes: Theorizing Coalition against Multiple Oppressions
 by María Lugones
Why Privacy Isn't Everything: Feminist Reflections on Personal Accountability
 by Anita L. Allen

Forthcoming books in the series by

Amy R. Baehr; Joan Mason-Grant; Diana Tietjens Meyers; Robin Schott

Pilgrimages/Peregrinajes

Theorizing Coalition against Multiple Oppressions

María Lugones

ROWMAN & LITTLEFIELD PUBLISHERS, INC.
Lanham • Boulder • New York • Oxford

ROWMAN & LITTLEFIELD PUBLISHERS, INC.

Published in the United States of America
by Rowman & Littlefield Publishers, Inc.
A Member of the Rowman & Littlefield Publishing Group
4501 Forbes Boulevard, Suite 200, Lanham, Maryland 20706
www.rowmanlittlefield.com

P.O. Box 317, Oxford OX2 9RU, United Kingdom

British Library Cataloguing in Publication Information Available

Library of Congress Cataloging-in-Publication Data

Printed in the United States of America

♾ ™ The paper used in this publication meets the minimum requirements of
American National Standard for Information Sciences — Permanence of Paper for
Printed Library Materials, ANSI/NISO Z39.48-1992.

To the memory of Alejandro Lugones, *hermano, testigo fiel, corazón tierno, espíritu revolucionario.*

Recompongo lo poco que fue quedando y al fin, armando los pedazos del descarte, voy juntando, juntando, hasta que me queda un manojo bonito de piolines usados y sin embargo voy a tejer un abrigo nuevo que me cubra el corazón, y que no tenga ningún remiendo.

[Alejandro Lugones]

~

Contents

~

Preface

This book represents many years of theoretical reflection within grass-roots radical political work. It is my attempt to grasp a thematic for that work. The paths that I have taken in popular education, issue organizing, and movement politics have found roadblocks at the crucial moment of taking up oppressions as intermeshed. Practicing and theorizing resistance to oppressions as intermeshed became the focus of the work, what made it most radical, and what made it work on coalition in a deep sense of the term. So understood, this work requires a metamorphosis of self in relation as well as a metamorphosis of relations in defiance of both individualism and privacy as the domain of one's affective longings. It also requires a reconception of socialities that have stood in resistance to oppression in a univocal mode, a reimagining that understands that socialities are both more complex and more permeable. And it requires a humbling and honing of perception. That humbling and honing is sensorially rich, up close, in the midst of one's contemporaries, people who are historically interrelated. Coalition is always the horizon that rearranges both our possibilities and the conditions of those possibilities.

Because the work is theoretico-practical in every respect, the book asks for a theoretico-practical reading. It is neither a contemplative, nor a visionary, nor a programmatic work. It rather takes up, from within, a feel for collectivity without presupposing its ways and constitution. It "takes up" in the sense that it responds with an appetite for moving against entrapment, being cornered, trapped, reduced, conceptually and sensually invaded. The reader can access the resistant writing from within or from outside the trap, the reduction of oppression. But the "outside" does not point to positioning oneself as an observer. It rather marks a dominant position in the relations of power constitutive of oppression. This book is addressed most pointedly to those of us living the entrapments of oppressions from within. The framework I am offering is meant to help us rethink the task of political philosophy.

The central movement in every chapter is resistance to intermeshed oppressions as an ongoing activity from which to understand liberatory possibilities. Resistance is also the active state from which to seek collectivity and coalition. Resistance hardly ever has a straightforward public presence. It is rather duplicitous, ambiguous, even devious. But it is also almost always masked and hidden by structures of meaning that countenance and constitute domination. "Reading" resistance is crucial for an alternative understanding of the realities of the oppressed. But that reading is done within enclosures and crossings that attest to a need for company. "Traveling" to worlds of sense that are not given in the daily "teachings" of dominant structures of meaning is one of the techniques, the arts, of moving from resistance to liberation.

I have had insightful, enriching, and enduring company in this theoretico-practical path. I could not have come to voice without it. I could not have sustained my voice without it, either. Optimism, a realist optimism, is a hard thing to maintain in this *Pilgrimage*. I have kept that alive only with company. Gratitude is not the word for my attitude regarding each person included in that heterogeneous company. It is rather a sense of shaping ground together, of standing because of each other's words and deeds, and the congruence between them. I would like to honor them.

The Escuela Popular Norteña is the most radical space I have inhabited with others seeking liberatory possibilities. In that space, a space we created together, I got to articulate and fashion my sense of possibilities with *compañeras* and *compañeros* who have a theoretico-practical disposition and who, as a group, have a wealth of experience taking that disposition into the popular education situation. Mildred Beltré, María Benfield, Laura Burns Levison, Geoff Bryce, Julia Schiavone Camacho, Laura Dumond Kerr, Aurelia Flores, Easa González, Nydia Hernández, Ricardo Herrera, Manuel Herrera, Sarah Hoagland, Paul Hyry, Gladys Jiménez-Muñoz, Cricket Keating, Suzanne LaGrande, Rafael Mutis, Rudiah Primariantari, Joshua Price, Rocio Restrepo, Sylvia Rodríguez, Kelvin Santiago Valles, Ricardo Santos, Rocio Siverio, Sunaryo, Lisa Tessman, Angelo Cisneros, Michelle Wiese, and Sarah Williams were all at some point members of the Escuela Popular Norteña, *compañeras* and *compañeros* who shaped and sustained that radical space, our voices within it, my own included.

Los compañeros de las luchas en Valdez created an environment where we taught each other solidarity, a solid ground for our own sense of possibility, solid ground for my theorizing resistance. They are Antonio Apodaca, Joseph Apodaca, Trinidad Apodaca, Victoria Apodaca, Bela Arellano, Romolo Arellano, Sabinita Arguello, Fermín Arguello, Billie Archuleta, Lee Archuleta, Teresa Archuleta, Cora Montoya Bennett, Ron Bennett, Geoff Bryce, Carolina Domínguez, Bobby Espinoza, Consuelo Espinoza, Elias Espinoza, Mark Espinoza, Stephanie Espinoza, David Fernández, Patricia Fernández, Dorothy García, Dennis García, Frank García, Louie García, Lloyd García, Lolo García, Luís García, Nancy García, Rafael García, Tom García, Amelina Gonzáles, Beatriz Gonzáles, Celestino Gonzáles, Gregorita Gonzáles, Francisco "El Comanche" Gonzáles, Lola Gonzáles, Phaedra Greenwood, Bjorn Halvorsen, Juanita Jaramillo Lavadie, Eduardo Lavadie, Charlie W. López, Julian Lucero, Octaviano (Tano) Lucero, Cirila Martínez, Ervin Martínez, Ezechiel Martínez, Eva Martínez, Dorotea Martínez, Magdalena Martínez, Margarito Martínez, Maxine Martínez, Paul Martínez, Sylvia Martínez, Vicente Martínez, Joyce Medina, Jerry Mondragon, Peggy Nelson, Laura Oest, Nora Herrera Oest, Ronald Oest, Adrian Ortega, Antonio Ortega, Guillerma Ortega, Melachias Ortega, Marcelino Ortega, Pacífica Ortega, Younice Ortega, Manuel Ortiz Sr., Adelia Padilla, Jerry Quintana, Carlos Rendón, Isabel Rendón, Anita Rodríguez, Sylvia Rodríguez, Fabi Romero, Marcia Romero, Feliberto Romero, Marcia Romero, Telesfor Salazar, Elena Salazar, Jesse Salazar, Robert Salazar, Maria Sánchez, Rodolfo Sánchez, Artie Sharfin, Ruth Sharfin, Beth Taintor, Ben Tafoya, Fabiola Teter, Richard Teter, Alfred Trujillo, Adelmo Valdez, Angela Valdez, Antonio Valdez, Ben Valdez, David Valdez, Lorraine Valdez, Gertrude Valdez, Tina Valdez, Andres Vargas, Kika Vargas, Ambrosio Varos, Debra Varos, Micelle Varos, Orlando Varos, Patsy Varos, Priscilla Varos, Elizario Varos, Soveida Varos, and Enriqueta Vásquez. Some of them have died and their memory holds the place of resistance together.

Within the university, I have been fortunate to find theoretico-practical company, in two groups: Radical Folk at Carleton College and the Methodologies of Resistant Negotiation working group at the State University of New York, Binghamton. Humberto Huergo, Dan Kerr, Ethan Lowenstein, Susie Putz, and Marcia Williams were among the many imaginative, articulate, and courageous companions in Radical Folk. The second group has explored ways to understand practices of resistance to oppressions. I have been given enormous sustenance by the group in an environment that goes against the grain of our task. The essays in this work have benefited greatly from those discussions. The members, local and long distance, have included Joshua Price, Tabor Fisher, Gabriela Veronelli, Mazi Allen, Sarah Hoagland, Jackie Anderson, Shireen Roshanravan, Alejandro de Acosta, Ricardo Santos, Lillian de Paula, Anne Leighton, Laura Dumond Kerr, Chris Cavanagh, Rudiah Primariatari, Sunaryo, Mohatma, Eli Morrison, Vik Chaubey, Michael Hames-García, Jane Drexler, Julia Glanville, Kai Lundgren Williams, and Jenn Lutzenberger.

The Society for Women in Philosophy, Midwestern Division, has been the place where I began to conceive of myself as a philosopher with something to say. I have presented most of my work there, but most importantly I have heard and taken in the voices of many outstanding thinkers. The creation of a radical, experimental, and solidarious environment for the formation and discussion of ideas in a philosophical vein, against all forms of patriarchal domination in all their complexity, is the accomplishment of a group of women who favored me with great support and attention. Their teachings have been deeply instructive. I keep close to my heart and ears the words of Jeffner Allen, Jackie Anderson, Suparna Bhaskaran, Claudia Card, Chris Cuomo, Victoria Davion, Marilyn Frye, Sarah Hoagland, Alison Jaggar, Amber Katherine, Anne

Leighton, Crista Lebens, Naomi Scheman, Alison Bailey, Kim Hall, and Linda Lopez McAlister. The Women of Color Caucus, which Jackie Anderson and I founded, has been a particularly freeing space, one in which, as a Woman of Color, I learnt to think without the mediation of white interlocution.

While I was teaching at Carleton College, I had the enormous luck of having Elizabeth Spelman as a colleague for one term. The long-lasting conversation I initiated with her then has been enormously sustaining. I do not think I would have ever begun to write for an intellectual audience without her company.

Leonor Lugones, Monica D'Uva, Vanessa Ragone, and Andrea Roca participated vigorously in ground-breaking discussions on pluralist feminism in Buenos Aires and accompanied me in the development of my voice.

Con las compañeras sin nombre de la Clínica quiero compartir una lágrima y una carcajada larga que nos acompañe en el frío de las noches sin descanso.

Among the resistant women who have woven the fabric of my possibilities, Mercedes, my mother, has occupied a central place in my praxical thinking. She gave me the ways to live a life that, with her every gesture, undid the meanings that were supposed to tie her to subordination.

Mi adorable compañera Zohar, de patitas suaves y aliento tranquilo me alegró la escritura con la finura de su campañía.

Finally, I honor Joshua Price, Geoff Bryce, and Laura Dumond Kerr for their uncompromising theoretico-practical company, care, attention, and sustaining love.

I thank Dianne Ewing for her intelligence and patient editing. Finally, I thank Hilde Nelson and Sarah Ruddick for including *Peregrinajes* in this fine series, for their encouragement and thoughtful comments.

Introduction

The "pilgrimage" that the title of the book calls forth moves through different levels of liberatory work in company forged through a practice of *tantear** for meaning, for the limits of possibility; putting our hands to our ears to hear better, to hear the meaning in the enclosures and openings of our praxis.[1] I say different levels to try to accommodate levels of comprehension and incomprehension, as well as levels of opening ourselves to each other, levels of intimacy, and large and sometimes dispersed solidarity. Sometimes it has been many people together — hundreds of us talking and acting out our sense of the possible — and sometimes it has been very tentative connections inside the walls of very strictly guarded, normed, repressive domains.

> *"I am busy" she said, when they brought out the electro-shock machine, "I am busy." In a repetitious chant that we (not they) could understand, a busying of the mind that disrupts the brutal meddling, reminding oneself, after all, that one form of efficacious resistance lies in not being open to being "cured."*
>
> *She went "outside," around the streets, freely asking people to come "inside" her home and take all the furniture with them, the refrigerator, the stove, the bed, everything was up for grabs. She was put "inside" a different repressive enclosure. Her lack of sense consisted in believing her husband turned*

---

* I use the Spanish word "tantear" both in the sense of exploring someone's inclinations about a particular issue and in the sense of "tantear en la oscuridad," putting one's hands in front of oneself as one is walking in the dark, tactilely feeling one's way.

into a "lobizón" [werewolf] at night. The spatiality of her sense violated what could be tolerated as public discourse.

But I also mean levels in what counts as political. As you dare to witness police arresting people, or dare to ask a woman who is saying "no" to a man's hold whether she's all right, whether she wants to leave, you notice that it is quite different to do that than to organize a demonstration against Anglo takeover of land and water in the U.S. Southwest. It is all beyond the pale, but the latter is more easily understood as political—it is afforded a kind of sociality—that the others may lack. So, there are levels of disruption, levels of resistance, in terms of the political sense that the act makes. Foundations that fund political projects often look for political activity that makes a particular kind of "within-bounds" sense. It is important to take stock of the ease of acceptance, since there is a need to try to roam more deeply into the social to understand who's paying for one's acceptability.

I also mean levels of motility: sometimes you are stuck in a chair and the tiny movements in your hands are a level of intense resistance that requires a closeness of understanding to sense tactually the forcefulness of the motility. Sometimes you walk miles in a closeness of people giving birth to an intention that was not in any of us alone, with banners and other crafted signs of our impudence. Everyone in the crowd sensing in the sounds coming out of our bodies and our feet hitting the ground, and the bumping into each other, the carrying of the signs still fresh or used over and over, but made from our own cloth, the forcefulness and largeness of our motility.

"La bandera de Valdez," each Valdeño put his or her own blood on the double-size bed sheet, little kids rushing at an injury to augment their contributions, the bar filled with beer drinking men having their fingers pricked and sharing their blood on the banner. A conejo slaughtered, taking the chicken's place because the chicken began laying eggs again, its blood a big splotch at the top of the sign: "La Sangre de la Gente de Valdez." Of course, our marching behind that sign had an incarnate intentionality, like blood brothers and sisters, made anew out of love and anger.

Sometimes I also mean emotional levels, depths of anger, making one large to oneself and to others, gesticulating and expressing a commitment to be understood even if it is at the cost of giving rise to a sense of fear in another. Sometimes it is an extreme of intimate tenderness, getting very close to hear the sense in the sounds or speaking very softly, expressing a sense that can barely be entertained.

Sometimes it is not how far one moves but how one moves, within what complexities and against what simplifications of histories, geographies, and meanings. If oppressions intermesh but are represented as interlocking,[2] oppressed people are categorially lumped together and categorially broken from each other. Then, if the resistances are not going to follow the logic of the representation — a logic tied to purity as an instrument of social control — the resisters must be ready to intervene in the categorial separations and the categorial lumping together of peoples in a struggle to connect with each other. But it isn't just categorial enclosures and exclusions without a history, it is also histories of fragmentation and resistance. Getting ready to intervene at the level of meaning is one of the strands that I am putting out to worlds of resistance, to be taken up or transformed, but I hope to be considered.

Sometimes it is levels in the sense of meanings that erase other meanings, which, in turn, seek an intersection to find a worldly voice.

A meeting of the community takes place with representatives of a governmental office dealing with water issues. It is a public meeting. It is a bilingual state. So we ask for translators since there are community members who do not speak English. But, of course, they are not accustomed to that demand, so they cannot provide translation. But by law, we remind them, the meeting cannot proceed without translation, if people request it. So it is agreed that some of "us" will translate. This is another level of the political, one that lives in an intersection that is rarely made public, and once it is, its public quality is understood in completely divergent ways by those present. The opportunity is one of understanding by "translation" a much larger act, a much more faithful act, a more loving act, a more disruptive act, a more deeply insurgent act than the finding of linguistic "equivalences."[3] "No se desanimen por el idoima* que esta gente esta usando. Están tratando de silenciarnos con palabras científicas"[4] *is a bilingual message directed to both those who speak both languages and to those who are Spanish-only speakers. The translation interprets what is happening and gives voice to it in the subaltern language.*

Once I knew a young Hmong woman who had been instructed by the Minnesota courts to translate "word for word" what the lawyers and judge were saying. In the middle of the trial, the accused kept on pleading to the translator, "What do I do?" "What do I say?" The young woman translated word for word. At the end of the session, when the young woman was passing next to her leaving the court room, the defendant seized the opportunity to tell her: "You are no Hmong."

The time and spatiality of the praxis is always very particular. Sometimes, the history of the activities goes back hundreds of years in the consciousness of everyone who is acting up, a double sense of time: both forgotten, erased time by the oppressor and time in which "progress" will cure all ills and alter the vivid history of abuse and resistance to those in struggle. Time is reread over and over in the course of living outrageously in defiance of limits and limitations. The possibility of many senses to the past that one takes up in struggle is sometimes quieted down by anesthetizing and mythologizing history and place. Indeed, this pilgrimage is a walking against and away from that hushing of the manyness of the past in the present by both dominators and those resisting domination. But sometimes the history is of me and you, life history in the flesh, moods, tendencies, and dispositions to live big or small, to tame and trash someone's spirit or to live side by side in the task of overcoming incomprehension—all levels of the political.

She told us that when she is down, when things get to be too much, her husband gone on a drunken spree, all her children getting on her nerves, too little money, too much pressure, well, when she is down, she dresses up as a clown and she goes to the streets, la plaza, and she talks to people, mostly kids, and she feels fine again. She got some instruction on how to make herself up at Mujeres Latinas, but she would never work as a clown: "No one can own my clown," she said.

The places and spaces themselves are conceived quite differently by those who are part of the proceedings, as it were. There is the bird's-eye view — the perspective from up high, planning the town, the takeover, or the analysis of life and history. There is the pedestrian view — the perspective from inside the midst of people, from inside the layers of relations and institutions and practices. There is the understanding of place that sees it as already lost, next to the understanding of place in a mythologizing of its eternal meaning, next to the understanding that seizes its endurance in the possibilities of resisting both myth and erasure.

The chapters are cut of that cloth, of many levels, from within possibilities made in the making, not presupposed. I have taken my time in putting them together as a book, since the meaning of this act is, in itself, one that I approach cautiously. Each chapter has come from within political praxis among people held in the fragility of our connectedness. Each also has gone back to praxis often informing popular education[5] "situations." I have written the chapters and given words to what I learned in the engagement with others, guided by a maxim I developed so as not to be persuaded by the flights of fancy offered to me in the U.S. academy: I won't think what I won't practice. This is also a commitment against utopianism, which seems to me what keeps one out of despair when one cannot act, at all. I have tended, instead, to find activity in the movements of the hand of someone rendered frozen by acts of extreme violation. The commitment is to live differently in the present, to think and act against the grain of oppression. I write from the belief that it is only from that ground that the next possibility can be entertained socially, at the edge of realism. My perspective is in the midst of people mindful to the tensions, desires, closures, cracks, and openings that make up the social.

I am keen on theorizing what, from the standpoint of liberalism, would look like an almost inconsequential or attenuated sense of agency. What looks like a very attenuated sense of agency by the standards of liberal morality is a very powerful one, if one understands it as fitting:

a variegated,
dominated,

> *in resistance to a variety of intermeshed and interlocking*
> *oppressions, aggregate that*
> > *pulls in different ways,*
> > *sometimes in unison,*
> > *but more often in many directions,*
> > *dispersed*
> > *but "intent," in a loose sense of intentionality, on overcoming*
> > > *social fragmentation,*
> > > *the purity of language,*
> > > *disembodiment,*
> > > *a unilinear history,*
> > > > *mythical attachments to place or communities of*
> > > > *the*
> > *same.*

In expressing this sense of intentionality, I am not trying to explain, but rather am trying to understand with, and in the midst of others, the problems that I → we encountered on the way to exercising our agency. The understanding of agency that I propose, which I call "active subjectivity" and which I contrast with the influential understanding of agency of late modernity, is highly attenuated. It does not presuppose the individual subject and it does not presuppose collective intentionality of collectivities of the same. It is adumbrated to consciousness by a moving with people, by the difficulties as well as the concrete possibilities of such movings. It is a sense of intentionality that we can reinforce and sense as lively in paying attention to people and to the enormously variegated ways of connection among people without privileging the word or a monological understanding of sense. We can reinforce and influence the direction of intention in small ways by sensing/understanding the movement of desires, beliefs, and signs among people.

The question I have asked myself from within the midst of multiple political relations is: *how much and what sort of "agency" do we need to move with others*
> *without falling into a politics of the same, a politics that values or assumes sameness or homogeneity;*
> *without mythologizing place;*
> *attempting to stand in the cracks and intersections of multiple histories of domination and resistances to dominations?*

That is the sense of agency I have tried to put into words, but also the sense that I am participating in as I write. I propose understandings, techniques, vantage points, languages, and tactical strategies that I mean to place in the multiple liberatory trajectories that I → we inhabit.

One way of imaging my concern with intentionality and active subjectivity is to focus on the "traveling" of our own against the grain, resistant, oppositional thoughts, movements, gestures among variegated, heterogeneous aggregates of subjects negotiating a life in the tensions of various oppressing ↔ resisting relations. The "carrying media" for their traveling are by no means permanently and solidly in place. Rather, they are always metamorphosing and in need of attention, the kind of attention that enables us to see deeply into the social. "They" cannot be reified.

Another way of understanding the pilgrimage is to think of it as also epistemic: I am providing ways of witnessing faithfully and of conveying meaning against the oppressive grain. To witness faithfully is difficult, given the manyness of worlds of sense related through power so that oppressive and fragmenting meanings saturate many worlds of sense in hard to detect ways. A collaborator witnesses on the side of power, while a faithful witness witnesses against the grain of power, on the side of resistance. To witness faithfully, one must be able to sense resistance, to interpret behavior as resistant even when it is dangerous, when that interpretation places one psychologically against common sense, or when one is moved to act in collision with common sense, with oppression. Faithful witnessing leads one away from a monosensical life. One ceases to have expectations, desires, and beliefs that fit one for a life in allegiance with oppression. The work I have done has been an exploration of many different ways of accessing meaning that is construed against the grain of oppression. "World"-traveling is one of those ways of keeping oneself focused on resistance, one that enables us to exercise the multiple visions, multiple sensings, and multiple sense makings that I pursue in this book.

Mamá would sometimes—often—say things that were nonsense or false, like the little vase that I was to give the fourth

grade teacher and I broke it before I got to school and she glued
it together and placed it on a shelf. "Well," she would say, "I
wonder when and how that broke," as if it had just happened
rather than forty years ago. Going around people and tasks
saying things that had no redemptive interpretation, unless
one was looking for resistance. After months of my asking her,
she said, "I do it to remind myself that no one is listening."
That was my mother, a powerful resister to any sort of cheap
love anyone offered her, easy love by folks who were not ready
to go the distance.

I chose "pilgrimage" as the way of movement because of
Victor Turner's understanding of pilgrimages as movements
of people that loosen the hold of institutional, structural descriptions in the creation of liminal spaces (Turner 1974). The
possibilities of antistructural understandings of selves, relations, and realities became important to me, not as a temporary, passing experience, but as a way to think of resisters to
structural, institutionalized oppressions. I think of antistructural selves, relations, and practices as constituting space and
time away from linear, univocal, and cohesive constructions
of the social.

Trespassing

In *Pilgrimages*, I introduce a vocabulary, an imagery, a set of
practices, and exercises in praxical thinking designed to convey the complexities of resistances to intermeshed oppressions. In this section, I begin to think through the spatiality of
resistances within and against the spatiality of dominations.
  Visualize, remember, and sense a map that has been drawn
by power in its many guises and directions and where there is
a spot for you. All the roads and places are marked as places
you may, must, or cannot occupy. Your life is spatially mapped
by power. Your spot lies at the intersection of all the spatial
venues where you may, must, or cannot live or move. Those
intersections also spatialize your relations and your condition
with respect to the asymmetries of power that constitute those
relations. This map is, in a sense, abstract since, in it, resistance
and domination are conceptually separated. It is also abstract
since the ways of power conceive domination through abstrac-

tion. There is no "you" there except a person spatially and thus relationally conceived through your functionality in terms of power. That you is understood as thoroughly socially constructed in terms of power. Thus, even if you is a spot and intersection of domination, and that gives you carte blanche as to where you may go, you may not go there in resistance to domination; that occupation of space is not mapped in this map. You may go places as boss, pleasure seeker on the labor of others, tourist, colonizer, and user of people's lives and labor without being touched by exercising yourself as apart from them, and you are ideologically constructed as having deserved your spot. And if "you" (always abstract "you") are one of the dominated, your movements are highly restricted and contained. And there may not be any you there under certain descriptions, such as "lesbian" or any other description that captures transgression. The abstract "you" has desires, thoughts, inclinations, and relations that are all constructed by power with their collaboration, the collaboration of the you. That is, every "you" is of the "system," logically speaking.

But though the map must contain this abstraction, in engaging in this embodied thought experiment, you (without quotes to indicate your concreteness rather than your "trueness"⁶) are sensing the geography looking for signs of power and of limitations, reductions, erasures, and functionalist constructions. This is, in terms of logical levels, the first transgression. And that is also a fundamental transgression, since you are sensing, recognizing, and moving through the spatiality of your everydayness as possibly reductive, demoralizing, containing, and eliminating your possibilities. Your having that double consciousness about yourself in space is transgressive. You recognize signs that you are familiar with or signs that you see for the first time in this exploration since they are nowadays, in many geographies, mostly hidden: too little time, unsafe, only for smart people who are seeking degrees, for whites only (except if you're going to serve or clean), too little money, not my community or my people, illegal, for heterosexuals only, or simply just private property ("keep out").

When you think about the map, you see that people are organized and channeled spatially in ways that contain them in a systematic way from getting together against the grain of power. Or, you may not quite realize that. You may not realize how you collaborate in the production of that spatiality. This latter possibility has to be investigated concretely, in the flesh, to the extent to which your motility and your desires are or are not of a piece in moving through your everydayness.[7] You may, from your vantage point (not from "up high") not recognize any containment; thus there may be no trespassing in your walking the map of oppression.

> I don't go into neighborhoods of color because that's to meddle where I am not wanted. That's their community. I could go if I had their permission or welcome, but I have never had either. [As if neighborhoods of color were not public space.]

Taking in the map is not to occupy a "from the top position," a bird's-eye view. It is rather to study one's spatiality, the spatiality of one's relations, of one's productions and their meaning in both a concrete and an abstract sense. You are concrete. Your spatiality, constructed as an intersection following the designs of power, isn't. This discrepancy already tells you that you are more than one.

In understanding this map, one can also begin to understand all the ways in which oneself and others violate this spatiality or inhabit it in great resistance, without willful collaboration. Indeed, it seems very important to count as resistance all those tensions whose logic belongs to a logic of resistance, even when they do not redraw the spatiality. Consider battering as a way to control women as an example. The inhabitation of the spatiality may be different in small things like ignoring the batterer's calls a little bit longer or withdrawing one's affection without his noticing. So, then, it is in noticing the tensions, the small deviations, the senseless communications within the spatiality of power that we begin to be able to speak to each other about resistance.

> I couldn't figure what else to do except to move with him to make him get off me a little bit faster. But all the while I despised him, there was not once a touch that didn't repel me. We lived together for years. He would fuck me always after beating me up or as part of beating me up. To figure out how to leave was something that took all my imagination. But you

*know how small your imagination gets after being beaten up
and fucked over and over for years. You know how hard you
have to try to make it grow. But all the while, I didn't make
myself like it. That's why my imagination could grow. I didn't
make myself like it.*

*I keep secrets. Even though I am told over and over by white
feminists that we must reveal ourselves, open ourselves, I keep
secrets. Disclosing our secrets threatens our survival.*

*We go into the museum. The woman says we have to pay an
entrance fee. Why, we say, should we pay money to see our
people's things? We will not look at anyone else's. We know it
is the last room. We all file in with our hands making up blind-
ers, all of us, quite a few of us, and we just move in and go
to the last room. Beautiful adobe room. Wish we could take it
home.*

It is in noticing resistance to oppressions in their complex
interconnections, including their interlocking to fragment people categorially, that we can sense each other as possible companions in resistance, where company goes against the grain
of sameness as it goes against the grain of power. Noticing the
tensions from within a logic of resistance enables one to acquire a multiple sensing, a multiple perceiving, a multiple sociality. As one understands the limits, erasures, violations, and
reductions of oppressions, one also begins to understand them
as they are resisted. Trespassing against the spatiality of oppressions is also a redrawing of the map, of the relationality of
space. Trespassing is very difficult to achieve, since there are a
great many ways to entice one back to the road of collusion
with power.

We can then put the two logics constructing the map together and sense the terrain in a tension of oppressing/being
oppressed ⇔ resisting, concrete beings abstractly constructed
refiguring their concreteness in complex dealings with abstraction. In the oppressing/being oppressed ⇔ resisting a refracted, heterogeneous, concrete, you may negotiate resistantly
in the company of others, your own being imagined, ab-
stracted, reduced, debased, demoralized, muted. You understand your own fragmentation and your own multiplicity in
these movements. Since there are histories of resistance, resisting ⇔ oppressing/being oppressed does not presuppose or re-

quire any underlying "I" that is the "true" self. Rather, to understand the spatiality of our lives is to understand that oppressing/being oppressed ⇔ resisting construct space simultaneously and that the temporality of each, at their infinite intersections, produces multiple histories/stories. This is central to this book. This is an emancipatory investigation of this tense oppressing/being oppressed ⇔ resisting of beings both fragmented and multiple.

The movements that this book imagines, describes, and exercises are all in this vein. They are forms of trespassing in the sense of violating the spatiality and logic of oppression. In particular, I am eager to move against social fragmentation. World-traveling, streetwalker theorizing, curdling, and trespassing are all different and related forms of noticing oppression *at* its logic and moving against it. Some of the movements are emphatically epistemic; all include an epistemic shift.

If we think of people who are oppressed as not consumed or exhausted by oppression, but also as resisting or sabotaging a system aimed at molding, reducing, violating, or erasing them, then we also see at least two realities: one of them has the logic of resistance and transformation; the other has the logic of oppression. But, indeed, these two logics multiply and encounter each other over and over in many guises. I want to consider them here in the two moments of resistance and oppression.

When one is acting in accordance with the logic of resistance, one may act with intentions that are incompatible with the logic of oppression and that may thus be very difficult to communicate in an oppressive reality. Sustained use of a logic of resistance will result in the development of character and personality traits that are incompatible with the traits of someone who follows a logic of oppression. The feminine virtues, for example, may be nurtured by a logic of oppression, while rudeness at treatments that anticipate and request servility or subservience is at home in a logic of resistance to give a very obvious example, but the differences become extremely nuanced. Yet one act may be intended from a logic of resistance and be understood with the logic of oppression.

And one may count on the oppressed reading. One may also aim at an ambiguous reading and may intend ambiguously. Thus, the logics of oppression and resistance construct people's movements, interactions, desires, and intentions. A person may be both oppressed and resistant and act in accordance with both logics. Such a person will have a character and personality traits, relations to others, and histories that have interwoven lines with contradictory logics and that are understood by, revealed to, and recognizable by different socialities. Thus, the social is itself crisscrossed with these contradictory, in tension, temporo-spatialities defined and defining multiple intersections that constitute different social beings who are some of the time "you" *and* you.

Given the tension, incompatibility, or oddity between the perceptions produced by the two logics, the perceptions are hard to sustain in conjunction with each other. If you see oppression, you tend not to see resistance. It is not just that it is epistemically difficult to understand the intention constitutive of resistant behavior and see the same behavior as responding to the motivational structure of oppression. And here we need to note that all resistance understands and responds to oppression. But it is one thing to see oppression and another to understand a bit of one's behavior or someone else's as "issuing" from a resistant *and* an oppressed motivational structure. So, there is an epistemic tendency, unless one has cultivated a resistant multiple interpretive vein, to see behavior as either resistant or oppressed.

The person who is resisting, when understood as resisting, is not understood as someone with subservient or servile intentions, while the person understood as acting oppressed — within the logic of oppression — is assumed to be responsive to the oppressor's orders, wishes, desires, suggestions, or expectations. If it can be read either as a mistake or as sabotage, there are many reasons why someone may read it as a mistake, much of the time to their detriment. But the act may be read both ways. Both readings may coexist and one person may read the act both ways and, importantly, intend the act to be read both ways. As one intends the sabotage, one may avail oneself of the reading of the act as incompetent because that hides it and makes one less vulnerable. If the act is one of sabotage and it is read as incompetence, the reading makes it incompetent if done by people who have the power to declare something to be real. It makes it incompetent in at least one reality — one that emphasizes the logic of oppression. But such people hardly ever have the power to erase resistance because they find themselves in the double bind of not being willing or able to see resistance since that would require seeing oppression.

There is also a sense of integrity, moral integrity included, that is lived as violated by the duplicitous interpretation, if one's understanding of the moral presupposes the unification of the self, as much of mainstream, institutionalized morality does. And there are other difficulties related to questions of character. It is difficult to look at one's oppressed behavior in the flesh and the face. Even if the oppressed readings confront one as constructing a reality that one struggles to undermine, or dismantle, the power of the reading in constructing us is often inescapable. It inhabits us from within, it is us, in a servile, subordinate, perverse, criminal, subhuman, or "lost" construction. We can inhabit that construction in enormous tension, but that we can do so is an apparent conundrum that I will return to often in this book. The reading of the act as incompetent has significant consequences since it conforms to the justification of subordination. So the oppressor has a lot to gain from not seeing sabotage and resistance. But then the oppressor cannot erase resistance, because to be erased, resistance needs to be seen.

Perceiving oneself as an oppressor is harder to sustain morally than deception. There is often a lapse, a forgetting, a not recognizing oneself in a description, that reveals to those who perceive multiply that the oppressor is in self-deception, split, fragmented. Self-deception appears to require the unification of the self to be conceivable, that is, it is one self that deceives him- or herself. But one can understand self-deception without this presupposition. The oppressor can be seen to inhabit multiple realities all in the first person. As a self-deceiving multiple self, the oppressor does not remember across realities. Self-deception lies in this disconnection of memory. Thus, I understand that when someone is self-deceiving, there is one incarnate being who animates two co-temporaneous behaviors in the first person without any cross-referencing, without first person memories of him- or herself in more than one reality. It is of great interest for emancipatory work that we can cross-reference different realities. We may indeed have good reason to fear doing that because we may be revealed as vile or as servile. The one in self-deception could, but does not, cross-reference.

To say that someone "intends" in a particular way is a shorthand for a more complex, more social understanding of intention that I will pursue in chapter 10 (see "Streetwalker Theorizing" p. 222). Intentions that affect the organization of power need a sociality in order to move. That is, the formation of those intentions is social. The success of intentions that lack sociality is of a different order. They succeed in keeping one from being exhausted by oppressive readings. They are indeed not worldly. There may even be a reluctance to have them acknowledged, a fear of the risk of publicity at any level. Indeed, it is very difficult to distinguish intending from wishing in those cases, yet it involves complicated tactical strategies to reinforce one's unshared world of sense. But many people sustain themselves against oppression in this wishing to be creative and lively, as they also inhabit a subservient being. Enacting resistance as social and worldly requires an interactive understanding of intentions.

This stepping into the map of oppression/map of resistance logics exhibits two interwoven interests that I pursue in the chapters of this book: an interest in motivational structure at the level of persons and readings of particular acts and an interest in the larger social movement of intentions. This back and forth is important to me as I intend the pieces to be read as praxical. As such, one needs to beware of the tendency to assume others to be such and such or so and so, without paying attention to the particularities of the characters and personalities, the complexities of them, and the manyness of them and of the worlds they inhabit. At the same time, it would be a mistake to construe the movement of the social as cut from that cloth. That movement is a great deal more dispersed, and intentionally complex, between chaotic and of uncertain "constitution," extraordinarily difficult to navigate communicatively. I understand both the movements at the level of selves and relations and the larger movements of the social as inextricably related and resolutely political.

One advantage of the map is that the thought exercise/practice can enable you to become perspicacious in sensing/understanding the spatiality of social fragmentation as it is lived by you and others in great detail.

Traveling

I have repeatedly used spatial vocabulary to engage a logic of resistance in reading histories, geographies, selves, relations, possibilities. One such term is "traveling," as in "'world'-traveling." When I first wrote "Playfulness, 'World'-Traveling, and Loving Perception," I abstained from reading any of the literature on space, including work on travel. Indeed, I abstained from new conversations on the subject with text. I departed from the philosophical literature that had emphasized to me a nonspatial way of perception and conception of life, a unity of the self, a linear way of telling, and an abstract rhetoric. Instead, I lived the exercise as an exposure of psychic multiplicity and I strove to make sense of it by locating the multiple self in space, conceiving of space itself as multiple, intersecting, co-temporaneous realities.

It also seemed to me that I could make use of a spatial account in elucidating disruptions of isolating exclusions. The politics is one of striving for located connection among multiple locations fluidly conceived without the walls that make boundary crossing inconceivable or an exercise in betrayal of "one's own." So, what I wrote is on the logic of connection that is attentive to a deep multiplicity of "worlds." I did not want then, and I do not want now, to eliminate the quotes. I am keen on not reproducing an atomistic understanding of heterogeneous reality; worlds are indeed permeable. Rather, I want to understand reality as heterogeneous, and the heterogeneity to lie not just in interpretation.

A long time after writing that piece I became aware of the politically radical contemporary interest in travel and spatiality. And I became interested in the literature on travel, particularly in Janet Wolff's (1992) and Caren Kaplan's work (1994, 1996). I have come to greatly appreciate their critique of discourses on travel as a set of practices that have inscribed in them the logic of power. I have also come to see why my understanding of travel is itself subversive. Here, I want to revisit my own use of travel and other terms of displacement in conversation with Wolff and Kaplan.

Wolff is interested in the proliferation of travel metaphors in cultural criticism: nomadic criticism, traveling theory, critic as tourist, maps, billboards, hotels and motels, as well as a growing literature on travel itself. She thinks these metaphors are gendered. By travel, she has in mind "a Western, middle-class idea of the chosen and leisured journey" (1992:225), because she thinks this is the sense at play in these discourses. She acknowledges that "the ways in which people travel are very diverse, ranging from tourism, exploring and other voluntary activity to the forced mobility of immigrant workers and 'guest workers' to the extremes of political and economic exiles" (Wolff 1999:224). Wolff focuses on the link between women's exclusion from travel and uses of notions of travel in cultural analysis. Wolff argues that metaphors of unrestrained mobility do not decenter masculinity since unbounded mobility and masculinity are intrinsically connected.

In the sense of travel that I use in "'world'-travel," all people who have been subordinated, exploited, and enslaved have been forced to travel to "worlds" in which they animate subordinate beings. This forced shift to a reality that reduces and contains one's subjectivity and possibilities as it arrogates one's substance is not restricted to women. Indeed, the mobility of those who are forced to travel to spatialities produced with their own substance—substance consumed in the production—is rigidly disciplined. It is only men of a certain class and race who are in a position to exercise their mobility without restriction.

The tension of being oppressed ⇔ resisting oppression "places" one *inside* the *processes* of production of multiple realities. It is from within these processes that the practice of shifting to different constructions, different spatialities, is created. One inhabits the realities as spatially, historically, and thus materially different: different in possibilities, in the connections among people, and in the relation to power. The practice of "world"-traveling involves "simultaneous placement and displacement that acknowledges multiple locations, locations that are not necessarily equally accessible, assimilable or equivalent" (Kaplan 1994:150). I am interested in freeing this practice from its connection with subordination, shifting the directionality and intentionality of travel. Racism and sexism have a vested interest in obscuring and devaluing the complex skills involved in "world"-traveling.

> By traveling to other people's "worlds," we discover that there are "worlds" in which those who are the victims of arrogant perception are really subjects, lively beings, resisters, constructors of visions even though in the mainstream construction they are animated only by the arrogant perceiver and are pliable, foldable, file-awayable, classifiable. [chapter 4]

The question that both Wolff's and Kaplan's work have posed for me is whether travel is so tainted a concept that one cannot succeed in deploying it against its tie with domination. I agree with Kaplan's claim that in my usage I "reject the conventional myth of travel as a quest for rapport and unconditional acceptance" (1994:150). In rejecting the myth, I want not only to differentiate the sense of travel I have in mind from tourism and colonial exploration, I also want to unmask the politics and conceptions of time/space that are intrinsic to them through unveiling an insurgent practice that the myth necessarily veils. I think that it is precisely the case that tourists and colonial explorers, missionaries, settlers, and conquerors do not travel in the sense I have in mind. That is, there is no epistemic shift to other worlds of sense, precisely because they perceive/imagine only the "exotic," the "Other," the "primitive," and the "savage," and there is no world of sense of the exotic, the Other, the savage, and the "one in need of salvation" separate from the logic of domination. Those conceptions of others are inextricably connected to epistemic imperialism and aggressive ignorance. The search for the "authentic" in an alienation from the familiar is a self-regarding, narcissistic search from a position of power. To travel to the worlds of those who are also oppressed but who are categorially isolated from us through the interlocking of oppressions involves acute fluency in the mechanisms of oppression and insight in resisting those mechanisms. That practice of travel is indeed in great tension with the Western, middle-class idea of the chosen and leisured journey:

> *Viaja una por colectivo, por tren, en carro, a pie. Viaja una cu-briendo distancias de muchas clases con y sin compañía.* One travels by bus, by train, by car, on foot. One travels covering various sorts of distances with and without company.
>
> *Una viaja con bolsas llena de fruta, verduras, ropa barata comprada en el border town, con los niños pequeños porque no puede dejarlos con nadie.* One travels with bags full of fruits, vegetables, cheap clothing bought in the border town, the smaller children coming along because there isn't anyone with whom they can stay.
>
> *Una viaja escapando a la violencia, o por el jale, lejos y cerca, el dinero siempre un problema.* One travels escaping violence, or to go to work, far and near, money always an issue.
>
> *Una viaja porque la idea de un lugar seguro donde una tiene el corazón y el pan abrazados en un lazo, es un cuento para niños pequeñitos, pero no para mujeres en edad de cuidar niños.* One travels because the idea of a safe place where one's heart and bread embrace each other is a story for small children, not for women old enough to take care of children.
>
> I relocated to the United States from violence. My location is that of someone who relocated away from battering, systematic rape, extreme psychological and physical torture, by those closest to me. I relocated in the sense of going for a new geographical place, a new identity, a new set of relations. Of course the geographical places, the identity (or identities), the relations were not for me to choose. Choice, in the liberal sense of the word, had nothing to do with any of it. But though they were not for me to choose, I didn't just become overwhelmingly and irrevocably and passively inscripted by them. The relocation has become necessarily a transgressive and resistant negotiation with, rather than away from violence and abuse. But I have looked for migrations and positionings and rehearsals that give me more room or more ground for maneuvering. Going back and forth gives me a possibility of tenderness with those that I am destined to hate.

Thus, the question of why the particular coloration of the word "travel" as a middle-class leisurely individualized journey has come to dominate modernist discourses in favor of other terms of displacement is tied — as Kaplan carefully argues — to the veiling of the oppressive commitments of exploration, tourism, and other practices of displacement that are practices of domination. That is why I insist on the use of these terms against the grain of this production.

I agree with Kaplan that the modern and the postmodern discourses of displacement that center on nomadism, exile, tourism, and expatriation hide these discourses' ties to domination. So, I think it is important to unveil their ties to domination by making clear that these personages of modern and postmodern displacement do not travel epistemically to different realities but are rather involved in narcissism. My sense and understanding of travel enable me to say that. In this sense, these personages do not travel. I also agree that it is important to unveil the existence of other displacements and the connection between those displacements and colonialism and global imperialism. But I also think it's important to unveil practices of resistance that are concocted in the intersection between oppressive practices of displacement and discourses of displacement.

Worlds

The logic of "as if" presupposes the distinction between actual and possible worlds. When I speak of different worlds, I do not have the logic of "as if" nor the implied distinction between possible and actual worlds in mind. Rather, I focus tenaciously on actual worlds. These worlds are all lived and they organize the social as heterogeneous, multiple. I think of the social as intersubjectively constructed in a variety of tense ways, forces at odds, impinging differently in the construction of any world. Any world is tense, not just in tense inner turmoil but also in tense acknowledged or unacknowledged contestation with other worlds. I think that there are many worlds, not autonomous, but intertwined semantically and materially, with a logic that is sufficiently self-coherent and sufficiently in contradiction with others to constitute an alternative construction of the social. Whether or not a particular world ceases to be is a matter of political contestation. No world is either atomic or autonomous. Many worlds stand in relations of power to other worlds, which include a second order of meaning.

I introduce the notion that there are many worlds in chapter 4 and I use it in many of the other chapters in this book. The notion of a world enables me to understand social heterogeneity, in both its oppressive and resistant forms. To further clarify my own usage, I will compare my understanding of a world to Arthur Danto's use of it (Danto 1998). His use is interestingly close to but distinct from mine. The comparison avoids the containment of a definition but guides usage. It is crucial to notice that it is not Danto's purpose to understand resistance to oppression, though his aim includes resistant symbolic expressions.

In *The Wake of Art*, Danto (1998) offers an understanding of interpretation that connects symbolic expression to communication, communication to community, and both communication and community to the self of the author of symbolic expressions. In introducing the notion of a symbolic expression, he distinguishes expressions from manifestations and symbols from signs. In drawing the distinctions he uses the concept of a world.

Danto begins to draw the distinction between expression and manifestation through an example. He depicts a disordered room, one that could only have gotten that way "if it is lived that way" (Danto 1998:99). The disordered room could express something about the occupant or be a manifestation of the domestic culture to which the occupant belongs. If it is a manifestation, it tells something about the occupant's world, but nothing much about her (Danto 1998:99). It is an expression when the occupant has decided to live that way for *reasons*. Danto goes on to suggest that the occupant might be a woman repudiating the tidiness associated with the social prototype of femininity. In that case, the room is a "political statement in symbolic form" (Danto 1998:99). To understand the disordered room as a symbolic expression is to interpret it rather than explain it since symbolic expressions do not point to causes but reasons. Indeed, "it gets to be an expression when explanations under which it is a manifestation fail" (Danto 1998:99).

The key ingredient in Danto's understanding of interpretation is his use of possible worlds. "The formula for interpretation is: find the world in which what is an expression in this world would be a sign in that one. Then the expression is a symbol of that world" (Danto 1998:102). Interpreting the expression asks that one imagine a possible world in which the disordered room, instead of being an expression, is a manifestation; instead of a symbol, it is a sign. One is to imagine a world culturally organized in such a way that in that world the disordered room is a mere sign, a cultural manifestation, a world in which "disordered rooms are no longer indexed to gender" (Danto 1998:101). But, indeed, that world is not actual.[8] "The expression symbolizes the reality in which it would have been a manifestation, or a mere sign, if that world instead of this one were real" (Danto 1998:101). Thus, the symbolic expression brings a fragment from that alternative world into the actual world, a fragment from that world that embodies it. "It is a symbol because it is *only* a fragment. It stands encapsulated in a world against which it bears witness" (Danto 1998:102). Symbolic expressions need not be "altogether transparent to the subject" (Danto 1998:104). Indeed, Danto understands Freud's teaching in terms of the manifestation/symbolic expression distinction. Forgettings, misinscriptions, and slips may be symbolic expressions and done for reasons.

The protesting feminist belongs to the world—which she regards as her true world—in which her disordered room is a sign, an alternative world to the one in which she is a prisoner, that is, the actual world. She may be intent on changing the actual world through *symbolic enactment* and she may even recognize that her only recourse is symbolic expression since she is "impotent to change the realities in any large way." She is changing it in a small way since she is "bringing the preferred reality into the bedroom" (Danto 1998:103). When two worlds intersect, it is to be expected that "content undergoes transformations" (Danto 1998:104).

Danto goes on to analyze symbolic expressions as communications that presuppose a code accessible to those to whom the communication is addressed. When the woman disorders the room or allows it to be become disorderly, she is repudiating gender injustice symbolically. She expresses this symbolically to those who expect that she will abide by standards of feminine behavior. "It is a mode of symbolic expression her culture, and then her station within that culture, make available to her imagination, and it can be read by those conversant in the code of "ordering rooms" (Danto 1998:111). "Symbolic expressions function as ways of saying what cannot be said, or saying more effectively what can be said, and they demonstrate the degree to which every item of culture is penetrated by meaning"(Danto 1998:111). So, as I understand Danto, the interpretation of her political statement is accessible to those very members of the cultural community who expect her to behave in the ways of the world she inhabits as a prisoner. Imagining the possible world in which her symbolic enactment coheres as a sign is something they can do.

Danto must be making an implicit distinction between an audience of what he calls "implicit understanders" and an audience that may be less likely to access her meaning. Both are fluent in the customs and codes of the world the author of the symbolic expression inhabits as a prisoner. But an audience that expects her to behave in accordance with the codes and customs of the culture may be less likely to want to access her meaning and may aggressively ignore it. Implicit understanders are described by Danto as "individuals whose feelings and thoughts will be modified upon grasping the meanings conveyed or transformed by the expressions" (Danto 1998:112). Danto understands the self, as the author of symbolic expressions, as "defined reciprocally by the community that may be expected to grasp the symbolic expressions the culture makes available to the self. The self *is* that community, internalized" (Danto 1998:113). I am unclear as to whether, for Danto, that community includes both audiences.

Ranahit Guha (1988:45) reads the tendency in dominant (counterinsurgent) histories to see peasant uprising as "caused" as an example of their reactionary character. He sees peasant uprisings as instead cultivated, through difficulty and elaboration, from a subaltern positionality taken over by the hegemonic logic of domination:

> When a peasant rose in revolt at any time or place under the Raj, he did so necessarily and explicitly in violation of a series

of codes that defined his very existence as a member of that colonial, and still largely semi-feudal society. For his subalternity was materialized by the structure of property, institutionalized by law, sanctified by religion and made tolerable—even desirable—by tradition. To rebel was indeed to destroy many of those familiar signs that he had learned to read and manipulate in order to extract a meaning out of the harsh world around him and live with it. The risk in "turning things upside down" under these conditions was indeed so great that he could hardly afford to engage in such a project in a state of absent-mindedness. [Guha 1988:45]

The description "rose in revolt" may be too large and too vague to serve as a description of a symbolic expression for Danto. Nevertheless, his theory of interpretation would coincide with Guha that rising in revolt in violation of a series of codes cannot be accounted for in terms of causes external to the "peasant's consciousness"(Danto 1998:47). Since the peasant's subalternity was highly institutionalized by law, religion, economics, and tradition, his revolt could not be understood in Danto's terms as a sign or a manifestation of semifeudal colonial India. The issue is whether his revolt is to be understood by appeal to a possible world in which the structure of property, law, and religion was egalitarian. Part of the issue here is whether the peasant's revolt is historically inserted in a sociality that stands in resistance to oppression. But also at issue is whether the peasant's consciousness *must* contain a utopian blueprint. The egalitarian possible world fitting the acts that constitute "rising in revolt" is a blueprint. Danto's interpretative schema cannot be used to understand resistance, as it does not make room for the historicity of resistance. Possible worlds are not historical, but logical entities. If one is to understand the actual world constituted by multiple spatio-temporalities in tense power relations and in tense semantic relations, Danto's schema seems insufficient. Another way of making the point is to say that Danto's depiction of the context of acts of symbolic expression—an actual world organized through custom, codes, "things one grows up with"—is insufficient as it leaves out the tensions and fractures of social power. The appeal to a possible world in interpretation—the blueprint — precisely escapes the tense historical intersection of two lived social arrangements. Danto depicts the actual world in terms of custom and culture, muting power relations as constitutive of custom and culture and thus failing to understand that world in its tense multiplicity.

What rides on whether we think of the feminist gesture as a fragment of a possible gender-just world that stands in a semantic relation to a gender-unjust actual world or as a fragment indicative of interworld contestation between actual, cotemporaneous, overlapping constructions of social relations, including relations of power? I introduce the interpretation of the social as heterogeneous in terms of multiple actual worlds because I am interested in theorizing resistance to intermeshed oppressions and to the interlocking of oppressions not as merely symbolic but as inserted in complex, tense, relational networks. Resistant networks are often historically muted or distorted. Communication is complex. Expressive gestures, acts, movements, and behaviors are often incommunicative with respect to some audiences and communicative with respect to others; meaning is often conveyed obliquely, indirectly, sometimes in ways hard to access but always differentially accessible to audiences related in terms of social power. Danto's interpretive formula, "find the world in which what is an expression in this world would be a sign in that one. Then the expression is a symbol of that world" (Danto 1998:102), cannot interpret resistance faithfully as it separates contestations of power in historical/spatial tense locations from contestations of meaning. The relation between worlds in Danto's schema is semantic; the intersection between worlds is not understood in terms of power.

Danto thinks of the self as defined by "the symbolic field within which it expresses itself" (Danto 1998:113) and with the community "that may be expected to grasp the symbolic expressions the culture makes available to the self" (Danto 1998:113). Culture is understood as what orders the world of meaning. Danto concludes his meditation with the striking claim that different cultures have different selves as products. Unlike his, my use of "world" does not identify world with culture. My use of the word "world" understands meaning and communication to be both less coded and less determined by cultural codes. And it understands the existing codes as less ossified and, as the result of ongoing transculturation, interworld influencing and interworld relations of control and resistance to control. Again, no world can be understood as monistic, homogenous, or autonomous. Communication across worlds is complex not because of impermeable cultural boundaries but because domination fragments the social and resistance takes power differentials, collaborations, and betrayals as well as solidarities in its communicative and incommunicative directions, its tactical strategies of resistant sense making. In this book, I explore some of those communicative difficulties and creativities.

The question of inter- and intraworld communication is central to this book and to the introduction of the notion of a world. Resisting the interlocking of oppressions involves rejecting practically the insurmountable walls built by ideological mechanisms that produce atomic understanding of social groups. Categorial understandings of oppressions; unilinear, univocal, unilogical understandings of history; and abstract understandings of space are all mechanisms that produce atomic understandings of social groups and block interworld and intraworld communication. I use worlds against the grain of atomic, homogeneous, and monistic understandings of the social in any of its dimensions.

Playfulness

If "playfulness" brings to mind the search for frivolous fun, *aturdimiento*, then it is grotesque to suggest that the crossings that would initiate deep coalitions be done playfully. Rather, when one considers the many crossings, I think it is important to cross, to go through, in uncertainty, open to risking one's own ground, including one's own self-understanding. An openness to uncertainty, which includes a vocation not bound by the meanings and norms that constitute one's ground, is characteristic of what I identify as a playful attitude. It is that openness to uncertainty that enables one to find in others one's own possibilities and theirs.

When I was a child, my sister, my brothers, and I were small enough to use the metal grid of the tall door shutters as steps to go up to the roof. Once on the roof we were in a land that enabled us to practice "seeing the neighbors with extraordinary eyes." We would look at the houses and people, at openings that we would never cross and cross them in imagination and make up tales about the neighbors' characters, lives, secret desires, and powers. My sister came up with the name "bichar" for what we did, a word that has another meaning in the caló [argot] of Buenos Aires. Whenever anyone would call to us to locate us as out of danger and ask us "What are you doing?" we would answer "Estamos bichando."

Fear is called for by crossing, because there is an impending sense of loss: loss of competence and loss of a clear sense of oneself and one's relations to others. A playful attitude is a good companion to fear; it keeps one focused on the crossing, on the process of metamorphosis.[9]

Methodology

None of the examples I use in this book are uses of the hypothetical, nor are they ever used as counterexamples. Yet, though my examples are temporally and geographically located (i.e., they are never tenseless or in no-place), I do not use them as a historian or social scientist might. I usually zoom onto a slice of larger histories and geographies, always thinking of the open-ended quality of the "story," and I exhibit its logic. I exhibit the logic of the story/example with a possible modality in mind: oppressive, resistant, reactive, and so on.

I use the modalities to have an edge into the story, but my task is really to enrich, complicate, give texture, and concretize the modalities, making them temporally and spatially concrete. That is accomplished through a multiplicity of stories/ examples into which I look for what makes their logic, for example, a logic of resistance. That is not accomplished by fitting the story into the modality resistance, as a particular fits into a universal. Rather, resistance gives one an edge but getting into the logic of the story requires reaching for what makes the story move in a context at which the story hints. The resistant logic is exhibited, gotten out of the story. Thus, the example always needs to be interpreted; it never stands in our face, showing us anything without intervention. Indeed, part of the methodology of this book is to make clear how and why no slice of "reality" can have a univocal meaning. Unless one begins with a possible movement as what tickles the story on, the story stands in its opacity. Given that one begins with a possible movement, there is a circularity here, as in all logical reasoning — practical reasoning included — but not a vicious one.

The stories not only give texture to the modalities, they also concretize them. The advantage of concretizing is that one does not overdetermine the story to one particular point, in which case the story shows us nothing new. And indeed, what is new is the articulation of what the story revealed through the meanderings and moves of the investigation. The investigation is of complex, concrete, open-ended stories, and the investigation, itself a political act, puts us in a position of intersubjective attention, possibly a dialogical situation. For much of the time, the possibility of dialogue is not something given through transparency of communication. The navigation of the communicative complexities that would make dialogue possible is an aspect of coming to understand the logic of the story.

Indeed, by the logic of the story, I do not mean its point, but its inner works — what thought paths lead where. So, much like the syllogism or the propositional argument, which unfold what is contained in a set of states of belief or desire or in a set of propositions, I seek to unfold the story line, not by exhibiting it in a temporal sequence, but through dwelling in the meanings that one can reveal going in this or that tactical-strategic line. The trick in telling the story lies in revealing its logical intricacies.

Whenever my mother would ask for something, she would say "It is on that thing next to that thing." If you were not in the habit of following her in her moves — maybe that was not what your relation to her asked of you or what you put into it — you would never be able to bring her "that thing." My father was related to her in such a way that not knowing how to follow her in her moves through the cleaning and the cooking and the making of a life for us was to his advantage and part of his patriarchal position. He would not bring her "that thing." For him to risk coming to know was to risk the lack of reciprocity, which was central to the relationship. And he did not risk it.

Late in life when he wanted to spend part of his day "ordering" his own things, things my mother had always ordered for him, my mother saw a threat to her order and her order had served her well. Because he could not follow her into it, she was in that sense, out of his reach. But if you did follow her into her moves, as we kids had to,[10] you could easily get her "that thing." You see, she—someone who was to be unimportant, the perfection of whose makings was to lie in the making not being visible—managed to make herself important and to keep the makings both visible and invisible. "This," "on that," next to it," were stations in her path, she was the pivotal directional subject.

Pilgrimages is, to an important extent, an exploration of the logic of resistance in its multifarious concreteness. I want to dispel any sense that the logic(s)[11] of resistance lies in reaction. To think of the logic(s) of resistance only in terms of reaction is to reduce it in a dangerous way, since reaction does not add anything creative to the meanings contained in that which is resisted, except some form of "no." When resistance is reduced to reaction, it is understood in the physical model and thus as contained in action. But resistance is not reaction but response—thoughtful, often complex, devious, insightful response, insightful into the very intricacies of the structure of what is being resisted.

Thus, it is not sufficient to say that what there is to resistance is what is already contained in oppression plus an excess. That keeps too much of the logic of reaction. The responses do not have that character a great deal of the time. Indeed, there are reactive resistances, but to interpret all resistances as reactive is to go at the investigation with too crude a logical imagination. I am interested in this book in resistance to the interlocking of intermeshed oppressions.[12] Logic is about connection among meanings. In that sense, even though I converse with and have benefited enormously from scholars who work in a variety of disciplines, this is a philosophical investigation.

I have also written each chapter as an exhortation to practice. I believe that the logic of resistance cannot be appreciated and thus cannot be critiqued from outside resistance, without following its logic, which is praxical. I have engaged in rhetorical exploration, giving each piece a layering that shows me where it is located *within* the logic(s) of resistance. One of the pilgrimages here is rhetorical, as it is about learning to write from within resistance rather than about it. Developing that way of writing/reading is one of the paths I/you move through in writing/reading the book. The earlier chapters are very different from the latter ones in this respect, in part because in the earlier chapters I was learning to depart from the tradition of philosophical writing in which I was schooled.[13] But they are also different because the latter writings dwell on movements of resistant intentions at the level of collectivities in formation, while the earlier ones emphasize the movements of resistant intentions between people at closer range, two connecting levels of the political. And there is also an important shift in interlocution.

The earlier chapters are mainly in conversation with contemporary American feminist philosophers, a conversation that has been vital to me. I have conversed with feminist philosophers from inside a heterogeneous collectivity, that of Women of Color. I understood Women of Color to stand for a coalition of differences grounded not in coincidences of individual or group interests but in multiple understandings of oppressions and resistances. That sense of coalition is still very much with me and in many ways it has formed the politics of this book. No one spoke that coalition better than Audre Lorde. I found company in her writings and in the writings of many Chicanas and Asian American, Native American, and African American women. The later chapters evidence a deeper interdisciplinarity. I have particularly benefited from writings on space and coloniality. These conversations have affected the rhetorical experimentation, since there is a greater complexity to the logical strands that I am juggling.

Moving through the Text

I invite you to read the text praxically, in the spirit of disruption, taking up the nonscripted possibilities in the cracks in domination. The intent is not to glorify resistance to oppressions, but rather to understand resistance as adumbrating our possibilities. Taken in that vein, the text is rather dense. Since the text is wordy, Mildred Beltré and I accompany each other, "reading" each other's different expressive modalities and interspersing them on the page, for you to take up as you move.

I have placed the pieces in an order that is in part suggested by my own activist theorizing within particular socialities and levels of meaning. Though the pieces can be read in isolation from each other and in a variety of orders, they articulate with each other. Under the weight of oppression, with little room to maneuver, I attempt to intervene in the conceptual traps that constitute us as oppressed.

In *"Hablando Cara a Cara"* (chapter 1), I enact the difficulties of communication that constitute racism as interactive, dwelling on the very different possibilities of the different terms of an interaction charged with power. As I characterize ethnocentric racism, I inhabit it mockingly, trying out my voices and making clear the presuppositions of understanding them. At the same time, I travel to the other term of the conversation, and meet the ethnocentrist-racist subject and her techniques of incomprehension. I unveil those techniques as self-deprecating. Exercising a poli-vocality in the face of ethnocentric racism in the direction of multiple communicative logics keeps me sensical, as I must search for the sociality of my sense and for the sociality of its muting.

"Structure/Anti-structure and Agency under Oppression" (chapter 2) is my first exploration into oppressed subjectivity and the subjective possibility of liberation. It introduces themes that remain important throughout the book, in their first formulation. There is a timid hint of moving inside plurality as I write, but there is no full inhabitation. In many ways, I remain outside as if producing "descriptions" and suggesting logical shifts that push the descriptive toward the political. The descriptions central to the chapters are related to lives lived under oppression, but I had not found my way into writing from within the oppressing ⇔ resisting tension. Also, as the book develops, the spatio-temporality of plurality is explored from within. The complex spatio-temporalities hinge on the relations between multiplicity and fragmentation. Because intention formation and intention enactment are spatio-temporal, the negotiations of the relation between fragmentation and multiplicity by resistant subjects become central to an understanding of resistant subjectivity.

"Structure/Anti-structure" works in a logic that lacks the complexities revealed by a full recognition of the obscuring of oppressions as intermeshed by the interlocking of oppressions. I came to complicate the logic with which I was working by moving progressively further into writing within the oppressing ⇔ resisting tension and thus also within the sociality of that tension. But the chapter introduces the importance of the relation between intention formation, plurality/multiplicity, and liberation as it argues for a historicized understanding of the multiplicitous subject of liberation. By the end of *Pilgrimages*, the importance of memory in multiplicity is unveiled in its more fully social, if dispersed and uncertain, dimension.

In this Introduction I have discussed the central concepts at work in "Playfulness, 'World'-Traveling, and Loving Perception" (chapter 4). As I introduce the chapter further, I want to think of both my motivation and my relations to other women as woven into the movements performed in this writing. In "Playfulness" I wanted to express the actuality and possibilities of relations among women as nonlinear: women standing on the oppression of other women, women colluding with the reduction of other women, women colluding with the blocking of other women's possibilities, women standing in resistance against those reductions in oneself, women standing with other women making their possibilities.

The lack of linearity quarrels with any clean separation between oppressors and oppressed. In *"Hablando Cara a Cara,"* I am speaking to white/Angla women. In "Boomerang Perception and the Colonizing Gaze" (chapter 7), I am speaking with and to Women of Color. In "Playfulness," I am doing both, but my emphasis is on the sociality of holding on to *my own* possibilities: my possibilities lie in my interdependence in resistance. As I am pained, terrified of ending up someone created by oppression or reduced by the tense inhabitation of oppressive spaces into a hard woman (the warrior face), I come to understand that my possibilities may lie with other women. I want to chisel more nuances into my face. So, playfulness in me, for me, is not a frivolous, disposable quality in me or in my loving. It is at the crux of liberation, both as a process and as something to achieve. I think there is something important in the relation between playfulness and tenderness. I attempt to unravel the connection arguing for a sense of playfulness that is tied to risk: we risk our ground as we prepare our ground, as we stand on a ground that is a crossing.

In "On the Logic of Pluralist Feminism" (chapter 3), I take stock of a deep difference between white/Angla women and Women of Color: Women of Color understand racism as a fully interactive phenomenon, while white/Angla women do not. Here I investigate what happens when we look at racism as an interactive phenomenon *once* reality is understood as multiplicitous *and once* one is accompanied in the navigation of multiple realities by the knowledge of one's company. I argue that in racist interactions, the racist fails to recognize, affirm, and understand the interaction. I offer the recognition and investigation of interaction across barriers of sense and power as necessary in any theorizing that will not simplify, reduce, or contain women's possibilities.

"Hard-to-Handle Anger" (chapter 5) is the first chapter in this book that is fully written *within* reality as multiple. Praxically, it presupposes the other chapters. In it, I open a conceptual space for a reconsideration of anger as a process of transformation. From within an understanding of selves and realities as multiple, it makes sense to ask which self is angry, in what world, and whether the anger is within or across worlds of sense.

I distinguish between communicative and incommunicative angers and first- and second-level angers. I am interested in the transformative and communicative possibilities of anger. The relation between communicative intent and transformation from subordination or oppression is revealed as complex from within multiplicity since intelligibility may contain one away from transformation. It may be that high-pitched anger, anger that pushes against the walls of sense, across domains of sense, has more potential for transformation. But, of course, as intelligibility cannot be presupposed, the intention to communicate cannot be understood as straightforward.

From within hard-to-handle anger, one may adumbrate the poverty of a Habermasian communicative ethics in reaching each other in resistance across worlds of sense. We may be able to be attentive to the emotional echoing of high-pitched anger in resistant communication across worlds of sense. To sustain the act of writing from within conscious multiplicity, I keep up multiple conversations with writers who have focused on the radical possibilities of anger.

In "Purity, Impurity, and Separation" (chapter 6), I draw a distinction between social fragmentation and multiple realities. I engage the ideological erasure of multiplicity through the production of social fragmentation. Fragmentation hides multiplicity. It masks the accomplished movement through permeable groups and identities by poli-vocal subjects in various forms of oppressing ⇔ resisting relations. Social subjects are rendered passive and reduced through exercises in purity. In a valorization of impurity, I call the resistant standing in the way of the production of social fragments "curdling" separation. Curdling separation is a form of solidarity that does not begin or end within the "safety" of communities of the same.

On a personal note, when I was invited to write on separation for an issue of *Signs*, I thought I had nothing to say on the topic that was pro-separation and new. I woke up having dreamed of mayonnaise curdling. Making mayonnaise is one of those tasks urban Argentinian women of my mother's generation delegated to boys and men—all manners of beating foodstuffs. My mother considered me a boy because of my physical prowess and good memory. She never tried to disambiguate me. So my knowing about curdled mayonnaise is one of those knowledges issuing from my ambiguity, my standing in the middle of either/or.

In "Boomerang Perception and the Colonizing Gaze" (chapter 7), I continue the work of traveling between worlds of resistant sense against the grain of social fragmentation. I stand among "people of color" in a coalition-making mood . In resistance to the logic of divide and conquer, men and women subjected through racism have built communities that distrust their own porosity and permeability, their own fuzzy edges. People of color, in its coalition sense, stands against that mistrust. I provide an understanding of its logic. I propose that openness to and inside understanding of the significant variety of resistant logics is not developed in creating a resistant sense of one's own people, those providing homegrown resistant senses of self.

The last three chapters in the book are the most frankly spatial. Movement through space includes the epistemological but also includes the production of spatial continuities and discontinuities and their liberatory and oppressive possibilities. In "The Discontinuous Passing of the *Cachapera/Tortillera* from the Barrio to the Bar to the Movement" (chapter 8), I spatialize the fragmentation of Latina and Latino homoerotic subjects. In this piece, my reflections are about geography, sexuality, and subjectivity in a society where the geographical memory of Latino homoerotic subjects is sharply discontinuous. My intent here is to disturb the complacencies that uphold the fusion of heterosexuality and colonization. I see these complacencies as unwitting or careless or tyrannical collaborations between Latino nationalisms and the contemporary U.S. Lesbian Movement in its various versions and enclaves.

In "Enticements and Dangers of Community and Home for a Radical Politics" (chapter 9), I return to the subject that I addressed in chapter 7, but this time I am more firmly planted against the logic of boundedness. I argue for intercommunalism from the midst of impure subjects, negotiating life transgressing the categorial understandings of a logic of binaries that produces hard-edged, ossified, exclusive groups. I understand the boundedness and isolation of particular groups as a fiction from within the midst of spatio-temporally concrete communities.

To turn that fiction around is one of the directions of affirming impure connections and it is guided by a duplicitous perception that understands the naturalizing of those communities as it sees the social heterogeneity bound, reduced by the fiction of isolation. This not just a question of history, it is also a question of geography, of the social construction of space. The naturalization of space serves to create the illusion of territorial boundedness and isolation; the histories of connected peoples become spatially fragmented. So I argue for the importance of spatial particularity. If the theorizing is from inside the midst of people spatially placed in a spatiality that is produced, the history of that production becomes crucial to an understanding of interrelations. The production of resistant spatiality, the spatiality of intercommunalism can be understood as impure, against the grain of fragmentation and naturalization.

In "Tactical Strategies of the Streetwalker" (chapter 10), I begin to develop a locus for activist theorists, a positionality committed to understanding our liberatory possibilities from within the thickness of body to body engagement at the pedestrian level. This is a locus that necessitates understanding what keeps us locked into the ephemerality of the tactical. It is also a locus that affords understanding the larger than individual perceptual, sensual, gestural capabilities as I → we move against despair.

This theorizing of resistance thus intermingles in the spatiality of the street. This pivoting of the spatiality of cognition radically alters what is conceivable. Done as a pedestrian, *una callejera, en compañía*, in the midst of company, and obliterating the theory/practice distinction, this theorizing seeks out, puts out, entrusts, invokes, rehearses, performs, considers, and enacts tactical-strategic practices of resistant/emancipatory sense making. Performing a rejection of theorizing the social from above, streetwalker theorizing understands and moves resistance to intermeshed oppressions.

The Images by Mildred Beltré

María invited me to make images for this book. In the spirit of friendship and political companionship, I accepted. Using her own vivid visual imagery as a starting point, I created a series of etchings that I feel are of a piece with the writing. These prints are not illustrations for the words in the book. Rather, they are meant to keep the words company and give your eyes and thoughts a different way to move as you go through the text. They are not interpretations of the text that translate in the sense of finding equivalences. They are another way of arriving at/moving meaning.

María and I had many discussions about the different ways of communication (visual, verbal, gestural, tactile), and I feel that our collaboration on this is a continuation of that ongoing discussion. There are themes and visual gestures in the prints that gain momentum and significance when they are viewed as a group within the text and would be lost if each print were viewed individually.

Mildred and María want to upset the authority of words taking our minds/bodies in this or that direction, a determinate direction. Indeed, if the text takes possession of the direction of your thoughts, there is no company, no sociality, no solidarity except one that is obedient. The sociality we would like to elicit is one that responds with its own movements, a sociality that is formed rather than coerced or presupposed. Some of the time, people are more accomplished at taking images rather than words in directions that are not within the logic of obedience, advertising not withstanding. In a praxical vein, we are offering environments that are thickly populated with meaning attempting to entice your resistance to domination.

Notes

1. I use the term "praxis" here to mark the indissoluble link between theory and practice that I have in mind in this book. I like the word "practice" better, but it is often read without the link to a thoughtful search for connection, for example. The book is written from within praxis in this sense. I don't mean any straightforward connection with what Gramsci called "the philosophy of praxis."

2. I draw this distinction in chapter 10, "Tactical Strategies of the Street-walker."

3. See Lydia Liu (1995) for an understanding of translation that goes against the equivalence presupposition.

4. "Do not get bogged down by the use of fancy terminology, they are trying to impress us into silence." This is an example of "bilanguaging" in Walter Mignolo's usage (Mignolo 2000). "Idoima" is New Mexican Spanish for "language."

5. Much of what I have learned among people, I have learned as a popular educator in the Escuela Popular Norteña.

6. In this project, I reject the tendency to think of any set of behaviors, character and personality traits, desires, and beliefs as constituting a "true" self.

7. Here the "*dérive*" as a method created by the Situationist International may be a useful way of investigating. But of course the *dérive* already transgresses against containment (Knabb 1981).

38 ～ Introduction

8. Throughout the work, Danto uses alternative cultural worlds that are consistently contrasted with the world inhabited by the author of the expression. In some of the examples, particularly in his interpretation of Boltanski's *Purim,* the alternative "cultural location" is not just possible but actual. But in many of the examples, the alternative world is merely possible.

9. In *Methodology of the Oppressed,* Chela Sandoval (2000) explores love in a vein related to my understanding of playfulness.

10. I do not want to suggest here that the "kids" were in a subordinate position and not in collusion with patriarchal oppression. We were all in a patriarchal relation to her but the relations were structurally different. The logic of service is not univocal.

11. I write "logic(s)" this way to capture both the "type" and the many textured concrete logical moves.

12. I explore the distinction between interlocking of oppressions and intermeshed oppressions in chapters 6 ("Purity, Impurity, and Separation"), 9 ("Enticements and Dangers of Community and Home for a Radical Politics") and particularly 10, "Tactical Strategies of the Streetwalker."

13. One can find the traces of conversations with Elizabeth Anscombe, the pragmatists (particularly James and Peirce), Aristotle, and rational moral philosophy (both modern and American twentieth century). I was not schooled in either nineteenth or twentieth century continental philosophy.

References

Danto, Arthur. 1998. *The Wake of Art.* Amsterdam: G + B Arts International.

Guha, Ranahit. 1988. The Prose of Counter-Insurgency. In *Selected Subaltern Studies,* edited by Ranahit Guha and G. C. Spivak, 45–88. New York: Oxford University Press.

Kaplan, Caren. 1994. The Politics of Location as Transnational Feminist Critical Practice. In *Scattered Hegemonies: Postmodernity and Transnational Feminist Practices,* edited by Inderpal Grewal and Caren Kaplan, 137–52. Minneapolis: University of Minnesota Press.

———. 1996. *Questions of Travel.* Durham, NC: Duke University Press.

Knabb, Ken, ed. 1981. *Situationist International Anthology.* Berkeley, Calif.: Bureau of Public Secrets.

Liu, Lydia. 1995. *Translingual Practice: Literature, National Culture, and Translated Modernity — China, 1900-1937.* Palo Alto, Calif.: Stanford University Press.

Mignolo, Walter. 2000. *Local Histories/Global Designs.* Princeton, N.J.: Princeton University Press.

Sandoval, Chela. 2000. *Methodology of the Oppressed*. Minneapolis: University of Minnesota Press.

Turner, Victor. 1974. *Dramas, Fields, and Metaphors*. Ithaca, N.Y.: Cornell University Press.

Wolff, Janet. 1993. On the Road Again: Metaphors of Travel in Cultural Criticism. *Cultural Studies* 7 (2): 224–39.

CHAPTER ONE

~

Hablando Cara a Cara/Speaking Face to Face: An Exploration of Ethnocentric Racism

Esta es escritura hablada cara a cara. This is writing spoken face to face. *Escritura solitaria por falta de compañía que busca solaz en el dialogo.* Writing that is solitary for lack of company and looks for solace in dialogue. *Monólogo extendido hacía afuera y hablado en muchas lenguas.* Monologue spoken outwardly and in tongues.*

Empezaré monologándoles en mi lengua ancestral para hacerle honor, para prepararme y prepararlas a hablar con comprensión† de las dificultades de nuestros diálogos y para recrearlas con el precioso son de una de las lenguas vivas de este país.

La soledad de mi escritura me pesa en la multitud de sus

*Inglés and several varieties of Spanish. If you do not read Spanish, see †.

†*Porque si compartes mis lenguas, entonces comprendes todos los niveles de mi intención.* And if you do not understand my many tongues, you begin to understand why I speak them. It is truly not just to be understood by you. I speak them because I want to point to the possibility of becoming playful in the use of different voices and because I want to point to the possibility of coming to appreciate this playfulness. Here, I exercise this playful practice. The appreciation of my playfulness and its meaning may be realized when the possibility of becoming playful in this way has been collectively realized, when it has become realized by us. It is here to be appreciated or missed and both the appreciation and the missing are significant. The more fully this playfulness is appreciated, the less broken I am to you, the more dimensional I am to you. But I want to exercise my multidimensionality even if you do not appreciate it. To do otherwise would be to engage in self-mutilation, to come to be just the person that you see. To play in this way is then an act of resistance as well as an act of self-affirmation.

significados. *Por eso, porque no quiero estar sola, invocaré a dos hermanas poetizas que me han guiado y acompañado en esta tarea. Marina Rivera, poetiza de Arizona, y Margarita Cota Cárdenas, poetiza de California, me espantaron la soledad de lejos.*

Dice Marina (1977):

> *Quedo solamente yo*
> *persona de en medio*
>
> *que luché en vida color de café*
> *luché en vida color blanco*
> *y me hice fuerte*
> *bastante para decir*
> *no me llamen por la chicana*
> *ni por el chicano*
> *ni por las mujeres*
> *llámenme por mi misma*

Y Margarita (1977):

> *Todas aguantaron*
> *. . . y yo*
>   *yo no quise*
> *no acepté*
>   *. . . no quería que una débil tarde*
> *vieras tus antiguas penas bordadas en mi cara*
>   *. . . yo quise*
>   *. . . volar altísimo*
> *definir mis entrañas*
>   *. . . yo ya no pude*
> *que mis hijas y sus hijas y sus hijas no*
> *dolorosa . . .*
> *di que comprendes*
>   *resucita conmigo*
>   *ya era tiempo*
> *de abortar los mitos*
> *de un solo sentido*

¡Qué bonita la coincidencia que no es azarosa! La relación íntima entre el abortar los mitos de un solo sentido y el romper espejos que nos muestran rotas, despedazadas. We want to be seen unbroken, we want to break cracked mirrors that show us in many separate, *unconnected* fragments.

Soy de la gente de colores, soy mestiza, latina, porteña, indita, mora, criollita, negra. Soy de piel morena y labios color ciruela. Soy vata, mujer, esa. To know me unbroken requires the kind of devotion that makes empathetic and sympathetic thinking possible. I think it is possible for white/Anglo women to think empathetically and sympathetically about those who are harmed seriously by racism and about their lives held in communities where culture flourishes through struggle. But I think that this takes the devotion of friendship. In becoming conscious and critical of the ways of thinking about racism and ethnocentrism, I thought it realistic to reserve sympathetic and empathetic thinking for the rarity of deep friendship. But anyone who is not self-deceiving about racist ethnocentrism can begin to see us unbroken through engaged thinking that takes seriously her own participation in an ethnocentric culture in a racial state. Such thinking requires that she become and think as a self-conscious critical practitioner of her culture and a self-conscious and critical member of the racial state. Furthermore, such thinking is possible because she is a participant in both.

Resucita conmigo y *llámame por mi misma.* Come back to life with me and call me for myself, or don't call me at all.

Racism and Ethnocentrism

To speak another language and another culture are not the same as being racialized. One can be ethnocentric without being racist. The existence of races as the products of racialization presupposes the presence of racism, but the existence of different ethnicities does not presuppose ethnocentrism, even if ethnocentrism is universal. So we should conclude that ethnicity is not the same as race and ethnocentrism is not the same as racism.

Ethnocentrism: the explicit and arrogantly held action-guiding belief that one's culture and cultural ways are superior to others'; or the disrespectful, lazy, arrogant indifference to other cultures that devalues them through not seeing appreciatively *any* culture or cultural ways except one's own when one could do otherwise; or the disrespectful, lazy, arrogant indifference that devalues other cultures through stereotyping them or through nonreflective, self-satisfied acceptance of such stereotypes.

Thus, if I lead you to recognize your own and my ethnicity, I would not yet have led you to recognize that we are differently racialized, that we occupy very different positions in the racial state, and that our ethnicities may be contaminated to some small or maximal degree with racism. But, on the other hand, unless there is a very high degree of assimilation, racism always seems to be accompanied and in part expressed by ethnocentrism.

Investigating collectively one's ethnocentrism and its roots may lead one to locate it in one's racism.

Racism: one's affirmation of, acquiescence to, or lack of recognition of the structures and mechanisms of the racial state; one's lack of awareness of or blindness or indifference to one's being racialized; one's affirmation of or indifference or blindness to the harm that the racial state inflicts on some of its members.[1]

Racist ethnocentrism: ethnocentrism that is expressive of racism.

Hablando Cara a Cara/Speaking Face to Face: Muting and Disengagement

I am thinking about cracked mirrors that reflect us falsely because I want to lead you into the spaces where I explore racist ethnocentrism with white/Anglas or with white-assimilated-to-Anglo women.[2] In this context, bilingualism and biculturalism or multiculturalism are very hard to express because they, as well as the racialization of everyone in the learning space, are muted: our ethnicities and races are muted. Since these mutings are not heard, they are not heard as related. This threefold muting is a central feature of the context of inquiry, one that needs to be overcome collectively simply because so long as it is present, we cannot really hear or speak about what is muted. Within this silence, white/Anglo women can see themselves as simply human or as simply women. I can bring you to your senses *con el tono de mi voz,* with the sound of my — to you — alien voice.

Precisely because thinking about this feature of the context of inquiry collectively presupposes a recognition of it, and because I cannot assume this recognition, I speak to you in tongues. But as I speak in tongues, *me siento separada como por una pared en el presentarme frente a los demás.* As I speak to you in the many incarnations of my native tongue, one of the live tongues of this country, I feel isolated from you as if by a thick wall. *Pero no lo hago para romper la pared, lo hago tan solo para reconocerla.* My intention is not to break the wall down, just to recognize it. This recognition is a first step to an honest understanding of ethnocentric racism and of the connections between the two.

So the central and painful questions for *me* in this encounter become questions of speech: *¿En qué voz,* with which voice, *anclada en qué lugar,* anchored in which place, *para qué y porqué,* why and to what purpose, do I trust myself to you . . . *o acaso juego un juego de,* cat and mouse just for your entertainment . . . *o por el mio?* I ask these questions out loud because they need to be asked. Asking them in this way *demands* recognition and places the burden (?) of answering them *actively* on your and not just on my shoulders.

So we can see that *si pudiera decir todo "derecho viejo,"* if I could say everything straightforwardly, *lo diría mal,* I would be saying it falsely, so I can't, *porque me hace mal,* because it harms me. It harms me to be clean and easy when it is a pretense, a pretense imposed on me because double talk is supposed to be more efficient and more educational than bilingual talk. So, for "our" sake, for the sheer possibility *de un "nosotras,"* I will swallow my tongue *"a medias,"* halfway.

We have begun to see that one cannot think well about racism and ethnocentrism or challenge and reconstruct the racial state or the ethnocentrism in one's culture and in oneself without an awareness of one's ethnicity, or of one's being racialized as well as of the ties between the two. It is one's competence and the competence of the other investigators as inquirers that are at stake. Being unaware of one's own ethnicity and racialization commits the inquirer to adopt a disengaged stance, one from outside the racial state and the ethnocentric culture looking in. *But it is one's culture and one's society that one is looking at.* Such a disengaged inquirer is committed either to dishonest study or to ignore deep meanings and connections to which she has access only as a self-conscious member of the racial state and as a sophisticated practitioner of the culture: she is committed to ethnocentric racism.

Everyone who is racialized is a member of and participant in at least one culture. One's position in the racial state may be maintained by beliefs of cultural superiority or by either active or passive devaluation, erasure, or stereotyping of cultures other than one's own.[3] That is, ethnocentrism may be one of the mechanisms of the racial state. Ethnocentrism may be part of the *ideology* of the racial state. Disengagement as a sanctioned ethnocentric racist strategy works as follows: you do not see me because you do not see yourself and you do not see yourself because you declare yourself outside of culture. But declaring yourself outside of culture is self-deceiving. The deception hides your seeing only through the eyes of your culture. So disengagement is a radical form of passivity toward the ideology of the ethnocentric racial state that privileges the dominant culture as the only culture to "see with" and conceives this seeing as to be done non-self-consciously.

Reading *Drylongso* (Gwaltney 1980), *White over Black* (Jordan 1971), *I Know Why the Caged Bird Sings* (Angelou 1969), *They Called Them Greasers* (De Leon 1983), *The Woman Warrior* (Hong Kingston 1976), *Invisible Man* (Ellison 1963), etc. is not helpful in exploring racism and ethnocentrism *unless* these works are read from this engaged position.[4] When read from the engaged position, these works can help the white/ Angla become self-consciously white/Anglo in the racial and ethnic senses of the words: they can help her unravel the connections between racism, ethnocentrism, white/Anglo self-esteem, polite arrogance, polite condescension, and a troubled sense of responsibility in the face of people of color.

> *Para interrupción, un son:*
> *Todo cada cual con su cada cuala*
> *doblando la espalda o volviendo la cara.*

*Miras en mis ojos y te ves mirada, me
tocas la mano y ya estás tocada.
Si no miras, vata, nunca verás nada.*

Lo Nuestro

Thinking back about the claim that ethnocentrism may be universal, as is sometimes claimed, I think it is worth making a distinction between two phenomena that, because they are expressed similarly, are often taken to exemplify ethnocentrism. I think one of them does not.

"*¡Ay qué linda mi gente (o mi cultura, o mi comunidad, o mi tierra), qué suave, si, la más suave!*""Ah, how beautiful my people (or my culture, or my community, or my land), how beautiful, the most beautiful!" I think this claim is made many times noncomparatively. It is expressive of the centrality that one's people, culture, community, or language have to the subject's sense of self and her web of connections. It expresses her fondness for them. In these cases, the claim does not mean "better than other people's," but "dearer to me than other people's communities, etc., are to me." It is like a mother saying "*¡Qué bella mi niña, la más bella!*" ("How beautiful my child, the most beautiful!") and expressing the centrality of this child in her affection. Many times, similar claims are made comparatively and invidiously, and I think that *only then* are they ethnocentric.

It is worth noticing that I have rarely heard white/Anglos make such claims in the first way, although I have heard similar claims used by white/Anglos to convey the second meaning. Many white/Anglos seem to me disaffected from, or indifferent to, or unaware of, or chauvinistically proud of their culture, people, or communities.

In making this distinction I do not mean to imply that one cannot make judgments about a people, culture, etc. that are not chauvinistic, not ethnocentric, and yet critical. Indeed, becoming aware of racism through an understanding of one's own ethnicity and the extent to which it is expressive of racism presupposes the possibility of making nonethnocentric critical judgments about one's own culture.

But sometimes Third World peoples in this country are ac-

cused of ethnocentrism and chauvinism when we are expressing our fundamental ties to *"lo nuestro."* Keeping this
distinction in mind may result in an undermining of the claim
that ethnocentrism is universal. It may also help white/Anglos
explore their ethnicity. In this exploration, it may be helpful to
see the extent to which white/Anglos do or can make the first
kind of claim. One may be too quick to assume an ethnocentric
interpretation of one's claims and too quick to see the whole
of one's culture and cultural ways as tainted with ethnocentrism. This distinction should be helpful in keeping that tendency in check.

Infantilization of Judgment

I think it is essential that in exploring racism and ethnocentrism, the white/Angla challenge and be challenged in her
own sense of incompetence. So far, I have directed my attention to the particular incompetence that results from the threefold muting mentioned at the beginning of this chapter and
that leads the inquirer, when the muting is not heard, to a disengaged position in the inquiry. I conclude by addressing another source of incompetence in the white/Anglo exploration
of racism and ethnocentrism: infantilization of judgment.

I have encountered this phenomenon so many times and in
so many people of good judgment in other matters that it is
frequently disconcerting: *Se han vuelto como niñas, incapaces
de juzgar, evitando el compromiso, paralizadas en tantos seres
responsables.* They have turned into children, incapable of
judgment, avoiding all commitment except against racism in
the abstract, paralyzed as responsible beings, afraid of hostility and hostile in their fear, wedded to their ignorance and arrogant in their guilty purity of heart.

Infantilization of judgment is a dulling of the ability to read
critically, and with maturity of judgment, those texts and situations in which race and ethnicity are salient. It appears to me
as a flight into a state in which one cannot be critical or responsible: a flight into those characteristics of childhood[5] that
excuse ignorance and confusion, and that appeal to authority.
If the description "child" is an appropriate description of
white/Anglas in the context of racism and ethnocentrism, then

to ascribe responsibility to them for the understanding and undoing of these phenomena is inappropriate. If a child, the white/Angla can be guilty of racism and ethnocentrism innocently, unmarked and untouched in her goodness, confused with good reason, a passive learner because she cannot exercise her judgment with maturity. But, of course, she is not a child. She is an ethnocentric racist.

Infantilization of judgment is a form of ethnocentric racism precisely because it is a self-indulgent denial of one's understanding of one's culture and its expressing racism. One of the features of this denial is the denial that racism is a two-party affair, an interactive phenomenon. In infantilization of judgment, the racist attempts to hide that she understands racism as a participant.

Infantilization is broken if one squarely and respectfully sets the white/Anglo inquirer in the position of seeing herself as a competent practitioner of her culture and a racialized member of the racial state and if one also blocks the possibility of escape into lack of engagement. She cannot then take refuge into incompetence, for this presupposes that racialization and the having of a culture are what happens to others who are not her people and whom she can know only abstractly. One cannot disown one's culture. One can reconstruct it in struggle.

One's experience of time, of movement through space, one's sense of others and of oneself are all culturally formed and informed:

> *Siempre hay tiempo para los amigos.*
> I'll see you next Tuesday
> at 5:15.
> *Vente y tomamos un café y charlamos*
> *mientras plancho la ropa.*
> I'll call you Monday
> evening to let you know for sure
> that I am coming.
> *Ay mujer, te ves triste, ¿te sientes bien?*
> *Me duele mucho la cabeza y*
> *estoy un poco sola y cansada.*
> *Dura la vida, ¿no?*
> Hi, how are you? Fine, and you?
> Fine, thank you.

My suggestions here are directed to breaking down traits in the inquirer that make the inquiry pointless, or an exercise in further domination, and adorn the inquirer with dishonesty.

Ya era tiempo de abortar los mitos de un solo sentido.

[Cota Cárdenas 1977]

Notes

1. We need to produce a theory of the racial state and its mechanisms. So far, the following seems to me true of the racial state:

  i. It produces a classification of people that gives rise to race.
  ii. The classification is not a rational ordering based on any "natural" phenomena.
  iii. The classification is historically variable.
  iv. The classification has a strong normative force in the form of custom or in the form of positive law.
  v. The classification is presupposed (explicitly or not) by many other legal and customary norms.
  vi. The classification imposes on people a false identity and arrogates the power of self-definition, even though the history of the classification may include the search and the hegemonical struggle for identity and self-definition by particular groups.
  vii. The classification is given meaning by particular organizations of social, political, and economic interaction that regulate relations among people who are differently classified.

2. I am thinking of the institutional academic classroom and other intellectual contexts that are predominantly white/Anglo. I also discuss racism and ethnocentrism in predominantly Chicano or Chicana contexts and in contexts that are predominantly peopled by Third World interlocutors. But this chapter is not located in the latter contexts. The understanding of racism and ethnocentrism in the latter contexts proceeds in a very different manner from the one delineated here.

3. When one's position in the racial state is that of a victim of racism, then that position may be partially maintained by beliefs of cultural inferiority or by either active or passive devaluation, erasure, or stereotyping of one's own culture.

4. I chose these texts because at the time of this writing, they have been canonized in the white/Angla bibliography on racism.

5. I use the word "child" here not because I think that young human beings are incapable of judgment, but because young human beings are

alleged to be incapable of judgment *and* because women have been thought to be like children in this respect. Any woman who rejects this attribution but falls into infantilization with respect to racism should be struck by the inconsistency of her stance. (I thank Sarah Hoagland for eliciting this note from me with her criticism of my use of the word "child" to make my point.)

References

Angelou, Maya. 1969. *I Know Why the Caged Bird Sings.* New York: Bantam Books.

Cota-Cárdenas, Margarita. 1977. A una madre de nuestros tiempos, *Noches despertando inconciencias.* Tucson, Ariz.: Scorpion Press.

De Leon, Arnoldo. 1983. *They Called Them Greasers.* Austin: University of Texas Press.

Ellison, Ralph. 1963. *Invisible Man.* New York: Vintage Books.

Gwaltney, J. 1980. *Drylongso: A Self Portrait of Black America.* New York: Random House.

Hong Kingston, Maxine. 1976. *The Woman Warrior.* New York: Vintage Books.

Jordan, Winthrop D. 1971. *White over Black.* Baltimore: Penguin Books.

Rivera, Marina Rivera. 1977. Mestiza: Poema en cinco partes. *Mestiza.* Tucson, Ariz.: Grilled Flowers.

~

CHAPTER TWO

Structure/Anti-structure and Agency under Oppression

I shall begin this exploration into oppressed subjectivity and the subjective possibility of liberation by briefly considering two examples of theories that portray oppression as inescapable *through* the. subjects' joint or separate exercise of their own volition, power, or agency. In neither case am I suggesting that the theorist does not offer also an account of liberation. But I claim that the account of oppression itself leaves the subject trapped inescapably in the oppressive system. The logic of the particular form of oppression leads me to understand it as inescapable.

I. Two Desiderata of Oppression Theory

Marx's alienated laborer (Marx and Engels 1971; Marx 1988), who does not have any control over the means of production, is one example of a systematically oppressed person whose oppression is not escapable through her agency. In the logic of capitalist oppression, proletarians are not free to do anything but sell their labor power. In so doing, they enter a terrain where their labor power belongs to someone else who dictates the terms of its exercise. As labor power is used, what is produced in its consumption becomes hostile to the laborer in the form of capital. Their own productive activity becomes alien to them, since—to put it in Aristotelian terms—the syllogism that ends with the consumption of the laborer's productive activity in production is not their syllogism, but the capitalist's.

The selling of labor power is the end of a syllogism of the proletarian. But this is also a peculiar syllogism, since the alternatives of the worker's choice have been manipulated. Laborers sell their labor power to obtain the means of subsistence that *under capitalism* they cannot obtain except through the alienation of their productive activity. The exercises that end with their alienation are the only exercises of their praxis—their conscious productive activity—open to them and these only further their alienation.

Marx also conveys clearly that proletarians must organize in the workplace against capital. He gives great importance to class struggle and the production of class consciousness. But, given his account of the logic of capitalism, I do not see how that is subjectively possible. I need to understand the subjective mechanisms of its possibility. If class consciousness is to be produced through necessities of particular unstable structures rather than through the subjects' exercises of their agency, such production is uninformative from the point of view advanced here. As produced in part by proletarian subjectivity, class consciousness is mysterious to me. The proletarian joining with other proletarians in class struggle is not countenanced by the logic of class oppression. I do not understand the subjective mechanisms of its production. It is particularly unclear how the self can be unified and contain and express both a liberating and an oppressed consciousness.

In her account of arrogant perception, Marilyn Frye (1983) depicts the arrogation of someone else's substance for one's own projects. The arrogant perceiver in Frye's work is a man. The end of arrogant perception is the "acquisition of the service of others. The means: variations on the same theme of disintegrating an integrated human organism and grafting its substance to oneself" (1983:64–65). In successful arrogant perception,

> The intelligent body ceases to be: intelligence and bodilyness are sundered, unable to ground or defend each other or themselves. Mind and body, thus made separate, are then reconnected, but only indirectly: their interactions and communications now mediated by the man's will and interest. Mind and body can preserve themselves only by subordinating each other to him. [Frye 1983:66]

As depicted, the arrogantly perceived woman cannot be an agent of her own liberation. In both "To Be and Be Seen" and "Separatism and Power" (1983), Frye depicts strategies to end the very oppression that she characterizes in "In and Out of Harm's Way." The logic of separation gives the lesbian—a nonarrogated woman, a woman who is not for men—agency. As the lesbian sees the woman from outside the logic of arrogation, she sees her as separate from men. But, given the logic of arrogation, it is unclear how it is possible for the arrogated woman to say "no" and separate, nor how the lesbian can be in her. The lesbian as the "outsider" changes the woman's self-perception because she is being seen as someone who is not arrogated. But how can the woman see the lesbian and see the lesbian seeing her?

It is a desideratum of oppression theory that it portray oppression in its full force, as inescapable, if that is its full force. I shall not critique Marx's account of class oppression or Frye's account of sexist oppression because they depict these forms of oppression as inescapable. I think much of the explanatory power of these theories of oppression resides in their depiction of the oppressions as inescapable.

But I also consider it a desideratum of oppression theory that the theory be liberatory. The ontological or metaphysical possibility of liberation remains to be argued, explained, uncovered. If oppression theory is not liberatory, it is useless from the point of view of the oppressed person. It is discouraging, demoralizing.

So, I recommend contradictory desiderata for oppression theory, desiderata that are in both logical and psychological tension. This recommendation, as well as the ontological possibility of liberation, depends on embracing ontological pluralism. Ontological pluralism is suggested by many oppression theorists. Nancy Hartsock's (1983) understanding of Marx as proposing different levels of reality that are both "real" suggests ontological pluralism; Frye's (1983) account of the lesbian and of the woman where the lesbian is also a woman suggests ontological pluralism; Sandra Bartky's (1977) concept of "double ontological shock" and Sarah Hoagland's (1982) account of femininity as resistance suggest ontological pluralism. Ontological pluralism is suggested vividly by theories of racial oppression presented by men and women of color: think of Ralph Ellison's *Invisible Man* (1972) and Gloria Anzaldúa's *Borderlands/La Frontera* (1987) as examples.

II. The Practical Syllogism

I understand the practical syllogism, as Aristotle understood it in *Nicomachean Ethics*, as reasoning that ends in action, not as propositions that entail other propositions. Because I am interested in oppression, I begin by paying attention to Aristotle's account of the slave keeping the practical syllogism in mind. Aristotle makes it clear that the slave can only obey or follow orders, but cannot reason his own syllogism. The master reasons and the slave does. For that reason, it is difficult to imagine the slave after working hours except as an animal: resting, eating, roaming around, copulating. But these are not human acts when performed by the after-hours slave since they are not acts that are the end of practical syllogisms and only these are open to the kind of evaluation that Aristotle offers when he talks of practical wisdom and moral virtue.

There is an interesting similarity and dissimilarity between the slave's action in relation to the practical syllogism and the action of the arrogantly perceived woman in relation to the practical syllogism. The act of arrogating someone's substance ends the possibility of the subject's giving a practical syllogism that she can put into action and is not severely affected by the practical syllogism of the arrogant perceiver.

Two practical syllogisms enter into actions performed by women who are successfully arrogantly perceived: hers and his. There is no denial here that the woman can engage in practical reasoning. But because she can, the alternatives from which she can choose and thus her conception of her well-being at the moment of action must be altered, manipulated. She then "chooses" between alternatives that she would not have chosen except for the arrogant perceiver's mediation. Once the arrogant perceiver manipulates her alternatives, she proceeds to reason practically and she chooses the alternative the arrogant perceiver wants her to choose. So, the effect is the same as in the case of the slave. But for there to be that coincidence, since the woman does reason practically, he has to eliminate choices that could not be "mediated by his will and interest" — for example, lesbian choices, loving perceivers' choices. In a world tightly and inescapably structured by arrogant perception, lesbian reasoning, woman-loving reasoning, lacks authority or is impossible.

I am interested in the practical syllogism as explaining action or failure to act in the case of oppressed persons. I am interested in the formation of intentions, in the blocking between intention and action and in the production of what I shall call "subservient" or "servile" syllogisms, of which the syllogism of the arrogantly perceived woman is an example. I am also interested in the open-endedness of oppressed persons' acting in terms of appropriate practical syllogisms, given the context(s) or background(s) of the acting. This open-endedness is possible because the self is not unified but plural.

III. Pluralism

I give up the claim that the subject is unified. Instead, I understand each person as many. In giving up the unified self, I am guided by the experiences of bicultural people who are also victims of ethnocentric racism in a society that has one of those cultures as subordinate and the other as dominant. These cases provide me with examples of people who are very familiar with experiencing themselves as more than one: having desires, character, and personality traits that are different in one reality than in the other, and acting, enacting, animating their bodies, having thoughts, feeling the emotions, in ways that are different in one reality than in the other. The practical syllogisms that they go through in one reality are not possible for them in the other, given that they are such different people in the two realities, given that the realities hold such different possibilities for them. If one can remember the intentions of the person one is in the other world and tries to enact them in the other, one can see that many times one cannot do so because the action does not have any meaning or has a very different sort of meaning than the one it has in the other reality.

It is very important whether one remembers or not being another person in another reality. In that case, of course, one has first-person memories of that person in the other reality. There are lots of reasons why one may not remember. In the case of people who dominate others, they may not remember the persons they are in the reality of the dominated. For example, many times people act in front of their maids as if there were no one in the room. They say things and behave in ways that one can imagine are said or done only in private. When people behave this way, they do not see themselves as the maid sees them and they do not want to remember or recognize the persons who are seen by the maids, of whom the maids are witnesses. The maids can testify only in the world of the dominated, the only world where that testimony is understood and recognized. There are many reasons why the employers do not remember themselves as maids know them. One of these reasons concerns their own sense of moral integrity since, as they are witnessed by the maids, they lack it. So a phenomenon such as self-deception becomes very important in this way of seeing things in ontological pluralism.

The relation between the practical syllogism and the rejection of the "each person is one" claim is complex. At least some of the syllogisms of the different person one is in one world will be different in kind from those in another world: they may be servile syllogisms, or syllogisms that have intentions that cannot be understood in the world in which they are being put into action. One can see that the very same person may remember herself in another reality and thus be able to form practical syllogisms that have intentions that the person she is in another reality would have. But, of course, her actions would not be visible or heard or understood in the reality in which she performs them in that case. That is the meaning of invisibility. That is why it is connected to responsibility. Visibility, faithful intelligibility, are necessary conditions for responsibility. In the reality in which the person is functioning, the person is not thought of, and it is hard for that person to animate herself as a person capable of practical syllogisms that are not subservient to the syllogisms of her dominator.

So, the liberatory experience lies in this memory, on these many people one is who have intentions one understands because one is fluent in several "cultures," "worlds," realities. The liberatory possibility lies in resistant readings of history that reveal unified historical lines as enacting dominations through both linearity and erasure. One understands oneself in every world in which one remembers oneself to the extent that one understands that world. This is a strong sense of personal identity, politically and morally strong. The task of remembering one's many selves is a difficult liberatory task. One may indeed inhabit a world and a self one fails to recognize as oneself because one has no understanding of that world. It may be that in that world one is familiar to others but not to oneself. Self-deception and mystification are among the many forms of control of our memory of our other selves. All oppressive control is violent because it attempts to erase selves that we are that are dangerous to the maintenance of domination over us.

But one may also inhabit the limen, the place in between realities, a gap "between and betwixt" universes of sense that construe social life and persons differently, an interstice from where one can most clearly stand critically toward different structures. Other worlds provide one with syllogisms that one can attempt to make actual in the worlds in which one is oppressed, given one's critical understanding of each world. The critical understanding is made possible, in part, by the going into the limen when one "travels" to the other worlds. The limen is the place where one becomes most fully aware of one's multiplicity.

My sense is that one of the factors that makes oppression inescapable in many theories that portray oppression as inescapable is the inability to form liberatory syllogisms in the world of the oppressor, given the logic of oppression. It is also my sense that the limen is a place where one can form liberatory syllogisms. But many of the syllogisms formed in the limen that would inform the fabric of everyday life cannot be completed. So one will have very good reason to attempt to understand why the syllogisms cannot be completed and attempt to correct what blocks action. So, the connection between the practical syllogism, ontological plurality, and liberatory oppression theory lies in the fact that the oppressed know themselves in realities in which they are able to form intentions that are not among the alternatives that are possible in the world in which they are brutalized and oppressed.

IV. Structure and Anti-structure

Victor Turner (1974) uses the distinction between structure and anti-structure to study pilgrimage. He borrows the term "structure" and its definition from Robert Merton, who uses the term for "patterned arrangements of role-sets, status sets and status sequences consciously recognized and regularly operative in a given society and closely bound up with legal and political norms and sanctions" (Turner 1974:237).

Although structures are not closed, ordinary life presents structures as systematic, complete, coherent, closed socio-political-economic institutions or normative systems that construe persons. Structures construct or constitute persons not just in the sense of giving them a facade, but also in the sense of giving them emotions, beliefs, norms, desires, and intentions that are their own. That is, the person does not just wear a mask, but that person is the person who the structure constructs. Even the experience of putting on a mask or enacting a role is structure dependent. The husband putting on his physician's coat does not move on to another structure even if he feels that, as he is putting on the coat, he is "changing faces," changing roles. Both roles occur within the same structure, and are articulated, connected in the same structure. I disagree in this respect with Turner's understanding of the person within a structure as a persona, a role mask, not "the unique individual" (Turner 1974:237). Turner seems to me to commit himself unnecessarily to a transcendental self that "plays the roles," puts on the masks but is distinguishable from them.

Anti-structure is characterized by Turner as constituted by liminality and communitas (Turner 1974:202). Liminality is a term that was introduced by the anthropologist Van Gennep in his study of rites of passage, and Turner analyzes and uses it in the study of pilgrimage. It is the phase between separation and reaggregation in transition rites (Turner 1974:231), the moment when the initiand is "betwixt and between successive lodgments in jural political systems" (Turner 1974:13). "In this interim of liminality, the possibility exists of standing aside not only from one's own social position but from all social positions and of formulating unlimited series of social arrangements" (Turner 1974:14). In the liminal phase, there are no structural descriptions, so the liminal subject does not stand with respect to others in the limen as in a hierarchy. "In liminality, the symbolism almost everywhere indicates that the initiand, novice, neophyte is structurally if not physically invisible in terms of his culture's standard definitions and classifications" (Turner 1974:232). The experience of victims of ethnocentric racism of moving across realities, of being different in each, and of reasoning practically differently in each, can be understood as liminal. To do so is to understand its liberatory potential because, when the limen is understood as a social state, it contains both the multiplicity of the self and the possibility of structural critique. Both are important components of the subjective possibility of liberation. I think that to experience oneself in the limen is significantly to experience oneself as multiple. As such, liminality is threatening to any world or any aspect of a world that requires unification, either psychologically, morally, politically, or metaphysically.

What I find interesting and helpful in Turner is both that he describes experiences that are of a piece with the experience of victims of ethnocentric racism and that he claims that liminal states are social states, just as much as structural states are.

If we use the concept of structure and anti-structure,

and understand structure as construing real persons and not just the masks of persons,

and we acknowledge that there is more than one structure in which the in-some-sense the same person lives,

and we acknowledge that people can go in-between structures, *and* that it is possible to be without structure and thus without structural construction,

then we do not have to appeal to the ahistorical, acultural, asexual, without race or gender, without a system of production within which her productive activity has meaning transcendental to ego in order to understand liberation from oppression.

We also succeed in offering a noncontradictory account of the escape from inescapable oppression.

Seeing structural invisibility as an important aspect of liminality makes clear why victims of ethnocentric racism are never seen as liminal subjects. But, of course, that the liminal state is structurally invisible does not necessitate that liminal states not be sociohistorical states. The social transcends the structural without metaphysical transcendence. The historical subject is multiplicitous and sometimes liminal.

Liminality is also of a piece with my account of the multiplicitous person reasoning practically within and across worlds. But if multiplicitous persons reason within and across worlds, one need not see a person at any one point as offering or enacting or intending just any *one* practical syllogism. The practical syllogisms may be many and thus her acting may be completely ambiguous. It may be that, at the same time, she is acting in accordance with the norms of one reality, one structure, and acting with the norms of another reality, or in accordance with the possibilities that lack of structure bring up for her. This is what I see as useful for liberatory theory in Turner's insight that anti-structure is social. A thoroughgoing critique of one's own situation may be a part of or inform one's practical syllogism, and that may be possible because of a structural gap and because one remembers oneself in the anti-structure.

But, of course, merely remembering ourselves in other worlds and coming to understand ourselves as multiplicitous is not enough for liberation: collective struggle in the reconstruction and transformation of structures is fundamental. But this collective practice is born of dialogue among multiplicitous persons who are faithful witnesses of themselves and also testify to, and uncover the multiplicity of, their oppressors and the techniques of oppression afforded by ignoring that multiplicity.

References

Anzaldúa, Gloria. 1987. *Borderlands/La Frontera*. San Francisco: Spinsters/Aunt Lute.

Bartky, Sandra. 1977. Toward a Phenomenology of a Feminist Consciousness. In *Feminism and Philosophy*, edited by Mary Vetterling-Braggin, Frederick A. Elliston, and James English, 22–34. Totowa, N.J.: Littlefield, Adams & Co..

Ellison, Ralph. 1973. *Invisible Man*. New York: Vintage.

Frye, Marilyn. 1983. *The Politics of Reality*. New York: Crossing Press.

Hartsock, Nancy. 1983. The Feminist Standpoint: Developing the Ground for a Specifically Feminist Historical Materialism. In *Discovering Reality*, edited by Sandra Harding and Merrill Hintikka, 283–310. Boston: Reidel.

Hoagland, Sarah. 1982. Femininity, Resistance and Sabotage. In *Femininity, Masculinity & Androgyny: A Modern Philosophical Discussion*, edited by Mary Vetterling Braggin, 85–99. Savage, Md.: Rowman & Littlefield.

Marx, Karl. 1988. *The Economic and Philosophic Manuscripts of 1844*. Amherst, N.Y.: Prometheus Books.

Marx, Karl, and Frederick Engels. 1971. *German Ideology*. New York: International Publishers.

Turner, Victor. 1974. *Dramas, Fields, and Metaphors*. Ithaca, N.Y.: Cornell.

CHAPTER THREE

~~~

On the Logic of Pluralist Feminism

This is written from a dark place: a place where I see white/
Angla women as "on the other side," on "the light side." It is
written from a dark place where I see myself dark but do not
focus on or dwell inside the darkness but rather focus on "the
other side."

To me, it makes a deep difference where I am writing from.
It makes a profound difference whether I am writing from the
place of our possibilities as companions in play or from the
place "in between," the place of pilgrimage, of liminality; from
the place of resistance, the place "within," or from across "the
other side," where light and dark are highlighted.

I inhabit the place from across "the other side" with anger,
pain, urgency, a sense of being trapped, pounding the walls
with a speech that hurts my own ears. It is from across "the
other side" that I want to explore the logic of pluralist feminism.

I am rereading Lorraine Bethel's (1979) "What Chou Mean
We, White Girl?" and June Jordan's (1980) "Where Is the
Love?" ten years after their publication. A layering of voices
of women of color comes to my mind, crowding my thinking
space: voices that I have heard keenly, attended to with the
gladness that fills one when one learns really good news,
voices that have accompanied me sweetly. The voices all
speak this knowledge to me: One just does not go around
alone (lonely maybe), but not individual-style alone making
or remaking anything, ignoring the relations one has, the ones
one does not have, the good about the good ones, the bad
about the bad ones and the good ones. To know oneself and

65

one's situation is to know one's company or lack thereof, is to know oneself with or against others.

I want to surround you with some of the voices that commit me to this knowledge and ask you to keep them with you as I explain the difference that lacking this knowledge makes while theorizing. When Audre Lorde (1984) tells us that "interdependency between women is the only way to the freedom which allows the 'I' to 'be,' not in order to be used, but in order to be creative" (Lorde 1984:111), she is offering us her visionary turn on this knowledge. Interdependency between women is the being with others that is necessary if we are to remake ourselves into active, creative selves. Lorde knows the company she wants to keep and why.

Lorraine Bethel (1979:86) also knows the company she wants to keep, what comes from keeping this or that company, who she wants to be, and how that is related to the company she keeps. Bethel says:

I am so tired of talking to others
translating my life for the deaf, the blind,
. . . while we wonder where the next meal, job, payment on our
    college loans and other bills,
apartment, the *first* car, Black woman-identified bookstore,
    health center, magazine,
bar, record company, newspaper, press, forty acres and a mule, or
    national conference
are going to come from.
They will come from us loving/speaking *to* our Black Third
    World sisters, not *at* white women.

In a calm refusal to assimilate, Ines Hernandez Tovar (1977) tells us about patient, painstaking, interactive self-knowledge and self-affirmation. She tells us of the creation of a reality that is good to the self that is interactively known and affirmed. She says,

And we will take our time
to make our time
count
clocks
do not intimidate us.

She speaks of a collective action, a patient action ("*we* will take *our* time"). It is an act of collective creation ("to *make* our time"). The act of collective creation is performed within another reality, and it is the collective creation of a reality where *we* count.

June Jordan's (1980:176) understanding of anyone's "life supportive possibilities" is highly interactive. She says:

> And it is against such sorrow, and it is against such deliberated strangulation of the possible lives of women, of my sisters, and of powerless peoples — men and children — everywhere, that I work and live, now, as a feminist trusting that I will learn to love myself well enough to love you (whoever you are), well enough so that you will love me well enough so that we will know, exactly, where is the love.

Genny Lim (1981:25) knows woman as a "house with echoing rooms" only through this knowledge: the knowledge of one's company:

Sometimes I stare longingly at women who I will never know
Generous, laughing women with wrinkled cheeks and white teeth
Dragging along chubby, rosy-cheeked babies on fat, wobbly legs
Sometimes I stare at Chinese grandmothers
getting on the 30 Stockton with shopping bags
Japanese women tourists in European hats
Middle-aged mothers with laundry carts
Young wives holding hands with their husbands
Lesbian women holding hands in coffee-houses
Smiling debutantes with bouquets of yellow daffodils
Silver-haired matrons with silver rhinestoned poodles
Painted prostitutes posing along MacArthur Boulevard
Giddy teenage girls snapping gum in fast cars
Widows clutching bibles, crucifixes

I look at them and wonder if
They are a part of me
I look in their eyes and wonder if
They share my dreams.

What U.S. women of color know is something that I want to find in feminist theorizing. To make clearer what it is that we know and what difference it makes in theorizing, I will take us back to Bethel's question "What Chou Mean *We,* White Girl?" I will take you through my understanding of white/ Angla feminist theorists' answers to it. In doing so, I want to see if I can answer three questions: What is the "problem of difference"? How do we theorize once we recognize "the problem of difference"? And does the "problem of difference" affect only some feminist theorizing? I hope that this chapter will make clear that the logic of all theorizing is affected by a recognition of difference. This is one of the lessons uncovered by the knowledge of women of color, the knowledge of one's company. If I am right, it is not just those who theorize about difference who need to worry about it when theorizing. Difference makes the kind of difference that makes inappropriate the theoretical division of labor between those of us who work on difference and those of us who don't.

White women used to simply and straightforwardly ignore difference. In their theorizing, they used to speak as if all women *as women* were the same. Now they recognize the problem of difference. Whether they *recognize* difference is another matter. As white women are beginning to acknowledge the problem in their theorizing, it is interesting to see that the acknowledgment is a noninteractive one, or at least there is no clear emphasis on interactive acknowledgment. I hope this claim will become clearer. If the acknowledgment is noninteractive, the knowledge that I want to see in feminist theorizing is missing.

The initial claim seems to be that "there are many ways of being, but we can still theorize about women if we acknowledge in some way or other that not everything we say is true of all women." One way of doing this is through the disclaimer. When I read theories about mothering, constructions of the moral domain, constructions of the self, and so on, that are prefaced by disclaimers about the universality of the theoretical claims, I am at sea as to whether I am to take what I am reading as anthropological or sociological field reports. After the disclaimer, nothing again indicates that difference has been recognized. The logic of the discourse emphasizes ignoring difference and acknowledging a singularity of practice, discipline, or construction.

One such disclaimer puts it interestingly, and I choose it not because what I have to say applies only to this author, but because the way the author puts the disclaimer captures the situation so well. The author announces that she is working within "the limits of her own particular social and sexual history" (Ruddick 1984:215). The disclaimer leaves the reader either within or without these limits. From within these limits, everything seems complete and rounded, the discourse gentle and comfortingly safe. From without these limits, the theoretical construction appears dangerous. The responsibility for corrections, Ruddick tells us, is left to the reader or interlocutor who is outside these limits, as if the logic of correcting views from outside these limits were clear. So, the disclaimer just serves as an announcement that the author will not accept responsibility for the effects of her own particular "social and sexual history" on others.

Most of the time what the theory proposes is not just a description of a particular practice or a particular construction or reconstruction of people. Most of the time a prescription is included. But a prescription *for whom*? How is one who lies outside the limits to correct the prescription? How is one to tell that the discourse that produced this prescription is friendly to oneself? Who is the author in her own eyes with respect to us? Who is the author in our eyes? Who are we in the author's eyes? Why does the author think that all we need to do is to correct the prescription? Why does the author just leave us to write another paper on the subject, but one that is *dependent* on hers even though she does not really acknowledge us? Why does she think she is justified in doing that? Why doesn't she realize that what she is doing is exercising authority and that the authority she would exercise, if we are not careful, is *authority over* us?

I hope it is becoming clearer to you that what I think is significantly missing in much of the work that attempts to acknowledge difference is the *interactive* step. I began by pointing out to you how much difference exists between the work of U.S. women of color and the work of white women in this respect. U.S. women of color know we are different, we have never attempted to tell white women that women are all alike, we have not had the imperialist eye. U.S. women of color have always had an interactive emphasis in our interest in difference: we recognize racism and racism is an *interactive* phenomenon. At the international level, *cultural and economic imperialism* are the interactive phenomena. I think the two are quite different. Among other things, it is possible not to quite notice cultural imperialism when you are a victim of it, because it is so impersonal. There is no person-to-person mistreatment to make it clear that one is about to be erased from the discourse by being asked to speak in or to listen to a universal voice.

There are other interactions where difference plays a significant part. I think they all need to be thought about *in their own right.* These interactions cannot be conflated and confused with each other under the label "difference." What interests many U.S. women of color is the formation of a feminism that overcomes racism, and racism is an emphatically interactive phenomenon that includes face-to-face interaction. Our interest in theorizing is importantly guided by this concern.

In hearing the "What Chou Mean *We,* White Girl?" question, white/Angla women theorists did not really hear an interactive demand, a demand for an answer. Looking at the resulting theoretical responses, it seems to me that what they heard was a radical attack on the activity of white women theorizing. This attack seemed justified to them, but it also seemed to them to undermine fundamentally the possibility of any theorizing to the extent that theorizing requires generalization. I think that this interpretation of the question generated the "problem of difference." In hearing the "What Chou Mean *We,* White Girl?" question and in uttering our many versions of it, U.S. women of color heard and uttered an attack on white racism: racist feminism does not see the violence done to women of color in denying that we are women or in requiring (the alternative is conceptually forced on us) that we assimilate if we are to be women at all. I think the difference in emphasis is significant. I think the logic of the difference in emphasis is theoretically significant.

What is the theoretical significance of the difference in understandings of the question? And why did white/Angla feminist theorists hear the demand for an answer in this way? I think that racism played and plays tricks on white women theorists who theorize about difference or who theorize and are aware that they should attempt to overcome the alleged problem of difference in their theorizing. I hope to answer both of these questions by describing these tricks. I have chosen not to exhibit the tricks in particular cases because I want to remain "outside the limits."

In saying that racism plays tricks on white women theorists, I mean not only the contextual racism in which they theorize but also the racism within, *the one from which they theorize.* So, the racism and the theorist are not separable just as the theorist and the context of theorizing are not quite separable.

To prepare the ground, I will begin by describing a trick that predates hearing the "What Chou Mean *We,* White Girl?" question. This trick is easy to describe, and it is familiar to most women theorizing about women: Women of color always knew that white women and women of color were different; white women all knew that they were different from women of color. But white women never considered the differences important, because they did not really *notice* us. So they theorized as if all women were the same. One can try to explain away this lack of noticing in many ways related to the received methodologies, but if white women theorists had noticed us, they would have rejected the methodologies. There are, of course, many reasons for this failure to notice us, but they all seem constitutive of racism. Elizabeth Spelman's work is remarkable among white feminist theorists in uncovering the many faces of feminist racism's resilience in this respect. "I look at you" Spelman (1988:12) says, "and come right back to myself. White children in the U.S. got early training in boomerang perception when they were told by well-meaning white adults that Black people were just like us—never, however, that we were just like Blacks."

The second trick that racism played/plays on white women theorists is conceiving this lack of noticing us as a theoretical problem, which they have labeled the "problem of difference." This is a more complicated trick. Notice that many white women theorists have heard the "What Chou Mean *We,* White Girl?" loud and clear and are attempting to *interpret* the question and find an answer to it. But white women theorists seem to have worried more passionately about the harm the claim does to theorizing than about the harm the theorizing did to women of color. I say this because even when they heard this claim, they did not notice us. Thus, white theorists interpreting the question saw a problem with the way they were theorizing: The "problem of difference" refers to feminist theories — these theories are the center of concern. So, the attempted solutions to the "problem of difference" try to rescue feminist theorizing from several possible pitfalls that would render it false, trivial, weak, and so on. The focus of the solutions is on how to generalize without being guilty of false inclusion. The solutions seem incorrect to me because they are addressing the wrong problem.

But the white theorist has been and is also tricked by racism in another way that accompanies the second trick. The white woman theorist did not notice us yet, her interpretation of the question placed the emphasis on theorizing itself, and the generalizing and theorizing impulse led the white theorist to *think of all differences as the same,* that is, as underminers of the truth, force, or scope of their theories. Here, racism has lost its character and particular importance — a clear sign that we have not been noticed. This trick does not allow the theorist to see, for example, the need to differentiate among racism, colonialism, and imperialism, three very different interactive phenomena.

But what would it be to be noticed? We are noticed when you realize that we are mirrors in which you can see yourselves as no other mirror shows you. When you see us without boomerang perception, to use Spelman's wonderful phrase. It is not that we are the only faithful mirrors, but I think we *are* faithful mirrors. Not that we show you as you *really* are; we just show you as one of the people you are. What we reveal to you is that you are many — something that may in itself be frightening to you. But the self we reveal to you is also one that you are not eager to know, for reasons that one may conjecture.

You block identification with that self because it is not quite consistent with your image of yourself. As Marilyn Frye puts it in "White Woman Feminist": "Whitely people have a staggering faith in their own rightness and goodness, and that of other whitely people" (Frye 1992:154). But you do not expect us to show a self that is good, decent, sensitive, and careful in your attending to others. You block identification because remembering that self fractures you into more than one person. You know a self that is decent and good, and knowing your self in our mirror frightens you with losing your center, your integrity, your oneness.

You block identification with that self because that person you are is also a mirror for us and that person constructs us as people whose standpoint you find disquieting: angry phantoms or pliable puppets. But whether phantoms or puppets, we are beings whose rules cannot be yours because your rules are used against us.

You block identification with that self we mirror for you because knowing us in the way necessary for you to know that self requires self-conscious interaction. Your fear of duplicity directs you to forget all interaction that we have had because that interaction, when lived and remembered as interaction, reveals yourself to yourself as a duplicitous being. So you are inattentive to our interactions. You are not keenly attentive to what our interactions might reveal.

You block identification with that self because knowing us in the way necessary to know that self would reveal to you that we are also more than one and that not all the selves we are make you important. Some of them are quite independent of you. Being central, being a being in the foreground, is important to your being integrated as one responsible decision maker. Your sense of responsibility and decision-making capacity are tied to being able to say exactly who it is that did what, and that person must be one and have a will in good working order. And you are very keen on seeing yourself as a decision maker, a responsible being: It gives you substance.

You block identification with that self because you are afraid of plurality: Plurality speaks to you of a world whose logic is unknown to you and that you inhabit unwillingly. It is a world inhabited by beings who cannot be understood given your ordinary notions of responsibility, intentionality, voluntariness, precisely because those notions presuppose that each person is one and that each person (unless mad or in a mad-like state or under someone's power) can effectively inform her actions with preferred descriptions that include intentionality, and do so all by herself. All other ways of being are outside value, outside worth, outside goodness, outside intelligibility.

In blocking identification with that self, you block identification with us and in blocking identification with us, you block identification with that self. You are in part what we make you up to be, and we are in part what you make us up to be. You may not "identify" with that self, but you can't help animating it. You may not want to think about that self, but not thinking about that self leads you not to know what U.S. women of color know: that self-knowledge is interactive, that self-change is interactive. You cannot shake that self and you cannot infuse that self with the trappings of responsibility. But you can acknowledge her and imbue her fully with ambiguity. We can't shake the selves that we are in your eyes or in your worlds; we do not just animate them *in spite* of ourselves. We are them, too: beings with a peculiar lack of substance or lack of credibility, or too frightening and intimidating, too dramatic, too predictable, with too much or too little authority: all out of proportion, not fully real. I can't will not to animate that being. That's not up to me. But I can imbue that being with ambiguity; I can imbue myself with ambiguity. In doing that, I can thereby enact a creative strategy of resistance only when ambiguity is understood and appreciated.

When I do not see plurality stressed in the very structure of a theory, I know that I will have to do lots of acrobatics—like a contortionist or tight-rope walker—to have this theory speak to me without allowing the theory to distort me *in my complexity.*

When I do not see plurality in the very structure of a theory, I see the phantom that I am in your eyes take grotesque forms and mime crudely and heavily your own image. Don't you?

When I do not see plurality in the very structure of a theory, I see the fool that I am mimicking your image for the pleasure of noticing that you know no better. Don't you?

When I do not see plurality in the very structure of a theory, I see the woman of color that I am speaking precisely and seriously in calm anger as if trying to shatter thick layers of deafness accompanied by a clean sense of my own absurdity. Don't you?

When I do not see plurality in the very structure of a theory, I see myself in my all-*raza* women's group in the church basement in Arroyo Seco, Nuevo Mexico, suddenly struck dumb, the theoretical words asphyxiating me. Don't you?

When you do not see plurality in the very structure of a theory, what do you see?

References

Bethel, Lorraine. 1979. What Chou Mean *We,* White Girl? Conditions: Five 11(2):86–92.

Frye, Marilyn. 1992. *Willful Virgin.* Freedom, Calif.: The Crossing Press.

Hernandez Tovar, Ines. 1977. On Hearing UT Football Fans on the Drag. *Ta Cincho.*

Jordan, June. [1980] 1990. Where Is the Love? In *Making Face, Making Soul*/Haciendo Caras: *Creative and Critical Perspectives by Women of Color,* edited by Gloria Anzaldúa, 174–76. San Francisco: Aunt Lute.

Lim, Genny. 1981. Wonder Woman. In *This Bridge Called My Back: Writings by Radical Women of Color,* edited by Cherrie Moraga and Gloria Anzaldúa. New York: Kitchen Table/Women of Color Press.

Lorde, Audre. 1984. The Master's Tools Will Never Dismantle the Master's House. In *Sister/Outsider: Essays and Speeches*, 110–13. Trumansburg, N.Y.: Crossing Press.

Ruddick, Sara. 1984. Maternal Thinking. In *Mothering: Essays in Feminist Theory,* edited by Joyce Trebilcot, 213–30. Totowa, N.J.: Rowman and Allanheld.

Spelman, Elizabeth V. 1988. *Inessential Woman: Problems of Exclusion in Feminist Thought.* Boston: Beacon.

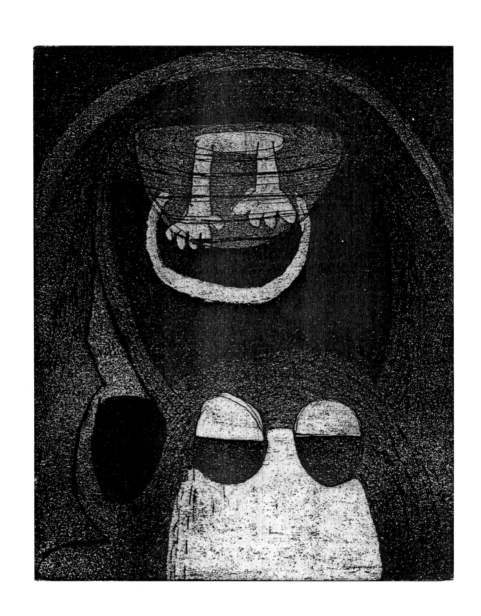

~

CHAPTER FOUR

Playfulness, "World"-Traveling, and Loving Perception

This chapter weaves two aspects of life together. My coming to consciousness as a daughter and my coming to consciousness as a woman of color have made this weaving possible. This weaving reveals the possibility and complexity of a pluralistic feminism, a feminism that affirms the plurality in each of us and among us as richness and as central to feminist ontology and epistemology.

The chapter describes the experience of "outsiders" to the mainstream of, for example, white/Anglo organization of life in the United States and stresses a particular feature of the outsider's existence: the outsider has necessarily acquired flexibility in shifting from the mainstream construction of life where she is constructed as an outsider to other constructions of life where she is more or less "at home." This flexibility is necessary for the outsider. It is required by the logic of oppression. But it can also be exercised resistantly by the outsider or by those who are at ease in the mainstream. I recommend this resistant exercise that I call "world"-traveling and I also recommend that the exercise be animated by an attitude that I describe as playful.

As outsiders to the mainstream, women of color in the United States practice "world"-traveling, mostly out of necessity. I affirm this practice as a skillful, creative, rich, enriching, and, given certain circumstances, loving way of being and living. I recognize that much of our traveling is done unwillingly to hostile white/Anglo "worlds." The hostility of these

77

"worlds" and the compulsory nature of the "traveling" have obscured for us the enormous value of this aspect of our living and its connection to loving. Racism has a vested interest in obscuring and devaluing the complex skills involved in it. I recommend that we affirm this traveling across "worlds" as partly constitutive of cross-cultural and cross-racial loving. Thus, I recommend to women of color in the United States that we learn to love each other by learning to travel to each other's "worlds." In making this recommendation, I have in mind giving a new meaning to coalition and propose "Women of Color" as a term for a coalition of deep understanding fashioned through "world"-traveling.

According to Marilyn Frye, to perceive arrogantly is to perceive that others are for oneself and to proceed to arrogate their substance to oneself (Frye 1983:66). Here, I make a connection between "arrogant perception" and the failure to identify with persons that one views arrogantly or has come to see as the products of arrogant perception. A further connection is made between this failure of identification and a failure of love, and thus between loving and identifying with another person. The sense of love is not the one Frye has identified as both consistent with arrogant perception and as promoting unconditional servitude. "We can be taken in by this equation of servitude with love," Frye says, "because we make two mistakes at once: we think of both servitude and love that they are selfless or unselfish" (Frye 1983:73). The identification of which I speak is constituted by what I come to characterize as playful "world"-traveling. To the extent that we learn to perceive others arrogantly or come to see them only as products of arrogant perception and continue to perceive them that way, we fail to identify with them—fail to love them—in this particular way.

Identification and Love

As a child, I was taught to perceive arrogantly. I have also been the object of arrogant perception. Though I am not a white/Anglo woman, it is clear to me that I can understand both my childhood training as an arrogant perceiver and my having been the object of arrogant perception without any reference to white/Anglo men. This gives some indication that the concept of arrogant perception can be used cross-cultur- ally and that white/Anglo men are not the only arrogant per- ceivers.

I was brought up in Argentina watching men and women of moderate and of considerable means graft the substance of their servants to themselves. I also learned to graft my moth- er's substance to my own. It was clear to me that both men and women were the victims of arrogant perception and that arrogant perception was systematically organized to break the spirit of all women and of most men. I valued my rural gaucho ancestry because its ethos has always been one of indepen- dence, courage, and self-reliance in the midst of poverty and enormous loneliness. I found inspiration in this ethos and committed myself never to be broken by arrogant perception. I can say all of this in this way only because of what I have learned from Frye's "In and Out of Harm's Way: Arrogance and Love" (1983). She has given me a way of understanding and articulating something important in my own life.

Frye is not particularly concerned with women as arrogant perceivers but as the objects of arrogant perception. Her con- cern is, in part, to enhance our understanding of women "un- touched by phallocratic machinations" (Frye 1983:53), by understanding the harm done to women through such machi- nations. In this case, she proposes that we could understand women untouched by arrogant perception through an under- standing of what arrogant perception does to women. Frye also proposes an understanding of what it is to love women that is inspired by a vision of women unharmed by arrogant perception. To love women is, at least in part, to perceive them with loving eyes. "The loving eye is a contrary of the arrogant eye" (Frye 1983:75).

I am concerned with women as arrogant perceivers because I want to explore further what it is to love women. I want to begin by exploring two failures of love: my failure to love my mother and white/Anglo women's failure to love women across racial and cultural boundaries in the United States. As a consequence of exploring these failures I will offer a loving solution to them. My solution modifies Frye's account of loving perception by adding what I call playful "world"-travel. Then I want to take up the practice as a horizontal practice of resistance to two related injunctions: the injunction for the oppressed to have our gazes fixed on the oppressor and the concomitant injunction not to look to and connect with each other in resistance to those injunctions through traveling to each other's "worlds" of sense. Thus, the first move is one that explores top down failures of love and their logic; the second move explores horizontal failures.

It is clear to me, that at least in the United States and Argentina, women are taught to perceive many other women arrogantly. Being taught to perceive arrogantly is part of being taught to be a woman of a certain class in both the United States and Argentina; it is part of being taught to be a white/Anglo woman in the United States; and it is part of being taught to be a woman in both places: to be both the agent and the object of arrogant perception. My love for my mother seemed to me thoroughly imperfect as I was growing up because I was unwilling to become what I had been taught to see my mother as being. I thought that to love her was consistent with my abusing her: using, taking her for granted and demanding her services in a far-reaching way that, since four other people engaged in the same grafting of her substance onto themselves, left her little of herself to herself. I also thought that loving her was to be in part constituted by my identifying with her, my seeing myself in her. Thus, to love her was supposed to be of a piece with both my abusing her and with my being open to being abused. It is clear to me that I was not supposed to love servants: I could abuse them without identifying with them, without seeing myself in them.

When I came to the United States I learned that part of racism is the internalization of the propriety of abuse without identification. I learned that I could be seen as a being to be used by white/Anglo men and women without the possibility of identification (i.e., without their act of attempting to graft my substance onto theirs rubbing off on them at all). They could remain untouched, without any sense of loss.

So, women who are perceived arrogantly can, in turn, perceive other women arrogantly. To what extent those women are responsible for their arrogant perceptions of other women is certainly open to question, but I do not have any doubt that many of them have been taught to abuse women in this particular way. I am not interested in assigning responsibility. I am interested in understanding the phenomenon so as to understand a loving way out of it. I am offering a way of taking responsibility, of exercising oneself as not doomed to oppress others.

There is something obviously wrong with the love that I was taught and something right with my failure to love my mother in this way. But I do not think that what is wrong is my profound desire to identify with her, to see myself in her; what is wrong is that I was taught to identify with a victim of servitude. What is wrong is that I was taught to practice servitude of my mother and to learn to become a servant through this practice. There is something obviously wrong with my having been taught that love is consistent with abuse, consistent with arrogant perception.

Notice that the love I was taught is the love that Frye (1983:73) speaks of when she says "We can be taken in by this equation of servitude with love." Even though I could both abuse and love my mother, I was not supposed to love servants. This is because in the case of servants one is supposed to be clear about their servitude and the "equation of servitude with love" is never to be thought clearly in those terms. So, I was not supposed to love and could not love servants. But I could love my mother because deception (in particular, self-deception) is part of this "loving."

In the equation of love with servitude, servitude is called abnegation and abnegation is not analyzed any further. Abnegation is not instilled in us through an analysis of its nature but rather through a heralding of it as beautiful and noble. We are coaxed, seduced into abnegation not through analysis but through emotive persuasion. Frye makes the connection between deception and this sense of loving clear. When I say that there is something obviously wrong with the loving that I was taught, I do not mean to say that the connection between this loving and abuse is obvious. Rather, I mean that once the connection between this loving and abuse has been unveiled, there is something obviously wrong with the loving given that it is obvious that it is wrong to abuse others.

I am glad that I did not learn my lessons well, but it is clear that part of the mechanism that permitted my not learning well involved a separation from my mother: I saw us as beings of quite a different sort. It involved abandoning my mother even while I longed not to abandon her. I wanted to love my mother, though, given what I was taught, "love" could not be the right word for what I longed for.

I was disturbed by my not wanting to be what she was. I had a sense of not being quite integrated, my self was missing because I could not identify with her, I could not see myself in her, I could not welcome her "world." I saw myself as separate from her, a different sort of being, not quite of the same species. This separation, this lack of love, I saw, and I think that I saw correctly, as a lack in myself (not a fault, but a lack). I also see that if this was a lack of love, love cannot be what I was taught. It has to be rethought, made anew.

There is something in common between the relation between me and my mother as someone I did not used to be able to love and the relation between women of color in the United States like me and white/Angla women: there is a failure of love. As I eluded identification with my mother, white/Angla women elude identification with women of color, identifications with beings whose substance they arrogate without a sense of loss. Frye helped me understand one of the aspects of this failure—the directly abusive aspect. But I also think that there is a complex failure of love in the failure to identify with another woman, the failure to see oneself in other women who are quite different from oneself. I want to begin to analyze this complex failure.

Notice that Frye's emphasis on independence in her analysis of loving perception is not particularly helpful in explaining these failures. She says that in loving perception, "the object of the seeing is another being whose existence and character are logically independent of the seer and who may be practically or empirically independent in any particular respect at any particular time" (Frye 1983:77). But this does not help me understand how my failure of love toward my mother (when I ceased to be her parasite) left me not quite whole. It is not helpful since I saw her as logically independent from me. And it also does not help me understand why the racist or ethnocentric failure of love of white/Angla women — in particular of those white/Angla women who are not pained by their failure — should leave me not quite substantive among them.

I am not particularly interested here in cases of white women's parasitism onto women of color but more pointedly in cases where the relation is characterized by failure of identification. I am interested here in those many cases in which white/Angla women do one or more of the following to women of color: they ignore us, ostracize us, render us invisible, stereotype us, leave us completely alone, interpret us as crazy. All of this *while we are in their midst.* The more independent I am, the more independent I am left to be. Their "world" and their integrity do not require me at all. There is no sense of self-loss in them for my own lack of solidity. But they rob me of my solidity through indifference, an indifference they can afford and that seems sometimes studied. But many of us have to work among white/Anglo folk and our best shot at recognition has seemed to be among white/Angla women because many of them have expressed a *general* sense of being pained at their failure of love.

Many times white/Angla women want us out of their field of vision. Their lack of concern is a harmful failure of love that leaves me independent from them in a way similar to the way in which, once I ceased to be my mother's parasite, she became, though not independent from all others, certainly independent from me. But, of course, because my mother and I wanted to love each other well, we were not whole in this independence. White/Angla women are independent from me, I am independent from them; I am independent from my mother, she is independent from me; and none of us loves each other in this independence. I am incomplete and unreal without other women. I am profoundly dependent on others without having to be their subordinate, their slave, their servant.

Identification and Women of Color

The relations among "Women of Color" can neither be homogenized nor merely wished into being as relations of solidarity. To the extent that Women of Color names a coalition, it is a coalition in formation against significant and complex odds that, though familiar, keep standing in our way. The coalition or interconnecting coalitions need to be conceptualized against the grain of these odds. To a significant extent that is the point of this book. Audre Lorde is attentive to the problem of homogenization in coalition formation when she tells us to explore our relations in terms of "non-dominant differences." This epistemological shift to non-dominant differences is crucial to our possibilities. To the extent that we are "created different" by the logic of domination, the techniques of producing difference include divide and conquer, segregation, fragmentation, instilling mistrust toward each other for having been pitted against each other by economies of domination, instilling in us the distinction between the real and the fake. Here I will not address each one of these techniques of keeping us focused on dominant differences among each other, that is differences concocted by the dominant imagination.[1] Rather, I will emphasize the epistemological shift to non-dominant differences.

To the extent that in resistance to oppressions, both men and women have historically fashioned resistant "communities," resistant socialities that have made meanings that have enabled us to endure as resistant subjects in the oppressing ⇔ resisting relation, we have created alternate historical lines that are in connection with each other — they do not exist in isolation — lines that we do not understand, as nothing requires that we understand the spatio-temporal differences among us. Systems of domination construct women of color as subordinate, inferior, servile. We can see each other enacting these dominant constructions, even when we do it against our own desire, will, and energy. We can see and understand these animations of the dominant imaginary, but we are not sufficiently familiar with each other's "worlds" of resistance to either cross, or travel to them, nor to avoid what keeps us from seeing the need to travel, the enriching of our possibilities through "world"-travel.

There is an important sense in which we do not understand each other as interdependent and we do not identify with each other since we lack insight into each other's resistant under-

standings. To put the point sharply, the resistant understandings do not travel through social fragmentation. Separatism in
communities where our substance is seen and celebrated,
where we become substantive through this celebration, combines with social fragmentation to keep our lines of resistance
away from each other. Thus, it is difficult for women of color
to see, know each other, as resistant rather than as constructed
by domination. To the extent that we face each other as oppressed, we do not want to identify with each other, we repel
each other as we are seeing each other in the same mirror.[2] As
resistant, we are kept apart by social fragmentation. To identify with each other, we need to engage in resistant practices
that appear dangerous. We have not realized the potential
lying in our becoming interdependently resistant. As resistant,
we appear independent from each other to each other. The coalition sense of "Women of Color" necessitates this identification that comes from seeing ourselves and each other
interrelating "worlds" of resistant meaning. To the extent that
identification requires sameness, this coalition is impossible.
So, the coalition requires that we conceive identification anew.
The independence of women of color from each other performed by social fragmentation leaves us unwittingly colluding with the logic of oppression.

"Worlds" and "World"-Traveling

Frye (1983:75) says that the loving eye is "the eye of one who
knows that to know the seen, one must consult something
other than one's own will and interests and fears and imagination." This is much more helpful to me so long as I do not understand her to mean that I should not consult my own
interests nor that I should exclude the possibility that my self
and the self of the one I love may be importantly tied to each
other in many complicated ways. Since I am emphasizing here
that the failure of love lies in part in the failure to identify, and
since I agree with Frye that one "must consult something
other than one's own will and interests and fears and imagination," I will explain what I think needs to be consulted. It was
not possible for me to love my mother while I retained a sense
that it was fine for me and others to see her arrogantly. Loving

my mother also required that I see with her eyes, that I go into my mother's "world," that I see both of us as we are constructed in her "world," that I witness her own sense of herself from within her "world." Only through this traveling to her "world" could I identify with her because only then could I cease to ignore her and to be excluded and separate from her. Only then could I see her as a subject, even if one subjected, and only then could I see at all how meaning could arise fully between us. We are fully dependent on each other for the possibility of being understood and without this understanding we are not intelligible, we do not make sense, we are not solid, visible, integrated; we are lacking. So traveling to each other's "worlds" would enable us to *be* through loving each other.

I hope the sense of identification I have in mind is becoming clear. But to become clearer, I need to explain what I mean by a "world" and by "traveling" to another "world." In explaining what I mean by a "world," I will not appeal to traveling to other women's "worlds." Instead, I will lead you to see what I mean by a "world" the way I came to propose the concept to myself: through the kind of ontological confusion about myself that we, women of color, refer to half-jokingly as "schizophrenia" (we feel schizophrenic in our goings back and forth between different "communities") and through my effort to make some sense of this ontological confusion.

Some time ago, I came to be in a state of profound confusion as I experienced myself as both having and not having a particular attribute. I was sure I had the attribute in question and, on the other hand, I was sure that I did not have it. I remain convinced that I both have and do not have this attribute. The attribute is playfulness. I am sure that I am a playful person. On the other hand, I can say, painfully, that I am not a playful person. I am not a playful person in certain "worlds." One of the things I did as I became confused was to call my friends, faraway people who knew me well, to see whether or not I was playful. Maybe they could help me out of my confusion. They said to me, "Of course you are playful," and they said it with the same conviction that I had about it. Of course I am playful. Those people who were around me said to me, "No, you are not playful. You are a serious woman. You just take everything seriously."[3] They were just as sure about what they said to me and could offer me every bit of evidence that one could need to conclude that they were right. So I said to my-self "Okay, maybe what's happening here is that there is an attribute that I do have but there are certain "worlds" in which I am not at ease and it is because I'm not at ease in those "worlds" that I don't have that attribute in those "worlds." But what does that mean?" I was worried both about what I meant by "worlds" when I said "in some 'worlds' I do not have the attribute" and what I meant by saying that lack of ease was what led me not to be playful in those "worlds." Be-cause, you see, if it was just a matter of lack of ease, I could work on it.

I can explain some of what I mean by a "world." I do not want the fixity of a definition at this point, because I think the term is suggestive and I do not want to close the suggestive-ness of it too soon. I can offer some characteristics that serve to distinguish between a "world," a utopia, a possible "world" in the philosophical sense, and a "world" view. By a "world" I do not mean a utopia at all. A utopia does not count as a "world," in my sense. The "worlds" that I am talking about are possible. But a possible "world" is not what I mean by a "world" and I do not mean a "world"-view, though some-thing like a "world"-view is involved here.

For something to be a "world" in my sense, it has to be in-habited at present by some flesh and blood people. That is why it cannot be a utopia. It may also be inhabited by some imaginary people. It may be inhabited by people who are dead or people that the inhabitants of this "world" met in some other "world" and now have in this "world" in imagina-tion.

A "world" in my sense may be an actual society, given its dominant culture's description and construction of life, in-cluding a construction of the relationships of production, of gender, race, etc. But a "world" can also be such a society given a nondominant, a resistant construction, or it can be such a society or a society given an idiosyncratic construction. As we will see, it is problematic to say that these are all con-structions of the same society. But they are different "worlds."

A "world" need not be a construction of a whole society. It may be a construction of a tiny portion of a particular society.

It may be inhabited by just a few people. Some "worlds" are bigger than others.

A "world" may be incomplete. Things in it may not be altogether constructed or some things may be constructed negatively (they are not what "they" are in some other "world"). Or the "world" may be incomplete because it may have references to things that do not quite exist in it, references to things like Brazil, where Brazil is not quite part of that "world." Given lesbian feminism, the construction of "lesbian" is purposefully and healthily still up in the air, in the process of becoming. What it is to be a Hispanic in this country is, in a dominant Anglo construction, purposefully incomplete. Thus, one cannot really answer questions like "What is a Hispanic?" "Who counts as a Hispanic?" "Are Latinos, Chicanos, Hispanos, black Dominicans, white Cubans, Korean Colombians, Italian Argentinians, Hispanic?" What it is to be a "Hispanic" in the varied so-called Hispanic communities in the United States is also yet up in the air. "We"[4] have not yet decided whether there is something like a Hispanic in our varied "worlds." So, a "world" may be an incomplete visionary non-utopian construction of life, or it may be a traditional construction of life. A traditional Hispano construction of northern New Mexican life is a "world." Such a traditional construction, in the face of a racist, ethnocentric, money-centered Anglo construction of northern New Mexican life, is highly unstable because Anglos have the means for imperialist destruction of traditional Hispano "worlds."

In a "world," some of the inhabitants may not understand or hold the particular construction of them that constructs them in that "world." So, there may be "worlds" that construct me in ways that I do not even understand. Or, it may be that I understand the construction, but do not hold it of myself. I may not accept it as an account of myself, a construction of myself. And yet, I may be *animating* such a construction.[5]

One can travel between these "worlds" and one can inhabit more than one of these "worlds" at the same time. I think that most of us who are outside the mainstream of, for example, the United States dominant construction or organization of life are "world" travelers as a matter of necessity and of survival. It seems to me that inhabiting more than one "world" at the same time and traveling between "worlds" is part and parcel of our experience and our situation. One can be at the same time in a "world" that constructs one as stereotypically Latina, for example, and in a "world" that constructs one as simply Latina. Being stereotypically Latina and being simply Latina are different simultaneous constructions of persons who are part of different "worlds." One animates one or the other or both at the same time without necessarily confusing them, though simultaneous enactment can be confusing if one is not on one's guard.

In describing my sense of a "world," I am offering a description of experience, something that is true to experience even if it is ontologically problematic. Though I would think that any account of identity that could not be true to this experience of outsiders to the mainstream would be faulty, even if ontologically unproblematic. Its ease would constrain, erase, or deem aberrant experience that has within it significant insights into nonimperialistic understanding between people.

Those of us who are "world"-travelers have the distinct experience of being different in different "worlds" and of having the capacity to remember other "worlds" and ourselves in them. We can say "That is me there, and I am happy in that "world." So, the experience is of being a different person in different "worlds" and yet of having memory of oneself as different without quite having the sense of there being any underlying "I." When I can say "that is me there and I am so playful in that 'world,'" I am saying "That is *me* in that 'world'" not because I recognize myself in that person; rather, the first person statement is noninferential. I may well recognize that that person has abilities I do not have and yet the having or not having of the abilities is always an "I have . . ." and "I do not have . . ." (i.e., it is always experienced in the first person).

The shift from being one person to being a different person is what I call traveling. This shift may not be willful or even conscious, and one may be completely unaware of being different in a different "world," and may not recognize that one is in a different "world." Even though the shift can be done willfully, it is not a matter of acting. One does not pose as someone else; one does not pretend to be, for example, someone of a different personality or character or someone who uses space or language differently from the other person. Rather, one is someone who has that personality or character or uses space and language in that particular way. The "one" here does not refer to some underlying "I." One does not *experience* any underlying I.

Being at Ease in a "World"

In investigating what I mean by "being at ease in a 'world,' I will describe different ways of being at ease. One may be at ease in one or in all of these ways. There is a maximal way of being at ease, viz., being at ease in all of these ways. I take this maximal way of being at ease to be somewhat dangerous because it tends to produce people who have no inclination to travel across "worlds" or no experience of "world"-traveling.

The first way of being at ease in a particular "world" is by being a fluent speaker in that "world." I know all the norms that there are to be followed. I know all the words that there are to be spoken. I know all the moves. I am confident.

Another way of being at ease is by being normatively happy. I agree with all the norms, I could not love any norms better. I am asked to do just what I want to do or what I think I should do. I am at ease.

Another way of being at ease in a "world" is by being humanly bonded. I am with those I love and they love me, too. It should be noticed that I may be with those I love and be at ease because of them in a "world" that is otherwise as hostile to me as "worlds" get.

Finally, one may be at ease because one has a history with others that is shared, especially daily history, the kind of shared history that one sees exemplified by the response to the "Do you remember poodle skirts?" question. There you are, with people you do not know at all and who do not know each other. The question is posed and then everyone begins talking about their poodle skirt stories. I have been in such situations without knowing what poodle skirts, for example, were, and I felt ill at ease because it was not *my* history. The other people did not know each other. It is not that they were humanly bonded. Probably they did not have much politically in common either. But poodle skirts were in their shared history.

One may be at ease in one of these ways or in all of them. Notice that when one says meaningfully "This is *my* 'world,'" one may not be at ease in it. Or one may be at ease in it only in some of these respects and not in others. To say of some "world" that it is "*my* world" is to make an evaluation. One may privilege one or more "worlds" in this way for a variety of reasons: for example, because one experiences oneself as an agent in a fuller sense than one experiences oneself in other "worlds." One may disown a "world" because one has first-person memories of a person who is so thoroughly dominated that she has no sense of exercising her own will or has a sense of having serious difficulties in performing actions that are willed by herself and no difficulty in performing actions willed by others. One may say of a "world" that it is "my world" because one is at ease in it (i.e., being at ease in a "world" may be the basis for the evaluation).

Given the clarification of what I mean by a "world," "world"-travel, and being at ease in a "world," we are in a position to return to my problematic attribute, playfulness. It may be that in this "world" in which I am so unplayful, I am a different person than in the "world" in which I am playful. Or it may be that the "world" in which I am unplayful is constructed in such a way that I could be playful in it. I could practice, even though that "world" is constructed in such a way that my being playful in it is kind of hard. In describing what I take a "world" to be, I emphasized the first possibility as both the one that is truest to the experience of "outsiders" to the mainstream and as ontologically problematic because the "I" is identified in some sense as one and in some sense as a plurality. I identify myself as myself through memory and I retain myself as different in memory.

When I travel from one "world" to another, I have this image, this memory of myself as playful in this other "world." I can then be in a particular "world" and have a double image of myself as, for example, playful and as not playful. This is a very familiar and recognizable phenomenon to the outsider to the mainstream in some central cases: when in one "world" I animate, for example, that "world"'s caricature of the person

I am in the other "world." I can have both images of myself, and, to the extent that I can materialize or animate both images at the same time, I become an ambiguous being. This is very much a part of trickery and foolery. It is worth remembering that the trickster and the fool are significant characters in many nondominant or outsider cultures. One then sees any particular "world" with these double edges and sees absurdity in them and so inhabits oneself differently.

Given that Latinas are constructed in Anglo "worlds" as stereotypically intense—intensity being a central characteristic of at least one of the Anglo stereotypes of Latinas—and given that many Latinas, myself included, are genuinely intense, I can say to myself "I am intense" and take a hold of the double meaning. Furthermore, I can be stereotypically intense or be the real thing, and, if you are Anglo, you do not know when I am which *because* I am Latin American. As a Latin American I am an ambiguous being, a two-imaged self: I can see that gringos see me as stereotypically intense because I am, as a Latin American, constructed that way but I may or may not *intentionally* animate the stereotype or the real thing knowing that you may not see it in anything other than in the stereotypical construction. This ambiguity is funny and not just funny; it is survival-rich. We can also make the picture of those who dominate us funny precisely because we can see the double edge, we can see them doubly constructed, we can see the plurality in them. So we know truths that only the fool can speak and only the trickster can play out without harm. We inhabit "worlds" and travel across them and keep all the memories.

Sometimes, the "world"-traveler has a double image of herself and each self includes as important ingredients of itself one or more attributes that are *incompatible* with one or more of the attributes of the other self: for example being playful and being unplayful. To the extent that the attribute is an important ingredient of the self she is in that "world" (i.e., to the extent that there is a particularly good fit between that "world" and her having that attribute in it, and to the extent that the attribute is personality or character central, *that "world" would have to be changed if she is to be playful in it*). It is not the case that if she could come to be at ease in it, she would be her own playful self. Because the attribute is personality or character central and there is such a good fit between that "world" and her being constructed with that attribute as central, *she* cannot become playful, she is unplayful. To become playful would be, for her, to become a contradictory being.

I suggest, then, that my problematic case, the being and not being playful, cannot be solved through lack of ease. I suggest that I can understand my confusion about whether I am or am not playful by saying that I am both and that I am different persons in different "worlds" and can remember myself in both as I am in the other. I am a plurality of selves. This explains my confusion because *it is to come to see it as of a piece* with much of the rest of my experience as an outsider in some of the "worlds" that I inhabit and of a piece with significant aspects of the experience of nondominant people in the "worlds" of their dominators.

So, though I may not be at ease in the "worlds" in which I am not constructed playful, it is not that I am not playful *because* I am not at ease. The two are compatible. But lack of playfulness is not caused by lack of ease. Lack of playfulness is not symptomatic of lack of ease but of lack of health. I am not a healthy being in the "worlds" that construct me unplayful.

Playfulness

I had a very personal stake in investigating this topic. Playfulness is not only the attribute that was the source of my confusion and the attitude that I recommend as the loving attitude in traveling across "worlds." I am also scared of ending up as a serious human being, someone with no multidimensionality, with no fun in life, someone who is just someone who has had the fun constructed out of her. I am seriously scared of getting stuck in a "world" that constructs me that way, a "world" that I have no escape from and in which I cannot be playful.

I thought about what it is to be playful and what it is to play and I did this thinking in a "world" in which I only remember myself as playful and in which all of those who know me as playful are imaginary beings. It is a "world" in which I am scared of losing my memories of myself as playful or have them erased from me. Because I live in such a "world," after I formulated my own sense of what it is to be playful and to play, I decided that I needed to look go to the literature. I read two classics on the subject: Johan Huizinga's *Homo Ludens* (1968) and Hans-Georg Gadamer's chapter on the concept of play in his *Truth and Method* (1975). I discovered, to my amazement, that what I thought about play and playfulness, if they were right, was absolutely wrong. Though I will not provide the arguments for this interpretation of Gadamer and Huizinga here, I understood that both of them have an agonistic sense of play. Play and playfulness have — in their use — ultimately, to do with contest, with winning, losing, battling. The sense of playfulness that I have in mind has nothing to do with agon. So, I tried to elucidate both senses of play and playfulness by contrasting them to each other. The contrast helped me see the attitude that I have in mind as the loving attitude in traveling across "worlds" more clearly.

An agonistic sense of playfulness is one in which *competence* is central. You'd better know the rules of the game. In agonistic play, there is risk, there is *uncertainty*, but the uncertainty is about who is going to win and who is going to lose. There are rules that inspire hostility. The attitude of *playfulness is conceived as secondary to or derivative from play.* Since play is agon, then the only conceivable playful attitude is an agonistic one: the attitude does not turn an activity into play, but rather presupposes an activity that is play. One of the paradigmatic ways of playing for both Gadamer and Huizinga is role-playing. In role-playing, the person who is a participant in the game has a *fixed conception of him- or herself.* I also think that the players are imbued with *self-importance* in agonistic play since they are so keen on winning given their own merits, their very own competence.

When considering the value of "world"-traveling and whether playfulness is the loving attitude to have while traveling, I recognized the agonistic attitude as inimical to traveling across "worlds." The agonistic traveler is a conqueror, an imperialist. Huizinga, in his classic book on play, interprets Western civilization as play. That is an interesting thing for Third World people to think about. Western civilization has been interpreted by a white Western man as play in the agonistic sense of play. Huizinga reviews Western law, art, and any other aspects of Western culture and sees agon in all of them. Agonistic playfulness leads those who attempt to travel to another "world" with this attitude to failure. Agonistic travelers cannot attempt to travel in this sense. Their traveling is always a trying that is tied to conquest, domination, reduction of what they meet to their own sense of order, and erasure of the other "world." That is what assimilation is all about. Assimilation is an agonistic project of destruction of other people's "worlds." So, the agonistic attitude, the playful attitude given Western man's construction of playfulness, is not a healthy, loving attitude to have in traveling across "worlds." Given the agonistic attitude, one *cannot* travel across "worlds," though one can kill other "worlds" with it.[6] So, for people who are interested in crossing racial and ethnic boundaries, an arrogant Western man's construction of playfulness is deadly. One cannot cross the boundaries with it. One needs to give up such an attitude if one wants to travel.

What, then, is the loving playfulness that I have in mind? Let me begin with one example: We are by the riverbank. The river is very low. Almost dry. Bits of water here and there. Little pools with a few trout hiding under the rocks. But it is mostly wet stones, gray on the outside. We walk on the stones for awhile. You pick up a stone and crash it onto the others. As it breaks, it is quite wet inside and it is very colorful, very pretty. I pick up a stone and break it and run toward the pieces to see the colors. They are beautiful. I laugh and bring the pieces back to you and you are doing the same with your pieces. We keep on crashing stones for hours, anxious to see the beautiful new colors. We are playing. The playfulness of our activity does not presuppose that there is something like "crashing stones" that is a particular form of play with its own rules. Instead, *the attitude that carries us through the activity, a playful attitude, turns the activity into play.* Our activity has no rules, though it is certainly intentional activity and we both understand what we are doing. The playfulness that gives meaning to our activity includes uncertainty, but in this case the uncertainty is an *openness to surprise.* This is a particular metaphysical attitude that does not expect the "world" to be neatly packaged, ruly. Rules may fail to explain what we are doing. We are not self-important, we are not fixed in particular constructions of ourselves, which is part of saying that we are *open to self-construction.* We may not have rules, and when we do have them, *there are no rules that are to us sacred.* We are not worried about competence. We are not wedded to a particular way of doing things. While playful, we have not abandoned ourselves to, nor are we stuck in, any particular "world." We *are there creatively.* We are not passive.[7]

Playfulness is, in part, an openness to being a fool, which is a combination of not worrying about competence, not being self-important, not taking norms as sacred, and finding ambiguity and double edges a source of wisdom and delight.

So, positively, the playful attitude involves openness to surprise, openness to being a fool, openness to self-construction or reconstruction and to construction or reconstruction of the "worlds" we inhabit playfully, and thus openness to risk the ground that constructs us as oppressors or as oppressed or as collaborating or colluding with oppression. Negatively, playfulness is characterized by uncertainty, lack of self-importance, absence of rules or not taking rules as sacred, not worrying about competence, and lack of abandonment to a particular construction of oneself, others, and one's relation to them. In attempting to take a hold of oneself and of one's relation to others in a particular "world," one may study, examine, and come to understand oneself. One may then see what the possibilities for play are for the being one is in that "world." One may even decide to inhabit that self fully to understand it better and find its creative possibilities.

Conclusion

There are "worlds" we enter at our own risk, "worlds" that have agon, conquest, and arrogance as the main ingredients in their ethos. These are "worlds" that we enter out of necessity and that would be foolish to enter playfully in either the agonistic sense or in my sense. In such "worlds," *we* are not playful. To be in those "worlds" in resistance to their construction of ourselves as passive, servile, and inferior is to inhabit those selves ambiguously, through our first-person memories of lively subjectivity.

But there are "worlds" that we can travel to lovingly, and traveling to them is part of loving at least some of their inhabitants. The reason I think that traveling to someone's "world" is a way of identifying with them is that by traveling to their "world" we can understand *what it is to be them and what it is to be ourselves in their eyes.* Only when we have traveled to each other's "worlds" are we fully subjects to each other. (I agree with Hegel that self-recognition requires other subjects, but I disagree with his claim that it requires tension or hostility.)

Knowing other women's "worlds" is part of knowing them and knowing them is part of loving them. Notice that the knowing can be done in greater or lesser depth, as can the loving. Traveling to another's "world" is not the same as becoming intimate with them. Intimacy is constituted in part by a very deep knowledge of the other self. "World"-traveling is only part of the process of coming to have this knowledge. Also, notice that some people, in particular those who are outsiders to the mainstream, can be known only to the extent that they are known in several "worlds" and as "world"-travelers.

Without knowing the other's "world," one does not know the other, and without knowing the other, one is really alone in the other's presence because the other is only dimly present to one.

By traveling to other people's "worlds," we discover that there are "worlds" in which those who are the victims of arrogant perception are really subjects, lively beings, resisters, constructors of visions even though in the mainstream construction they are animated only by the arrogant perceiver and are pliable, foldable, file-awayable, classifiable. I always imagine the Aristotelian slave as pliable and foldable at night or after he or she cannot work anymore (when he or she dies as a tool).[8] Aristotle tells us nothing about the slave *apart from the master.* We know the slave only through the master. The slave is a tool of the master. After working hours, he or she is folded and placed in a drawer until the next morning.

My mother was apparent to me mostly as a victim of arrogant perception. I was loyal to the arrogant perceiver's construction of her and thus disloyal to her in assuming that she was exhausted by that construction. I was unwilling to be like her and thought that identifying with her, seeing myself in her, necessitated that I become like her. I was wrong both in assuming that she was exhausted by the arrogant perceiver's construction of her and in my understanding of identification. I do not think I was wrong in thinking that identification was part of loving and that it involved in part my seeing myself in her. I came to realize through traveling to her "world" that she is not foldable and pliable, that she is not exhausted by the mainstream Argentinian patriarchal construction of her. I came to realize that there are "worlds" in which she shines as a creative being. Seeing myself in her through traveling to her "world" has meant seeing how different from her I am in her "world."[9]

So, in recommending "world"-traveling and identification through "world"-traveling as part of loving other women, I am suggesting disloyalty to arrogant perceivers, including the arrogant perceiver in ourselves, and to their constructions of women and to their constructions of powerful barriers between women. As Women of Color, we cannot stand on any ground that is not also a crossing. To enter playfully into each other's "worlds" of subjective affirmation also risks those aspects of resistance that have kept us riveted on constructions of ourselves that have kept us from seeing multiply, from understanding the interconnections in our historico-spatialities. Playful "world"-travel is thus not assimilable to the middle-class leisurely journey nor the colonial or imperialist journeys. None of these involve risking one's ground. These forms of displacement may well be compatible with agonistic playfulness, but they are incompatible with the attitude of play that is an openness to surprise and that inclines us to "world"-travel in the direction of deep coalition.

Notes

1. It is an important aim of this book to come to understand these barriers to the possibility of coalitions of understanding. Most chapters in the book are relevant to this question, but I call your attention in particular to the treatment of these difficulties in chapter 7 ("Boomerang Perception and the Colonizing Gaze"). I consider the failure of nationalisms and separatisms to escape these difficulties. The distinction between split-separation

and curdling-separation that I introduce in chapter 6 ("Purity, Impurity, and Separation") is also relevant. The distinction between intermeshing oppressions and the interlocking of oppressions that I develop in the Introduction and in "Tactical Strategies of the Streetwalker" (chapter 10) address the complexities of these barriers.

2. See Audre Lorde's treatment of horizontal anger in "Eye to Eye: Black Women, Hatred, and Anger" (Lorde 1996). Lorde understands black women seeing the servile construction of themselves in each other with anger, hatred.

3. It is important that I have been thought a person without humor by whites/Anglos inside the U.S. academy, a space where struggles against race/gender and sexual oppression require an articulation of the issues. I have been found playful by my companions in struggles against white/Anglo control of land and water in the U.S. Southwest. Those struggles have occurred in the space-time of Chicano communities. Being playful or not playful becomes in those two contexts deep traits, symptomatic of larger incongruities.

4. This "we" embraces the very many strands of Latinos in the United States. But this "we" is unusually spoken with ease. The tension in the "we" includes those who do not reject "Hispanic" as a term of identification.

5. Indeed people inhabit constructions of themselves in "worlds" they refuse to enter. This is true particularly of those who oppress those whose resistant "worlds" they refuse to enter. But they are indeed inhabitants of those "worlds." And indeed those who are oppressed animate oppressive constructions of themselves in the "worlds" of their oppressors.

6. Consider the congruities between the middle-class leisurely journey that Wolff describes and the agonistic sense of play (Wolff 1992). Consider also the discussion of travel in the Introduction.

7. One can understand why this sense of playfulness is one that one may exercise in resistance to oppression when resistance is not reducible to reaction. Nonreactive resistance is creative; it exceeds that which is being resisted. The creation of new meaning lies outside of rules, particularly the rules of the "world" being resisted.

8. But I can also imagine the Aristotelian slave after hours as an animal without the capacity to reason. In that case, roaming in the fields, eating, and copulating would be distinctly passionate activities where passion and reason are dichotomized. Imagining people who are taken into servility in this manner is what leads oppressors to think of those they attempt to dominate both as dangerous and as nonpersons.

9. The traveling also permitted me to see her resistances in plain view in my daily life. She did not hide resistance.

References

Frye, Marilyn. 1983. *The Politics of Reality: Essays in Feminist Theory.* Trumansburg, N.Y.: Crossing Press.

Gadamer, Hans-Georg. 1975. *Truth and Method.* New York: Seabury Press.

Huizinga, Johan. 1968. *Homo Ludens.* Buenos Aires, Argentina: Emecé Editores.

Lorde, Audre. 1984. Eye to Eye: Black Women, Hatred, and Anger. In *Sister Outsider,* edited by Audre Lorde. Trumansburg, N.Y.: Crossing Press.

Wolff, Janet. 1992. On the Road Again: Metaphors of Travel in Cultural Criticism. *Cultural Studies* 7 (2): 224–39.

CHAPTER FIVE

Hard-to-Handle Anger

Anger is a form that the passion for communication takes. It is a stirring form: an urgency wishing into being an extremely delicate possibility. Incommunicative anger expresses the state of transformation. It is a cocoon, an inward motion intent on sense making. The passion that I address at you in anger is neither really different nor separate from the passion of metamorphosis. It is in the same tonality and of the same cloth

Introduction

It is my sense that I can make more sense of anger if I capture it in its specificity. Some of the angers I am interested in share common features; they are addressed at the same group of people or they have the same tone, the tone of rage, for example, or they are resistant angers. But the angers I will consider are sufficiently different that I want to consider each in its own right. They give rise to and answer different questions, different preoccupations. They require significantly different interpretations and conceptual schemes. There is anger that is a transformation of fear; explosive anger that pushes or recognizes the limits of one's possibilities in resistance to oppression; controlled anger that is measured because of one's intent to communicate within the official world of sense; anger addressed to one's peers in resistance; anger addressed to one's peers in self-hatred; anger that isolates the resistant self in germination; anger that judges and demands respect; anger that challenges respectability. Many of these angers can be understood as "outlaw emotions": emotions that are conventionally unacceptable. "Outlaw emotions are distinguished by their incompatibility with the dominant perceptions and values"(Jaggar 1998). But although many of these angers are outlaw emotions, some are more outlawed than others.

Some of these angers appear irrational because it seems that *one* has been overcome by passion, that *one* is seized, possessed, in a fit. But that understanding presupposes that the self is unitary. The understanding of *one* being possessed, in a passionate, passive trance, assumes that there is only one person, the person who, in anger, tries to make sense within the limits of official interpretations of reality, who exercises herself in controlled anger, attentive to the official interpretation of her movements, voice, message, asking for respectability, judging those who have wronged her. But one can understand those angers that appear irrational, that appear as possession, as rather the anger of a self different from the one who is trying to makes sense within the confines of the official reality, a self who is doing the work of resistance. Doing so enables one to understand these angers as cognitively rich, the cognitive content understandable only in nonofficial, oppositional communities or universes of sense. In considering anger, I consider questions related to the self of the angry person. Who is angry? Is the angry self the subordinate self or the insubordinate self? Is the insubordinate self resistant or asking to be seen from within the official reality by those whose subordinate she is?

I am also interested in anger and communication. I do not think all anger has a communicative intent, but rather the point of some anger is to isolate the self from others. Gloria Anzaldúa (1987) gives us a striking understanding of this anger. For each sort of anger, I will consider how other-directed the anger is, to whom it is directed, and whether its intent is to communicate. I will ask how concerned the anger is with others' feelings or with the impression one makes on others.

It has become clear to me that some angers are second-order angers. They presuppose worlds of sense against which the anger constitutes an indictment or a rebellion, worlds of sense from which one needs to separate. These angers also presuppose or establish a need for or begin to speak from within separate worlds of sense. Separate, that is, from worlds of sense that deny intelligibility to the anger.

The anger of dominators slides over me as something of no consequence. I beware of and deal with its harm, the destruction it proposes and many times succeeds in bringing about, but I pay no attention to the emotion as a source of insight or companionship. I am also unconcerned from a theoretical point of view with the anger of dominators; anger that is connected with hatred; anger that is used to mold through instilling fear for the purposes of domination, that aims at transforming its target into a function of the angry dominator's needs[1]; anger that expresses displeasure at one's not having been able to exercise complete control over one's environment for the purpose of satisfying one's own needs. But it is important to think of the manipulative power of this anger. We need to learn to exercise indifference to it, since it is a psychological tool of domination, and part of its effect depends on one's paying attention to it.

We do need to think about the manipulative effects of our own anger. Anger creates an environment, a context, a tone, and it echoes. Anger needs to be trained but not necessarily toned down. We need to think what good the anger does us with respect to oppression.

In sum, as I think about anger, I keep in mind the self who is angry, the worlds of sense that make sense of her and of her anger, the worlds of sense in which she makes no sense as angry, and whether the anger has a communicative or an incommunicative intent. I also think about the training of our angers for the purposes of resistance or for self-care. Some of our angers may be harmful, but we still need to recognize them both in order to deal with them and to not confuse them with the work of our selves in angry resistance.

Why Am I Worried about Anger?

My anger has meant pain to me but it has also meant survival, and before I give it up I'm going to be sure that there is something at least as powerful to replace it on the road to clarity. [Lorde 1984:132]

One is made angry not simply by violation. The magic of anger

> is a response not to injustice, but to a frustrated political impulse to speak and be heard, and the existence of anger itself is evidence of the denial of a right to social participation. [Lyman 1981:71]

In part I think about anger because I have experienced anger as a problematic emotion: on the one hand, I find myself angrier and angrier; on the other, I have always disliked being overwhelmed by emotion. So I have tried to contain, mold, temper my own anger. I have distrusted anger uncontained as a source of knowledge, as the impetus for political action, as the tone for my interaction with other people. But most of all I have disliked myself in deep, overwhelming anger. I have disliked my bodily sense, my movements, the awesome quality of myself, the largeness of my occupying other people's interior space, the strong possibility of manipulation. I have also disliked the turmoil in myself during and after uncontrolled anger. I have most of all disliked its effectiveness, even as I have seen its political potential. It has made me think poorly of others as well as of myself, but for very different reasons. I am frightening when I am that angry and I feel somewhat possessed: the logic of my movements and of my use of space, of my use of my voice, of how I look at people is frenetic, rousing. I seem mad and sane at the same time because of the depth of my passion. I lose any concern with fitting in anywhere, with being appreciated, liked, respected. I am firmly marginal but I also manage to be threatening while most of the time I do not succeed in destabilizing the hold of the official on those around me or on myself. I haven't been that angry very often, but it seems to me that as years go by I am getting angrier and angrier in precisely that way. As I have a harder time containing this form of anger, I have begun to wonder about my own dislike of it and the extent to which my finding it unacceptable is not part of my indoctrination into subordination, which is of a piece with my concern with my respectability within the confines of the official, the normal.

I have witnessed women who lived this hard-to-handle anger in front of me and I found them extremely powerful, their faces expressive in extraordinary ways, their manners and words beyond containment. Awesome. Clear. This anger endangers one's hold over convention. It places one beyond the pale. It announces an emerging self toward whom the "one" tied to the official world of sense feels ill at ease. The official self wants to feel in control over her emotions; this is an important part of this self. But fury, hard-to-handle anger, feels to this self like a fit. Its vivid embodiment seems strange to the official "I": the gestures are wild or extremely hieratic, contained; the voice loud; the use of space extensive; the body flushed. The official self feels a fear of cognitive lack of control. I have been taught that in a fit of anger one is cognitively at a loss. Yet, when I have observed women in hard-to-handle anger, they have been outrageously clearheaded; their words clean, true, undiluted by regard for others' feelings or possible reactions.

Hard-to-Handle Anger

Having considered Aristotle carefully, I have spent a great deal of my life trying to feel anger in accord with the mean, even though I have not always known where the mean might lie. I have often thought that reality has to be fairly well defined, at least coherent, for one to be able to find the mean, so I have doubted the possibility of a mean when one's reality is crisscrossed by contradiction. But I have kept a sense that it is good to look for it and that it is good to retain a sense of control over my anger.

Elizabeth Spelman refers to the "mean" when she warns us about the conflation of anger with rage. She tells us that rage is the excess and anger the mean. She also tells us that subordinate people have been discouraged from looking positively at their anger through the conflation of rage and anger (Spelman 1989). I have certainly been discouraged from looking at rage positively, and maybe the point of view from which this conflation occurs is one that I have internalized. Maybe this point of view is one that devalues rage because it is troubled by the possibility of its being dismantled through rage. I will come back to this. I will prepare the way back.

Marilyn Frye tells us that anger can be an instrument of cartography. "By determining where, with whom, about what and in what circumstances one can get angry and get uptake, one can map others' concepts of who and what one is" (Frye 1983:94–95). Frye's claim reveals that she is concerned with first-order anger: anger that has a communicative intent and does or does not succeed in getting "uptake" within a particular world of sense. Frye's reflection on this type of anger leads her to an understanding that women's anger may succeed in its communicative intent in an "official" world of sense only within particular womanly domains. The fact that women's anger outside womanly domains in the official world of sense doesn't get "uptake" reveals to Frye that women are not included among those who can be wronged outside those domains, that women's claims to respect outside those domains are unintelligible. "In getting angry one claims that one is in certain ways and dimensions respectable. One makes a claim upon respect"(Frye 1983:90).

I think Frye's analysis is important because anger that doesn't get uptake is as interesting for what it reveals about the person who cannot countenance it as for what it reveals about the person who is angry. If she makes a claim on respect, the angry woman must make sense of herself to herself. She must inhabit a world of sense in which she is respectable, a world of sense different from the world the one addressed through anger inhabits. It is important both to inquire into this world of sense keeping anger in mind and to question whether all anger makes a claim upon respect. The angry woman may share the official sense and just demand her inclusion into it. The official *world* of sense is contradictory in this respect: it both includes her formally and excludes her in fact.

As Carole Pateman argues, even the formal story is contradictory. In liberal societies, Pateman argues, women are *officially* individuals, people who have property in their persons. As such they can enter into contracts and commit themselves voluntarily to subordination: they can voluntarily enter into the marriage contract. But women enter the marriage contract as women, not as individuals whose sex is irrelevant to the act of contracting. It is as women that they subordinate themselves to men in exchange for benevolence, something that cannot be exchanged, because it cannot be demanded as one's right. *Only* subordinates enter the marriage contract to become subordinates (Pateman 1989).

So, the angry woman may be demanding respectability as an individual, a resolution of this contradiction in liberal societies toward her inclusion in them as an individual. In doing so, she is expressing a different conception of who she is. If she succeeds in being given uptake, in making her anger intelligible, she will have changed. "To expand the scope of one's intelligible anger is to change one's place in the universe, to change another's concept of what one is, to become something different in that social and collective scheme that determines the limits of the intelligible" (Frye 1983:92).

Notice that her anger is not at her not making sense in that "social and collective scheme which determines the limits of the intelligible," the official world. Her anger is about something and at someone who has wronged her outside the womanly domain. Thus, her anger is first-level anger. Though it reveals that she inhabits two different domains of sense, her anger is not about this fact. The fact that she inhabits two different worlds of sense explains why her anger is not given uptake. The fact that the only, but extraordinary, difference between these worlds is that she is an individual in one but not in the other explains her communicative intent. The communicative act of anger exhibits her as someone who has the properties required for uptake. It "models" her as the right kind of person, someone who can get angry outside of womanly domains. This is one of Lyman's points when he says that "the existence of anger itself is evidence of the denial of a right to social participation" (Lyman 1981:71).

Spelman tells us that although in Western cultures reason has been associated with members of groups that are dominant politically, socially, and culturally, and emotion has been associated with members of subordinate groups, anger has been excluded from the dominant group's profile of subordinates. When one gets angry, according to Spelman, one regards the person whose conduct one assesses as one's equal. So, we can understand why anger has been excluded from the personality profile of the subordinate. In excluding anger from their personality profile, dominant groups exclude subordinates from the category of moral agents, since to be angry is to make oneself a judge and to express a standard against which one assesses the person's conduct, both of which are marks of a moral agent (Spelman 1989:271). In becoming angry, subordinates signal that they take themselves seriously; they believe they have the capacity as well as the right to be judges of those around them.

Spelman and Frye are talking about the same kind of first-level anger, anger that makes a claim on respect and signals one's own ability to make judgments about having been wronged, one's own respectability. I cannot understand this anger unless I pay attention to the oppressor, since it is a communicative act, and, as described by Frye and Spelman, it demands respect from the oppressor. From the inside, I know this anger in its demand for respectability and both in its effectiveness and its failures. Given the contradictory nature of the official world—it treats us as subordinates at the same time that it declares us equals—this anger is useful and resistant; it has a political dimension. Later, I will describe an anger that is a transformation of fear that makes clear the politically resistant import of "claim upon respect" anger, and I will interpret this anger in two ways, one of which makes it an example of claim upon respect anger.

But the demand for respectability can become a trap against inhabiting worlds of sense that are entirely antagonistic to the social and collective scheme that determines the limits of the intelligible, because from within them one may not be able to intend to present oneself as respectable to others who are outside of these limits. So if I am right in following Spelman's and Frye's analyses to my conclusion, their analyses reveal both the usefulness and the dangers of this kind of anger.

But imagine the angry woman thinking of herself as respectable in a world of sense that is entirely antagonistic to the official world of sense. The self that thinks of herself as respectable is a different self from the one she is in the official world. Her claims on respect make sense only if addressed to herself and to others who share this world of sense. But her anger across worlds cannot be understood as a demand on respect, because she does not respect the available domains. Her anger, then, must have a different meaning. It must be second-level anger, anger that contains a recognition that there is more than one world of sense. Anger across worlds of sense may well turn out to be rage precisely in lacking a communicative intent or in having a communicative intent of a very different, noncognitive sort, without itself being devoid of cognitive content.

Spelman understands rage as the "excess" in the continuum that has anger as a "mean." She thinks that dominant groups have included rage in the profile of the subordinate that allows for the identification of the subordinate with emotion. Rage is equated by dominators with hysteria or insanity. Though she does not say this outright, she implies that rage cannot be justified. She tells us that rage is an excess. She also tells us that subordinates "have been discouraged from looking positively or clearly at their anger through the conflation of rage and anger" (Spelman 1989:271). So, we can see now that the point of view from which rage is devalued is the dominator's point of view.

I find Spelman's concern with the interpretation of rage by those in the dominant group helpful in understanding our disagreement about rage, as well as in understanding my own devaluation of rage and its revaluation. She helps me understand that I had internalized the dominator's point of view in devaluing rage. As an excess, rage cannot justifiably express a judgment of having been wronged addressed to those who have wronged one, either because the manner of expression is not justifiable or the claim is not justified. I understand Spelman as suggesting that rage cannot express, in a justifiable manner, a judgment addressed to those who have wronged one. I could not agree more since, as a noncommunicative act, rage cannot be making a claim addressed to those who share the official sense. This anger echoes or reverberates across worlds. It is a second-level anger. It decries the sense of the world that erases it precisely since that world of sense stands in the way of its possibility. It recognizes this world's walls. It pushes against them rather than making claims within them.

This is the second interpretation I give to Lyman's claim that the "existence of anger itself is evidence of the denial of a right to social participation" (Lyman 1981:71). This anger speaks its sense within the official world of sense in enraged tones without the intention to make sense to those within it.

Its harshness attests to the hardness of the walls against which and over which it echoes. Its intimidating power indicates that it does echo. Its inspiring power indicates that it does echo. This is separatist anger.

Once one recognizes first- and second-order anger, one can see that some anger can be interpreted both ways. It may also be possible to intend both acts, both levels of anger, through the same expression of anger. I said earlier that I would consider anger that is fear transformed. This anger also seems to possess one because there is a personality change. The oppressed, subservient person is taken over by, possessed, and becomes again the assertive, resistant person. When I asked a northern New Mexican Chicano what knowledge he had gained from his oppressed condition that he could bring to liberatory struggle, he described this mysterious transformation of fear into anger. He told us that it had been very important to him to know that this happens in him. After the Moly mine closed and he was out of a job, he decided to go back to school on the G.I. bill. The money from the G.I. bill began to run out before he was finished with his schooling. That meant that he had to talk to numerous educated, polished bureaucrats about funds for his education. He entered every one of these situations in fear. Ill at ease because of his lack of polish in these contexts, he experienced both a lack of control over his situation and the total control of the bureaucrat through the latter's use of language that could be abusively refined. "You Chicanos are all the same" would flow into the bureaucrat's speech with ease. Reduced by the "mark of the plural" (Memmi 1965:85), and invaded by the logic of devaluation, the Chicano found himself at a loss for words, confused, facing the inevitability of the end of his education. At this time, as he had experienced it before, the transformation came. He became self-possessed in anger: clear-headed, no nonsense, going to the core of the racist matter, immovable, determined, his muscles and his voice tense, backing up his words. The logic and the weight of oppression no longer determining him. The logic and weight of resistance were fully inspiring.

I think that in expressing this kind of anger, the Chicano can be understood either as demanding uptake from the bureaucrat or as evoking a response from the bureaucrat through anger, provoking the bureaucrat into responding to his needs. He could also be intending both acts: he could be demanding respect from the bureaucrat in the terms of the bureaucrat's formal world of sense and decrying that world of sense. "I am to be treated as an equal, not as a subordinate," and "damn your world of sense which has my subordination at its core."

First-order anger seems to be consistently backward looking. In the case of subordinates, it remembers the past insubordinately. Second-order anger can be forward looking. First-order anger responds to someone's (oneself or another) having been wronged, harmed, enslaved. Audre Lorde is thinking of first-order anger when she tells us that "strength that is bred by anger alone . . . cannot create the future. It can only demolish the past" (Lorde 1984:152). But she is talking of second-order anger when she tells us of putting our anger at the service of our visions. Peter Lyman is thinking of first-order anger when he talks of "ressentiment," Nietzsche's term for anger that leads "beyond angry speech and aggressive action to a self-destructive adaptation to subordination through the internalization of rage." Lyman says that in that case "the past becomes a trauma that dominates the present and future, for every event recapitulates the unresolved injury" (Lyman 1981:5–13). Lyman is also talking about first-order anger when he distinguishes "being angry" from "being made angry" (Lyman 1981:62). The latter is politicized anger, in that it recovers the origin of the anger in a social relation and thus overcomes ressentiment. But in this recovery one may be led to second-order anger, because, he thinks, the emergence of authentic political anger requires "new speech for the experience of the angry'"(Lyman 1981:68).

It is as future-looking second-order anger that I interpret the anger that Gloria Anzaldúa points to in *Borderlands* (1987) and that Lorde describes in her "Uses of Anger," an anger that is "a grief of distortion between peers"(Lorde 1984: 82, 129).

Anzaldúa describes a self, the self in between, as a self that is intimately terrorized by two different worlds of sense, the Anglo world and the traditional Mexican world. The in-between self resists intimate terrorism — the being erased, rendered speechless, irresponsible, by the two worlds. She resists intimate terrorism by taking stock of the limits of these two worlds and inhabiting the in-between world squarely: in germination toward becoming the new mestiza. She—the self in between—uses rage to drive others away and to insulate herself against exposure. This is the reverse of what people do through anger when they can exercise their anger successfully within worlds of sense in which they are both intelligible and not subordinate. They use anger against other people and address them through anger. They engage through anger. They may attempt to dominate others through anger or rage or they may demand rectification of a wrong done to them. In both cases, intelligibility and agency are presupposed if the angry act is to succeed. There is an expectation of being understood.

But for the in-between self, rage is a way of isolating her self, of making space for her self, of pushing others back in creating oneself out of intimate terrorism. The in-between self cannot use rage to communicate rage: her rage is out of character and it is unintelligible. But for the in-between self, it is the making of space apart from harmful sense. This anger recognizes more than one world and recognizes the need for creating not just a different speech but a different self, and this self cannot develop under intimate terrorism. Its germination requires separation. Since this anger is about and rejects being terrorized intimately, it is a second-order anger.

So far we have seen first- and second-order angers within or across worlds of sense that involve the oppressor/oppressed relation. But there is also anger between oppressed people. Anger between peers. Audre Lorde paints for us two kinds of anger between peers, the "angers that lie between us": anger that is "a grief of distortion between peers" and anger that keeps peers separate. These two forms of anger are interestingly complex. The second form of anger is built from the outside, from racist hatred, but it invades the Black woman's self. "We have not been allowed to experience each other freely as Black women in America; we come to each other coated in myths, stereotypes, and expectations from the outside, definitions not our own" (Lorde 1984:170).

What is so interesting about this anger is that Lorde can recognize her love for other women as she understands it. To understand what the anger is and what is wrong with it is to understand her longing for the company of other Black women. She says that the anger masks "my pain that we are so separate who should be most together." Lorde explains the anger: "The deepest understructure of this anger [is] hatred, that societal death wish directed against us from the moment we were born Black and female in America. Echoes of it return as cruelty and anger in our dealings with each other" (Lorde 1984:146). This anger is first-order anger but it is a peculiar form of it since the judgment it exercises against Black women is at the service of the oppressor and it is not about the past. It is, rather, fixed in the present.

A Black woman turns away from another Black woman in angry judgment of her. She is "good for nothing" (Lorde 1984:168). The Black woman is the racist stereotype turned into flesh. She turns away because the judgment applies to her, too, unless she is separate from the one she judges. But this is not a judgment of having been wronged by the other woman. Rather the judgment presupposes a wrong done to her by the racist oppressor, so deep that it has rendered them both, in her eyes, beyond respect, and it leads them to avert their eyes when in each other's presence. "It is very hard to look absorbed hatred in the eye" (Lorde 1984:168). Understanding this form of anger reveals the damage of racism in us and how it keeps us apart when we need each other to heal the damage. But it is important to understand this anger to distinguish it from other, constructive anger between peers: the anger that is a grief of distortion.

This anger is particularly important to me because what has made me angriest in struggles has been the slow and terrible realization of the difficulties of working across oppressions. We are separate in difficult-to-overcome ways. This is the very subject of the anger that is a grief of distortion between peers. Lorde thinks that anger has a role to play in overcoming this separation. This is anger that echoes across different worlds of sense, sometimes across different resistant worlds that retain the oppression of others within them. Its content indicates that it is second-order anger. It recognizes the resistant world of sense of other oppressed people as resistant, but it also decries its distortion of oneself and one's own. It expresses grief at distortion in angry ways because the barriers across sense are hard to overcome. So this anger does not depend solely or mainly on recognition of cognitive content, but it calls for an emotional noncognitive response, and it further asks that the emotional response, the echo, acquire cognitive content, that is, that it become fully anger. The acquisition of cognitive content requires that we "listen to its rhythms," that we "learn with it, to move beyond the manner of presentation to the substance." This implies "peers meeting upon a common basis to examine difference, and to alter those distortions which history has created around our difference." This anger is thus also forward looking. Its object is change: "to tap the anger as an important source of empowerment." This anger "births change, not destruction, and the discomfort and sense of loss it often causes is not fatal, but a sign of growth" (Lorde 1984:129–130).

The propriety of this anger lies in one's expressing through it one's need for overcoming separation without distortion. It expresses love and an unwillingness to accept anything but love in return. This is a generous anger, completely extended outward over extraordinary obstacles.

Conclusions

I have interpreted anger across worlds of sense as producing emotional echoes, or emotional reverberations, in those worlds of sense. In doing so, I am following Claudia Card's lead in her work on "Homophobia and Lesbian/Gay Pride" (1990). Card characterizes emotional echoing as a "picking up and feeling in oneself the joy, or sadness of others surrounding us, without any perception of the basis of these feelings, or even awareness that what we are doing is reproducing the feelings of others." The "underlying reasons are not communicated with the feeling" (Card 1990:152–66).

Anger across worlds of sense may echo as anger or it may reverberate as fear or even sadness. The echoing anger may be contagious anger or it may be counteranger. Anger across worlds is unexpected much of the time, out of context, and out of character from the point of view of the oppressor. The oppressor may be caught emotionally off-guard.

The fact that the cognitive content of across-worlds anger is not understood does not mean that the anger is cognitively empty or expressed as cognitively empty. It means, rather, that it cannot be intended across worlds as cognitively straightforward, and as we saw, some across-worlds anger is precisely about lack of across-worlds intelligibility. Lorde's "grief of distortion between peers" anger demands understanding across worlds, but it depends on emotional echoing to communicate the need for understanding.

The investigation of different forms of anger shows us that since our situation requires that we move within, across, and apart from official worlds of sense, our anger strategies, the ways we train our angers, need to correspond to this feature of our situation. But since the training calls for such different ways of understanding, of feeling and expressing anger, we need to be careful with the emotional and cognitive tendencies that each produces in us. The "claim upon respect anger" creates in me a tendency toward demanding respectability as my work in liberatory struggle feeds my resistant anger away from respectability. So, I put my anger down, I tortured it, failing to understand it. In this, I colluded with the oppressors' logic that would understand my rage as madness and would "mythologize" much of Black women's anger as an "attitude"; my rage is a sickness that resides in me: Black women just are hostile — that's part of their personality, just as some people are funny.

I have considered several kinds of anger expressed by subordinates in different worlds of sense. The investigation has uncovered important differences between anger, differences that are important from a liberatory standpoint. Anger can be first order, resistant, measured, communicative, and backward looking. Or it can be second order, resistant, raging, uncommunicative, and forward looking. Anger across worlds of sense can be generous or forbidding. And so on. The investigation shows us that we cannot understand controlled, backward looking, communicative, insubordinate anger as the only model for anger. A beginning but significant step in the political work of training our angers is understanding ourselves and each other in anger.

Note

1. In *The Colonizer and the Colonized*, Albert Memmi (1965) characterizes the colonized as a function of the colonizer's needs.

References

Anzaldúa, Gloria. 1987. *Borderlands/La frontera.* San Francisco: Spinsters/ Aunt Lute.

Card, Claudia. 1990. Homophobia and Lesbian/Gay Pride. Unpublished manuscript.

Frye, Marilyn. 1983. A Note on Anger. In *The Politics of Reality.* New York: The Crossing Press.

Jaggar, Alison. 1998. Love and Knowledge: Emotion in Feminist Epistemology. In *Women, Knowledge, and Reality,* edited by Ann Garry and Marilyn Pearsall, 144–45. Boston: Unwin Hyman.

Lorde, Audre. 1984. Uses of Anger and Eye to Eye: Black Women, Hatred, and Anger. In *Sister Outsider,* edited by Audre Lorde. New York: The Crossing Press.

Lyman, Peter. 1981. The Politics of Anger: On Silence, Ressentment, and Political Speech. *Socialist Review* 11 (3): 55–74.

Memmi, Albert. 1965. *The Colonizer and the Colonized.* Boston: Beacon Press.

Pateman, Carole. 1989. *The Sexual Contract.* Palo Alto, Calif.: Stanford University Press.

Spelman, Elizabeth. 1989. Anger and Insubordination. In *Women, Knowledge, and Reality,* edited by Ann Garry and Marilyn Pearsall, 263–73. Boston: Unwin Hyman.

CHAPTER SIX

~~~~

Purity, Impurity, and Separation

Note to the reader: This writing is done from within a hybrid imagination, within a recently articulate tradition of Latina writers who emphasize mestizaje *and multiplicity as tied to resistant and liberatory possibilities. All resemblance between this tradition and postmodern literature and philosophy is co-incidental, though the conditions that underlie both may well be significantly tied. The implications of each are very different from one another.*

Voy a empezar en español y en la cocina. Two uses of the verb *separar. El primer sentido. Voy a separar la yema de la clara, separar un huevo.* I will *separate* the white from the yolk. I will *separate* an egg. I crack the egg and I now slide the white onto one half of the shell and place the egg white in a bowl. I repeat the operation until I have separated all of the egg white from the yolk. *Si la operación no ha sido exitosa, entonces queda un poquito de yema en la clara.* If the operation has not been successful, a bit of the yolk stains the white. I wish I could begin again with another egg, but that is a waste, as I was taught. So I must try to lift all the yolk from the white with a spoon, a process that is tedious and hardly ever entirely successful. The intention is to separate, first cleanly and then, in case of failure, a bit messily, the white from the yolk, to split the egg into two parts as cleanly as one can. This is an exercise in purity.

Part of my interest in this chapter is to ask whether separation is always or necessarily an exercise in purity. I want to investigate the politics of purity and how they bear on the politics of separation. In the process, I will take neither the domi-

121

nant nor the "standard" tongue as my anchor in playing with "separation," as those who separate may do so not in allegiance to but in defiance of the dominant intention. As I uncover a connection between impurity and resistance, my Latina imagination moves from resistance to *mestizaje*. I think of *mestizaje* as an example of and a metaphor for both impurity and resistance. I hold on to the metaphor and adopt *mestizaje* as a central name for impure resistance to interlocked, intermeshed oppressions.[1] Much of the time, my very use of the word "separate" exhibits a form of cultural *mestizaje*.[2]

> *If something or someone is neither/nor, but kind of both, not quite either,*
> *if something is in the middle of either/or,*
> *if it is ambiguous, given the available classification of things,*
> *if it is mestiza,*
> *if it threatens by its very ambiguity the orderliness of the system, of schematized reality,*
> *if given its ambiguity in the univocal ordering, it is anomalous, deviant, can it be tamed through separation? Should it separate so as to avoid taming? Should it resist separation? Should it resist through separation? Separate as in the separation of the white from the yolk?*

Segundo sentido. Estoy haciendo mayonesa. I am making mayonnaise. I place the yolk in a bowl, add a few drops of water, stir, and then add oil drop by drop, very slowly, as I continue stirring. If I add too much oil at once, the mixture *se separa*, it separates. I can remember doing the operation as an impatient child, stopping and saying to my mother "*Mamá, la mayonesa se separó.*" In English, one might say that the mayonnaise curdled. Mayonnaise is an oil-in-water emulsion. As all emulsions, it is unstable. When an emulsion curdles, the ingredients become separate from each other. But that is not altogether an accurate description: rather, they coalesce toward oil or toward water, most of the water becomes separate from most of the oil—it is instead, a matter of different degrees of coalescence.[3] The same with mayonnaise; when it separates, you are left with yolky oil and oily yolk.

> *Going back to mestizaje, in the middle of either/or, ambiguity, and thinking of acts that belong in lives lived in mestizo ways,*

thinking of all forms of mestizaje,
thinking of breaching and abandoning dichotomies,
thinking of being anomalous willfully or unwillfully in a world of
    precise, hard-edged schema,
thinking of resistance,
resistance to a world of purity, of domination, of control over our
    possibilities,
is separation not at the crux of mestizaje, ambiguity, resistance?
Is it not at the crux both of its necessity and its possibility? Separation
    as in the separation of the white from the yolk or separation as
    curdling?

When I think of *mestizaje,* I think both of separation as curdling, an exercise in impurity, and of separation as splitting,
an exercise in purity. I think of the attempt at control exercised
by those who possess both power and the categorial eye and
who attempt to split everything impure, breaking it down into
pure elements (as in egg white and egg yolk) for the purposes
of control. Control over creativity. And I think of something
in the middle of either/or, something impure, something or
someone mestizo, as both separated, curdled, and resisting in
its curdled state. *Mestizaje* defies control through simultaneously asserting the impure, curdled multiple state and rejecting fragmentation into pure parts. In this play of assertion and
rejection, the mestiza is unclassifiable, unmanageable. She has
no pure parts to be "had," controlled.

Inside the world of the impure
    There was a muchacha who lived near my house. La gente del
pueblo *talked about her being una de las otras, "of the Others." They*
said that for six months she was a woman who had a vagina that bled
once a month, and that for the other six months she was a man, had
a penis and she peed standing up. They called her half and half, mita
y mita, neither one nor the other but a strange doubling, a deviation
of nature that horrified, a work of nature inverted. [Anzaldúa
1987:19]

    and Louie would come through — melodramatic music, like in the
mono — tan tan taran! — Cruz
Diablo, El Charro Negro! Bogart smile (his smile as deadly as his
vaisas!) He dug roles, man, and names — like "Blackie," "Little
Louie . . ."

Ese, Louie. . .
   Chale, man, call me "Diamonds!" [Montoya 1972]

   Now my mother, she doesn't go for cleanliness, orderliness, static have-come-from-nowhere objects for use. She shows you the production, her production. She is always in the middle of it and you will never see the end. You'll have to follow her through her path in the chaotic production, you'll have to know her comings and goings, her fluidity through the production. You'll have to, that is, if you want to use any of it. Because she points to what you need in her own way, her person is the "here" that ensures her subjectivity, she is the point of reference, and if you don't know her movements, her location, you can't get to the end of the puzzle. Unless she wants you to, and sometimes, she'll do that for you, because she hasn't stored that much resistance. She doesn't have names for things (oh, she has them somewhere, but uses them very little), as if she always saw them in the making, in process, in connection, not quite separable from the rest. She says "it," "under that," "next to me." "These go in the thing for things." And if you follow her movements up to the very present, you know just what she means, just what her hand is needing to hold and just where she left it and her words are very helpful in finding it. Now, clean, what you call clean, you will not see clean either. You'll see halfway. Kind of. In the middle of either/or. She doesn't see things as broken, finished, either. It's rather a very long process of deterioration. Not a now you see it, now you don't, gone forever. Just because it fell on the floor and broke in half and you glued it and you have to fill it half way, so stuff doesn't drip from the side, it doesn't stop being a tureen (or a flower pot for "centros de mesa," or maybe it'll be good as one of those thingamajigs to put things in). It's still good. And it hasn't changed its "nature" either. She has always had multiple functions for it, many possibilities. Its multiplicity has always been obvious to her.

   Getting real close, like a confidence, you tell me, "Because certain individuals can get too accustomed to being helped." That snatch of mestizaje — "certain individuals" — the South American use of "individuos" chiseled into your English. Makes me feel good, in the know. I know what you mean mujer, South American style. Just like my "operation." Claro que se dice real close, it's not just for everyone's ears. You make me feel special. I know, I know about "certain individuals." Like the "apparatus" you borrow from me or I borrow from you.

"Culture is what happens to other people." I've heard some-thing like that. I'm one of the other people, so I know there is something funny there. Renato Rosaldo helps me articulate what is peculiar, paradoxical. As he is critiquing classic norms in anthropology marking off those who are visible from those who are invisible in a culture, Rosaldo articulates the politics underlying them: "Full citizens lack culture, and those most culturally endowed lack full citizenship" (1989:198).

Part of what is funny here is that people with culture are people with a culture unknown by full citizens, not worth knowing. Only the culture of people who are culturally trans-parent is worth knowing, but it does not count as a culture. The people whose culture it is are postcultural. Their culture is in-visible to them and thus nonexistent as such. But postcultural full citizens mandate that people with a culture give up theirs in favor of the nonexistent invisible culture. So, it's a peculiar status: I have "culture" because what I have exists in the eyes of those who declare what I have to be culture. But they declare it culture only to the extent that they know they don't know it except as an absence that they don't want to learn as a presence and they have the power not to know. Furthermore, they have the power to order me to cease to know. So, as I resist and know, I am both visible and invisible. Visible as other and in-visible as myself, but these aren't separable bits. And I walk around as both other and myselves, resisting classification.

Rosaldo criticizes the "broad rule of thumb under classic an-thropological norms . . . that if it's moving it isn't cultural" (1989:209). "The blurred zones within a culture and the zones between cultures are endowed by the norms with a curious kind of hybrid invisibility" (Rosaldo 1989:209). Paradoxically "culture" needs to be both static, fixed and separate, different from the "post-cultural" (Rosaldo 1989:199) to be seen. So, if it's different but not static, it isn't "culture." But if it's different, if it's what "other people do," it's cultural. If the people who do it are other but what they do is not static, it is and it isn't culture. It's in the middle, anomalous, deviant, ambiguous, im-pure. It lacks the mark of separation as purity. If it's hybrid, it's in the middle of either/or twice.

The play between feminine and masculine elements that we contain in heterosexist eyes;
the parody of masculine/feminine, the play with illusion that

*transgresses gender boundaries, the "now you see 'it' now you
don't" magic tricks aimed at destroying the univocal character
of the "it" that we disdain with playful intention;
the rejection of masculine/feminine in our self-understanding
that some of us make our mark;
all contain a rejection of purity.*

In every one of these examples there is curdling, *mestizaje,*
lack of homogeneity. There is tension. The intentions are curdled, the language, the behavior, the people are mestizo.

I. Control, Unity, and Separation

*Guide to the reader: I will presuppose that as I investigate the
conceptual world of purity, you will keep the world of mestizaje, of curdled beings, constantly superimposed onto it, even
when that is made difficult by the writing's focus on the logic
of purity. Sometimes the logic of purity dominates the text,
sometimes the logic of curdling does. But at other points, both
worlds become vivid as coexisting and the logic of what I say
depends on the coexistence. The reader needs to see ambiguity, see that the split-separated are also and simultaneously
curdled-separated. Otherwise, one is only seeing the success
of oppression, seeing with the lover of purity's eyes. The
reader also needs to, as it were, grant the assumptions of the
lover of purity to understand his world. The fundamental assumption is that there is unity underlying multiplicity. The assumption is granted for the sake of entering the point of view
and for the purposes of contestation. The questioning is done
from within la realidad mestiza and the intent of the questioning is to clarify, intensify, aid the contestation between the two
realities. As I enter the world of purity, I am interested in a
cluster of concepts as clustered: control, purity, unity, categorizing. Control or categorizing in isolation from this network
are not my concern.*

*My aim is to distinguish between multiplicity (mestizaje)
and fragmentation and to explain connections that I see between the terms of this distinction and the logics of curdling
(impurity) and of splitting (purity). Fragmentation follows the
logic of purity. Multiplicity follows the logic of curdling. The*

*distinction between fragmentation and multiplicity is central
to this essay. I will exhibit it within individuals and within the
social world.*[4]

*According to the logic of curdling, the social world is complex and heterogeneous and each person is multiple, nonfragmented, embodied. Fragmented: in fragments, pieces, and
parts that do not fit well together; parts taken for wholes, composite, composed of the parts of other beings, composed of
imagined parts, composed of parts produced by a splitting
imagination, composed of parts produced by subordinates enacting their dominators' fantasies. According to the logic of
purity, the social world is both unified and fragmented, homogenous, hierarchically ordered. Each person is either fragmented, composite, or abstract and unified—not exclusive
alternatives. Unification and homogeneity are related principles of ordering the social world. Unification requires a fragmented and hierarchical ordering. Fragmentation is another
guise of unity, both in the collectivity and the individual. I will
connect* mestizaje *in individuals to* mestizaje *in groups and
thus in the social world, and I will connect fragmentation
within individuals to the training of the multiple toward a homogeneous social world.*

*I do not claim ontological originality for multiplicity here.
Rather both the multiple-mestizo and the unified-fragmented
coexist, each have their histories, are in contestation and in
significant logical tension. I reveal the logics underlying the
contestation. Sometimes my use of language strongly suggests
a claim of originality for the multiple. I speak of the multiple
as trained into unity and of its being conceived as internally
separable. I could say that to split-separate the multiple is to
exercise a split imagination. But if what is imagined is to gain
a powerful degree of reality, unity must be more than a reading or interpretation. It must order people's lives and psyches.
The becoming of the order is a historical process of domination in which power and ideology are at all times changing
into each other.*

Monophilia and purity are cut from the same cloth. The
urge to control the multiplicity of people and things attains
satisfaction through exercises in split separation. The urge to
control multiplicity is expressed in modern political theory

and ethics in an understanding of reason as reducing multiplicity to unity through abstraction and categorization, from a particular vantage point.[5] I consider this reduction expressive of the urge to control because of the logical fit between it and the creation of the fragmented individual. I understand fragmentation to be a form of domination.

I see this reduction of multiplicity to unity as being completed through a complex series of fictions. Once the assumption of unity underlying multiplicity is made, further fictions rationalize it as a discovery. The assumption makes these fictions possible, and they, in turn, transform it from a simple assumption into a fiction.

The assumption of unity is an act of split separation; as in conceiving of what is multiple as unified, what is multiple is understood as internally separable, divisible into what makes it one and the remainder. Or, to put it another way: to conceive of fragmentation rather than multiplicity is to exercise a split-separation imagination. This assumption generates and presupposes others. It generates the fictional construction of a vantage point from which unified wholes, totalities, can be captured. It generates the construction of a subject who can occupy such a vantage point. Both the vantage point and the subject are outside historicity and concreteness. They are both affected by and effect the reduction of multiplicity. The vantage point is privileged, simple, one-dimensional. The subject is fragmented, abstract, without particularity. The series of fictions hides the training of the multiple into unity as well as the survival of the multiple. It is only from a historical enmeshing in the concrete that the training of the multiple into fragmented unities can be seen; that is, it can be seen from a different logic, one that rejects the assumption of unity. The ahistoricity of the logic of purity hides the construction of unity.

In understanding the fictitious character of the vantage point it is important that we recognize that its conception is itself derivative from the conception of reality as unified. If we assume that the world of people and things is unified, then we can conceive of a vantage point from which its unity can be grasped. The conception of the vantage point follows the urge to control; it is not antecedent to it, because unity is assumed.

The vantage point is then itself beyond description, except as an absence: "outside of" is its central characteristic. The vantage point is not of this world, it is otherworldly, as ideal as its occupant, the ideal observer. It exists only as that from which unity can be perceived.

The subject who can occupy such a vantage point, the ideal observer, must himself be pure, unified, and simple so as to occupy the vantage point and perceive unity amid multiplicity.[6] He must not himself be pulled in all or several perceptual directions; he must not perceive richly. Reason, including its normative aspect, is the unified subject. It is what characterizes the subject as a unity. A subject who in its multiplicity perceives, understands, grasps its worlds as multiple sensuously, passionately as well as rationally without the splitting separation between sense/emotion/reason lacks the unidimensionality and the simplicity required to occupy the privileged vantage point. Such a subject occupies the vantage point of reason in a pragmatic contradiction, standing in a place where all of the subject's abilities cannot be exercised and where the exercise of its abilities invalidates the standpoint. So a passionate, needy, sensuous, and rational subject must be conceived as internally separable, as discretely divided into what makes it one—rationality—and into the confused, worthless remainder—passion, sensuality. Rationality is understood as this ability of a unified subject to abstract, categorize, train the multiple to the systematicity of norms, of rules that highlight, capture, and train its unity from the privileged vantage point.

The conception of this subject is derivative from the assumption of unity and separability. The very "construction" of the subject presupposes that assumption. So, though we are supposed to understand unity in multiplicity as that which is perceived by the rational subject occupying the vantage point of reason, we can see that the logic of the matter goes the other way around. Control cannot be rationally justified in this manner, as the urge to control antecedes this conception of reason. Part of my claim here is that the urge for control and the passion for purity are conceptually related.

If the modern subject is to go beyond conceptualizing the reduction to actually exercising control over people and things, then these fictions must be given some degree of reality. The modern subject must be dressed, costumed, masked so as to appear able to exercise this reduction of heterogeneity to homogeneity, of multiplicity to unity. The modern subject must be masked as standing separate from their own multiplicity and what commits him to multiplicity. So, his own purification into someone who can step squarely onto the vantage point of unity requires that his remainder become of no consequence to his own sense of himself as someone who justifiably exercises control over multiplicity. Thus his needs must be taken care of by others hidden in spaces relegated outside of public view, where he parades himself as pure. And it is important to his own sense of things and of himself that he pay little attention to the satisfaction of the requirements of his sensuality, affectivity, and embodiment.

Satisfying the modern subject's needs requires beings enmeshed in the multiple as the production of discrete units occurs amid multiplicity. Such production is importantly constrained by its invisibility and worthlessness in the eyes of those who attempt to control multiplicity. To the extent that the modern subject succeeds in this attempt to control multiplicity, the production is impelled by his needs. Those who produce it become producers of the structuring "perceived" by the lover of purity from the rational vantage point as well as its products. So in the logic of the lover of purity they exhibit a peculiar lack of agency, autonomy, self-regulating ability.[7]

As the lover of purity, the impartial reasoner is outside history, outside culture. He occupies the privileged vantage point with others like him, all characterized by the "possession" of reason. All occupants of this vantage point are homogeneous in their ability to comprehend and communicate. So "culture," which marks radical differences in conceptions of people and things, cannot be something they have. They are instead "postcultural" or "culturally transparent."[8]

Since his embodiment is irrelevant to his unity, he cannot have symbolic and institutionalized inscriptions in his body that mark him as someone who is "outside" his own production as the rational subject. To the extent that mastering institutional inscriptions is part of the program of unification, there cannot be such markings of his body. His difference cannot be thought of as "inscriptions" but only as coincidental, nonsymbolic marks. As his race and gender do not identify him in his own eyes, he is also race and gender transparent.

Paradoxically, the lover of purity is also constituted as incoherent, as contradictory in his attitude toward his own and others' gender, race, culture. He must at once emphasize them and ignore them. He must be radically self-deceiving in this respect. His production as pure, as the impartial reasoner, requires that others produce him. He is a fiction of his own imagination, but his imagination is mediated by the labor of others. He controls those who produce him, who to his eyes require his control because they are enmeshed in multiplicity and thus unable to occupy the vantage point of control. They are marked as other than himself, as lacking the relevant unity. But the lack is not discovered, it couldn't be, since the unity is itself assumed. The lack is symbolically produced by marking the producers as gendered, racialized, and "cultured." The marking signifies that they are enmeshed in multiplicity and thus are different from the lover of purity. But he must deny the importance of the markings that separate them.

If women, the poor, the colored, the queer, the ones with cultures (whose cultures are denied and rendered invisible as they are seen as our mark) are deemed unfit for the public, it is because we are tainted by need, emotion, the body. This tainting is relative to the modern subject's urge for control through unity and the production and maintenance of himself as unified. To the extent that he is fictional, the tainting is fictional: seeing us as tainted depends on a need for purity that requires that we become "parts," "addenda" of the bodies of modern subjects—Christian white bourgeois men—and make their purity possible. We become sides of fictitious dichotomies. To the extent that we are ambiguous—nondichotomous—we threaten the fiction and can be rendered unfit only by decrying ambiguity as nonexistent—that is, by halving us, splitting us. Thus, we exist only as incomplete, unfit beings, and they exist as complete only to the extent that what we are, and what is absolutely necessary for them, is declared worthless.

The lover of purity is shot through and through with this

paradoxical incoherence. When confronted with the sheer overabundance of the multiple, he ignores it by placing it outside value when it is his own substance and provides his sustenance. So, he is committed both to an overevaluation and a devaluation of himself, a torturing of himself, a disciplining or training of himself that puts him at the mercy of his own control. The incoherence is dispelled through separation, his own from himself. As he covets, possesses, destroys, pleases himself, he disowns his own urges and deeds. So, he is always rescued from his own incoherence by self-deception, weakness of the will, aggressive ignorance. After he ignores the fundamental and unfounded presupposition of unity, all further ignoring becomes easier. He shuns impurity, ambiguity, multiplicity as they threaten his own fiction. The enormity of the threat keeps him from understanding it. So, the lover of purity remains ignorant of his own impurity, and thus the threat of all impurity remains significantly uncontaminated. The lover of purity cannot see, understand, and attempt to control the resistance contained in the impure. He can only attempt control indirectly, through the complex incoherence of affirming and denying impurity, training the impure into its "parts" and at the same time separating from it, erecting sturdy barriers both around himself and between the fictional "parts" of impure beings.

In *Purity and Danger,* Mary Douglas (1989) sees the impulse toward unity as characteristic of social structures, and she understands pollution behavior—behavior to control pollution, impurity—as a guarding of structure from the threat of impurity. According to Douglas, impurity, dirt, is what is "out of place" relative to some order. What is impure is anomalous and ambiguous because it is out of place. It threatens order because it is not definable, so separation from it is a manner of containing it. She also sees power in impurity. But it is not her purpose to distinguish between oppressive and nonoppressive structuring. Here, I want to precisely understand the particular oppressive character of the modern construction of social life and the power of impurity in resisting and threatening this oppressive structuring.

Part of what is interesting in Douglas is that she understands that what is impure is impure relative to some order and that the order is itself conventional. What is impure is anomalous. Douglas describes several ways of dealing with anomalies, but she does not emphasize that rendering something impure is a way of dealing with it. The ordering renders something out of place. Its complexity is altered by the ordering. The alteration is not only conceptual since its "life" develops in relation to this order. So, for example, the multiplicitous beings required for the production of the unified subject are anomalous as multiple. Unity renders them anomalous. So they are altered to fit within the logic of unification. They are split over and over in accordance with the relevant dichotomies of the logic of unity. As anomalous, they remain complex, defying the logic of unity. That which is multiplicitous metamorphoses over and over in its history of resisting alteration and as the result of alteration. Both the logic of control and unity and the logic of resistance and complexity are at work in what is impure. That is why I have and will continue to use *impure* ambiguously both for something complex that is in process and thus cannot really be split-separated and for that which is fragmented.

When seen as split, the impure/multiplicitous are seen from the logic of unity, and thus their multiplicity can neither be seen nor understood. But splitting can itself be understood from the logic of resistance and countered through curdling separation, a power of the impure. When seen from the logic of curdling, the alteration of the impure to unity is seen as fictitious and as an exercise in domination: the impure are rendered uncreative, ascetic, static, realizers of the contents of the modern subject's imagination. Curdling, in contrast, realizes their against-the-grain creativity, articulates their within-structure-inarticulate powers.[9] As we come to understand curdling as resisting domination, we also need to recognize its potential to germinate a nonoppressive pattern, a mestiza consciousness, *una conciencia mestiza*.[10]

Interrupción
Oh, I would entertain the thought of separation as really clean, the two components untouched by each other, unmixed as they would be if I could go away with my own people to our land to engage in acts that were cleanly ours! But then I ask

*myself who my own people are. When I think of my own peo-
ple, the only people I can think of as my own are transitionals,
liminals, border-dwellers, world-travelers, beings in the middle of either/or. They are all people whose acts and thoughts
curdle-separate. So as soon as I entertain the thought, I realize
that separation into clean, tidy things and beings is not possible for me because it would be the death of myself as multiplicitous and a death of community with my own. I
understand my split or fragmented possibilities in horror. I
understand then that whenever I desire separation, I risk survival by confusing split separation with separation from domination, that is, separation among curdled beings who curdle
away their fragmentation, their subordination. I can appreciate then that the logic of split-separation and the logic of curdle-separation repel each other, that the curdled do not
germinate in split separation.*

II. Split Selves

Dual Personality
What Frank Chin calls a "dual personality" is the production
of a being who is simultaneously different and the same as
postcultural subjects, a split and contradictory being who is a
product of the ethnocentric racist imagination (Chin 1991). It
is one way of dealing with the anomaly of being cultured and
culturally multiplicitous. The case I know best is rural Chicanos. *Chicano* is the name for the curdled or mestizo person.
I will name the dual personality *Mexican/American,* with no
hyphen in the name, to signify that if the split were successful,
there would be no possibility of dwelling or living on the hyphen.[11]

The rural Mexican/American is a product of the Anglo
imagination, sometimes enacted by persons who are the targets of ethnocentric racism in an unwillful parody of themselves. The Anglo imagines each rural Mexican/American as
having a dual personality: the authentic Mexican cultural self
and the American self. In this notion, there is no hybrid self.
The selves are conceptually different, apparently contradictory but complementary; one cannot be found without the

other. The Anglo philosophy is that Mexican/Americans should both keep their culture (so as to be different and not full citizens) and assimilate (so as to be exploitable), a position whose contradictoriness is obvious. But as a split dual personality, the authentic Mexican can assimilate without ceasing to be "cultured," the two selves complementary, the ornamental nature of the Mexican self resolving the contradiction.

The Mexican/American can assimilate because the *Mexican* in *Mexican/American* is understood to be a member of a superfluous culture, the culture an ornament rather than shaping or affecting American reality. A simple but stoic figure who will defend the land no matter what, the Mexican/American will never quite enter the twentieth century and will not make it in the twenty-first, given that in this scheme for the next century the land will no longer be used for farming but for the recreation of the Anglo upper class. The authentic Mexican is a romantic figure, an Anglo myth, alive in the pages of John Nichols's *Milagro Beanfield War* (1976): fiercely conservative and superexploitable.

As Americans, rural Mexican/Americans are not first-class citizens because the two sides of the split cannot be found without each other. The complementarity of the sides becomes clearer: the assimilated Mexican cannot lose culture as ornamental and as a mark of difference. So, a Mexican/American is not a postcultural American. The promise of postculturalism is part of what makes assimilation appealing, since the Mexican/American knows that only postculturals are full citizens. But assimilation does not make the Mexican/American postcultural. Making the Anglo ideals of progress and efficiency one's own only makes one exploitable but does not lead one to achieve full participation in Anglo life. Anglos declare Mexican/Americans unfit for control and portray them as men and women of simple minds, given to violence, drink, and hard work, accustomed to hardship and poverty, in particular.

The dual personality is part of the mythical portrait of the colonized (Memmi 1967). The split renders the self into someone unable to be culturally creative in a live culture. Thus "authentic" Mexican craft shops exhibit *santos, trasteros, colchas, reredos.* Mexican artists cannot depart from the formulaic; they are supposed to be producing relics for the Anglo consumer of the picturesque. The mythical portrait, therefore, has acquired a degree of reality that both justifies and obscures Anglo dominance. The portrait does not lack in appeal. It makes one feel proud to be *Raza* because the portrait is heroic. It also makes one stilted, stiff, a cultural personage not quite sure of oneself, a pose, pure style, not quite at ease in one's own cultural skin, as if one did not quite know one's own culture, precisely because it is not one's own but a stereotype and because this authentic culture is not quite a live culture: it is conceived by the Anglo as both static and dying. As Rosaldo says, part of the myth is that "if it moves, it is not cultural" (1989:212). This authentic Mexican culture bears a relation to traditional culture. It is tradition filtered through Anglo eyes for the purposes of ornamentation. What is Anglo, authentically American, is also appealing: it represents progress, the future, efficiency, material well being. As American, one moves; as Mexican, one is static. As American, one is beyond culture; as Mexican, one is culture personified. The culturally split self is a character for the theatrics of racism.

The dual personality concept is a death-loving attempt to turn *Raza* into beautiful zombies: an attempt to eradicate the possibility of a mestizo—a consciousness, of our infusing every one of our possibilities with this consciousness and of our moving from traditional to hybrid ways of creation, including the production of material life.

As split, Mexican/Americans cannot participate in public life because of their difference, except ornamentally in the dramatization of equality. If we retreat and accept the "between *Raza*" nonpublic status of our concerns, to be resolved in the privacy of our communities, we participate in the logic of the split. Our communities are rendered private space in the public/private distinction. Crossing to the Anglo domain only in their terms is not an option either, as it follows the logic of the split without the terms ever becoming our own; that is the nature of this—if not of all—assimilation. So, the resistance and rejection of the culturally split self requires that we declare our communities public space and break the conceptual tie between public space and monoculturally conceived Anglo-only concerns: it requires that the language and conceptual framework of the public become hybrid.

Fragmentation

In *Justice and the Politics of Difference* (1990a) and "Polity and Difference" (in 1990b), Iris Young highlights the concept of a group as central to her understanding of the heterogeneous public, a conception of the civic public that does not ignore heterogeneity through reducing it to a fictitious unity. Instead of a unified public realm "in which citizens leave behind their particular group affiliations, histories, and needs to discuss a general interest or common good," she argues for "a group differentiated citizenship and a heterogeneous public" (Young 1990b:121).

Young understands a social group as "a collective of persons differentiated from at least one other group by cultural forms, practices, or way of life" (1990a:43). Groups become differentiated through the encounter and interaction between social collectivities that experience some differences in their way of life and forms of association as well as through social processes such as the sexual division of labor. Group members have "an affinity with other persons by which they identify with one another and by which other people identify them" (1990b:122). Group identity partly constitutes "a person's particular sense of history, understanding of social relations and personal possibilities, her or his mode of reasoning, values and expressive styles" (Young 1990b:122). Their similar way of life or experience prompts group members "to associate with each other more than with those not identified with the group, or in a different way" (Young 1990a:43). A social group is not something one joins but, rather, "one finds oneself as a member of a group whose existence and relations one experiences as always already having been" (Young 1990b:122). But groups are fluid, "they come into being and may fade away" (Young 1990b:123). Though there is a lack of clarity in how Young identifies particular groups, as I understand her, African Americans, lesbians, differently abled women, Latinas, and Navajo are examples of social groups.

Young thinks that the "inclusion and participation of everyone in public discussion and decision making requires mechanisms of group representation" (Young 1990a:115). The "ideal of the public realm of citizenship as expressing a general will, a point of view and interest that citizens have in common and that transcends their differences . . . , leads to pressures for a homogeneous citizenry" (Young 1990a:116–17). In arguing for group representation as the key to safeguarding the inclusion and participation of everyone without falling into an egoistic, self-regarding view of the political process, Young tells us that "it is possible for persons to maintain their group identity and to be influenced by their perceptions of social events derived from their group specific experience and at the same time to be public spirited, in the sense of being open to listening to the claims of others and not being concerned for their own gain alone" (Young 1990a:120). She sees group representation as necessary because she thinks differences are irreducible: "People from one perspective can never completely understand and adopt the point of view of those with other group-based perspectives and histories" (Young 1990a:121). Though differences are irreducible, group representation affords a solution to the homogenization of the public because "commitment to the need and desire to decide together the society's policies fosters communication across those differences" (Young 1990a:121).

In Young's conception of the heterogeneous public, "each of the constituent groups affirms the presence of the others and affirms the specificity of its experience and perspective on social issues," arriving at "a political program not by voicing some 'principles of unity' that hide differences but rather by allowing each constituency to analyze economic and social issues from the perspective of its experience" (Young 1990a:123).

Young sees that each person has multiple group identifications and that groups are not homogeneous, but rather that each group has group differences cutting across it (Young 1990a:123, 1990b:48). Social groups "mirror in their own differentiations many of the other groups in the wider society" (Young 1990:48). There are important implications of group differences within social groups. Significantly, "individual persons, as constituted partly by their group affinities and relations, cannot be unified, themselves are heterogeneous and not necessarily coherent" (Young 1990a:48). Young sees a revolution in subjectivity as necessary. "Rather than seeking a wholeness of the self, we who are the subjects of this plural and complex society should affirm the otherness within ourselves, acknowledging that as subjects we are heterogeneous and multiple in our affiliations and desires" (Young 1990a:124).

Young thinks the women's movement offers some beginning models for the development of a heterogeneous public and for revolutionizing the subject through the practices it has instituted to deal with issues arising from group differences within social groups. From the discussion of racial and ethnic blindness and the importance of attending to group differences among women "emerged principled efforts to provide autonomously organized forums who see reason for claiming that they have as a group a distinctive voice that might be silenced in a general feminist discourse" (Young 1990a:162). Those discussions have been joined by "structured discussion among differently identifying groups of women" (Young 1990a:162–163).

Young's complex account suggests the problem but not the solution to what I understand as the fragmentation of the subject, a consequence of group oppression where group oppression follows the logic of unity, of purity. I think we need a solution to the problem of walking from one of one's groups to another, being mistreated, misunderstood, engaging in self-abuse and self-betrayal for the sake of the group that only distorts our needs because they erase our complexity. Young lacks a conceptual basis for a solution because she lacks a conception of a multiple subject who is not fragmented. I think she does not see the need for such a conception because she fails to address the problem of the interlocking of oppressions. Fragmentation is conceptually at odds with seeing oppressions as interlocked.

I do not disagree with Young's rejection of the individualism that follows from thinking of social groups as "invidious fictions, essentializing arbitrary attributes" (Young 1990a:46), nor with her rejection of an ideal of interests as common, of the universal, homogeneous subject, and of assimilation. I do not disagree with her account of social groups either, nor with her account of the problematic nature of one's subjectivity when formed in affiliation with a multiplicity of groups. But her account leaves us with a self that is not just multiplicitous but fragmented, its multiplicity lying in its fragmentation. To explain this claim, I need to introduce the concepts of thickness and transparency.

Thickness and transparency are group relative. Individuals are transparent with respect to their group if they perceive their needs, interests, and ways as those of the group and if this perception becomes dominant or hegemonical in the group. Individuals are thick if they are aware of their otherness in the group, of their needs, interests, ways, being relegated to the margins in the politics of intragroup contestation. So, as transparent, one becomes unaware of one's own difference from other members of the group.

Fragmentation occurs because one's interests, needs, and ways of seeing and valuing things, persons, and relations are understood not as tied simply to group membership, but as the needs, interests, and ways of transparent members of the group. Thick members are erased. Thick members of several oppressed groups become composites of the transparent members of those groups. As thick, they are marginalized through erasure, their voices nonsensical. The interlocking of memberships in oppressed groups is not seen as changing one's needs, interests, and ways qualitatively in any group but, rather, one's needs, interests, and ways are understood as the addition of those of the transparent members. They are understood with a "pop-bead logic," to put it as Elizabeth Spelman does in *Inessential Woman* (1988). The title *All the Women Are White, All the Blacks Are Men, But Some of Us Are Brave* (Hull, Scott, and Smith 1982) captures and rejects this logic. White women are transparent as women; black men are transparent as black. Black women are erased and fighting against erasure. Black women are fighting for their understanding of social relations, their personal possibilities, their particular sense of history, their mode of reasoning and values and expressive styles being understood as neither reducible to anything else nor as outside the meaning of being black and of being women. Black and women are thus conceived as plural, multiplicitous, without fragmentation.

The politics of marginalization in oppressed groups is part of the politics of oppression, and the disconnection of oppressions is part of these politics. Avoiding recognition of the interlocking of oppressions serves many people well, but no one is served so well by it as the pure, rational, full-fledged citizen. So I see a cross-fertilization between the logic of purity used to exclude members of oppressed groups from the civic public and the separation and disconnection of oppressions. Liberatory work that makes vivid that oppressions must be fought as interlocked is consistently blocked in oppressed groups through the marginalization of thick members.

So unless one understands groups as explicitly rejecting the logic of fragmentation and embracing a nonfragmented multiplicity that requires an understanding of oppressions as interlocked, group representation does most group members little good. It indeed fails at safeguarding the "inclusion and participation of everyone" in the shaping of public life. The logic of impurity, of *mestizaje*, provides us with a better understanding of multiplicity, one that fits the conception of oppressions as interlocked. I mean to offer a statement of the politics of heterogeneity that is not necessarily at odds with Young's, but its logic is different. Hers, though formulated in rejection of the logic of purity, is oddly consistent with though not necessarily tied to it. Mine is inconsistent with it. Communication across differences in her model may well fail to recognize that one is listening to voices representative only of transparents, voices that embody the marginalization of thick members and contain their fragmentation.

Social homogeneity, domination through unification, and hierarchical ordering of split social groups are connected tightly to fragmentation in the person. If the person is fragmented, it is because the society is itself fragmented into groups that are pure, homogeneous. Each group's structure of affiliation to and through transparent members produces a society of persons who are fragmented as they are affiliated to separate groups. As the parts of individuals are separate, the groups are separate, in an insidious dialectic.

Heterogeneity in the society is consistent with and may require the presence of groups. But groups in a genuinely heterogeneous society have complex, nonfragmented persons as members; that is, they are heterogeneous themselves. The affiliative histories include the formation of voices in contestation that reveal the enmeshing of race, gender, culture, class, and other differences that affect and constitute the identity of the group's members. This is a very significant difference in direction from the one suggested by the postmodern literature, which goes against a politics of identity and toward minimizing the political significance of groups.[12] The position presented in this chapter, a position that I also see in the literature on *mestizaje*, affirms a complex version of identity politics and a complex conception of groups.

Interrupción: Lesbian Separation

When I think of lesbian separation I think of curdle-separation. In this understanding of separation I am a lesbian separatist. We contain in our own and in the heterosexist construction of ourselves all sorts of ambiguities and tensions that are threatening to purity, to the construction of women as for use, for exploitation. We are outside the lover of purity's pale, outside his conceptual framework. Even the attempt to split ourselves into half man/half woman recognizes our impurity. In our own conception, we defy splitting separation by mocking the purity of the man/woman dichotomy or rejecting it.

But "Watchale esa!" doesn't resonate in its impurity implicitly in all lesbian ears, and not all lesbian hips move inspired by a Latin beat.

Lesbians are not the only transitionals, impure, ambiguous beings. And if we are to struggle against "our" oppression, Latina Lesbian cannot be the name for a fragmented being. Our style cannot be outside the meaning of Latina and cannot be outside the meaning of lesbian. So, our struggle, the struggle of lesbians, goes beyond lesbians as a group. If we understand our separation as curdle-separation, then we can rethink our relation to other curdled beings. Separation from domination is not split-separation.

III. Impurity and Resistance

People who curdle-separate are themselves people from whom others split-separate, dissociate, withdraw. Lovers of purity, controllers through split-separation not only attempt to split-separate us but also split-separate from us in ways I have discussed, such as ghettoization and conceptual exclusion. They also attempt to split-separate us from others who are themselves curdled through the logic of marginalization, of transparency. The logic of transparency shines in the constructed lover of purity himself, the modern subject, the impartial reasoner. He is the measure of all things. He is transparent relative to his position in the hetero-relational patriarchy, to his culture, race, class, and gender. His sense is the only sense. So curdled thoughts are nonsensical. To the extent that his sense is the instrument of our communication, we become susceptible to the logic of transparency and see split-separation from other curdled beings as sensical in our resistance to oppression. We also become susceptible to being agents of the lovers of purity in carrying out the oppression of other curdled beings, in constructing his made-to-order orderly world. Thus, curdle-separation is blocked, barred, made into a hard to reach resistant and liberatory possibility. It is also dangerous because curdled beings may adopt the logic of transparency in self-contradiction and act as agents of the lover of purity in coercing us into fragmentation and oppression. I think this is a risk that we can minimize only by speaking the language of curdling among curdled beings in separation and living its logic and by listening for, responding to, evoking, sometimes demanding, such language and logic. I think this is a risk we must take because the logic of split-separation contains not resistance but co-optation. So we have to constantly consider and reconsider the question: Who are our own people?

I don't think we can consider "our own" only those who reject the same dichotomies we do. It is the impulse to reject dichotomies and to live and embody that rejection that gives us some hope of standing together as people who recognize each other in our complexity. The hope is based on the possibilities that the unsettling quality of being a stranger in our society reveals to us, the possibilities that purification by ordeal reveals to us. I think this is Anzaldúa's point in thinking of a borderland: "It is a constant state of transition. The prohibited and forbidden are its inhabitants those who cross over, pass over, or go through the confines of the 'normal.' . . . Ambivalence and unrest reside there and death is no stranger" (Anzaldúa 1987:3–4). For her, "To live in the Borderlands means you are neither *hispana india negra española ni gabacha, eres mestiza, mulata,* half-breed . . . half and half—both woman and man, neither—a new gender. . . . In the Borderlands you are the battleground where enemies are kin to each other" (Anzaldúa 1987:194).

But, of course, that is thin ground for thinking of others as "our own": that we might be revealed to each other as possible through the tramplings and denials and torturings of our ambiguity. A more solid ground because it is a more positive ground is the one that affirms the lack of constraint of our creativity that is at the center of curdling; that holds on to our own lack of script, to our being beings in the making; that might contain each other in the creative path, who don't discount but look forward to that possibility.

Ambiguous, neither this nor that, unrestrained by the logic of this and the logic of that, and thus its course not mapped, traced already in movements, words, relations, structures, institutions; not rehearsed over and over into submission, containment, subordination, asceticism—we can affirm the positive side of our being threatening as ambiguous. If it is ambiguous it is threatening because it is creative, changing, defiant of norms meant to subdue it. So we find our people as we make the threat good, day to day, attentive to our company in our groups, across groups. The model of curdling as a model for separation is a model for worldly separation—the separation of border-dwellers, of people who live in a crossroads, people who deny purity and are looking for each other for the possibility of going beyond resistance.

IV. The Art of Curdling

Curdle-separation is not something that happens to us but something we do. As I have argued, it is something we do in resistance to the logic of control, to the logic of purity. Though transparents fail to see its sense, and thereby keep its sense from structuring our social life, that we curdle testifies to our being active subjects, not consumed by the logic of control. Curdling may be a haphazard technique of survival as an active subject, or it can become an art of resistance, metamorphosis, transformation.

I recommend cultivating this art as a practice of resistance into transformation from oppressions as interlocked. It is a practice of festive resistance:

> Bi- and multilingual experimentation;
> code-switching;
> categorial blurring and confusion;
> caricaturing the selves we are in the worlds of our oppressors, infusing them with ambiguity;
> practicing trickstery and foolery;
> elaborate and explicitly marked gender transgression;
> withdrawing our services from the pure or their agents whenever possible and with panache;
> drag;
> announcing the impurity of the pure by ridiculing his inability at self-maintenance;
> playful reinvention of our names for things and people, multiple naming;
> caricaturing of the fragmented selves we are in our groups;
> revealing the chaotic in production;
> revealing the process of producing order if we cannot help producing it;
> undermining the orderliness of the social ordering;
> marking our cultural mixtures as we move;
> emphasizing *mestizaje*;
> crossing cultures;
> etc.

We not only create ourselves and each other through curdling but also announce ourselves to each other through this art, our curdled expression. Thus, curdled behavior is not only creative but also constitutes itself as a social commentary. All curdled behavior, thought, and expression contain and express this second level of meaning, one of social commentary. When curdling becomes an art of resistance, the curdled presentation is highlighted. There is the distance of meta comment, auto-reflection, looking at oneself in someone else's mirror and back in one's own, of self-aware experimentation. Our commentary is not straightforward: the commentary underlines the curdling and constitutes it as an act of social creative defiance. We often intend and cultivate with style this social commentary, this meta meaning of our curdling. When confronted with our curdling or curdled expression or behavior, people often withdraw. Their withdrawal reveals the devaluation of ambiguity *as threatening* and is thus also a meta comment. It announces that, though we will not be acknowledged, we have been seen as threatening the univocity of life lived in a state of purity, their management of us, their power over us.

Notes

1. I thank Marilyn Frye for her criticism of the choice of *interlocking in interlocking oppressions.* I agree with her claim to me that the image of interlocking is of two entirely discrete things, like two pieces of a jigsaw puzzle, that articulate with each other. I am not ready to give up the term because it is used by other women of color theorists who write in a liberatory vein about enmeshed oppressions. I think *interwoven* or *intermeshed* or *enmeshed* may provide better images. At the time of this writing, I had not drawn the distinction between intermeshed oppressions and the interlocking of oppressions. See both the Introduction and chapter 10, "Tactical Strategies of the Streetwalker" for the relation between the two terms of this distinction.

2. This is the same form found in my use of *operation, apparatus,* and *individual.* Providing linguistic puzzles is part of the art of curdling.

3. For this use of *emulsion,* see Vogt-Schild (1991).

4. It is important to problematize the singularity of "social world" and the distinction between social world and individual.

5. I have based this description of the connection between the urge to control and modern political theory and ethics on Iris Marion Young's "Impartiality and the Civic Public" (in Young 1990b). Much of what I say in section I is a restatement and elaboration on sections 1 and 2 of Young's chapter. I have also benefited from Mangabeira Unger (1975) and Pateman (1988) in coming to this understanding.

6. The ideal observer, unified subject is male. This fictitious subject is not marked in terms of gender for reasons explained below.

7. See Smith (1974) and Hartsock (1988) for arguments backing this account.

8. See Rosaldo (1989:200, 203) for his use of *postcultural* and *culturally transparent.* I am using *postcultural* as he does. His use of *culturally transparent* was suggestive to me in reaching my own account.

9. See Douglas (1966): "In other words, where the social system is well-articulated, I look for articulate powers vested in the points of authority;

where the social system is ill-articulated, I look for inarticulate powers vested in those who are a source of disorder" (Douglas 1966:99).

10. See Anzaldúa (1987, especially pp. 41–51, on the Coatlicue state, and pp. 77–91, on *la Conciencia de la Mestiza*).

11. Sonia Saldivar-Hull used the expression "living on the hyphen" in the panel discussion "Cultural Identity and the Academy," at the tenth annual Interdisciplinary Forum of the Western Humanities Conference on Cultures and Nationalisms, University of California, Los Angeles.

12. Two examples that come vividly to mind are the positions suggested in Butler (1990) and Haraway (1990).

References

Anzaldúa, Gloria. 1987. *Borderlands/La Frontera: The New Mestiza.* San Francisco: Spinsters/Aunt Lute.

Butler, Judith. 1990. *Gender Trouble.* New York: Routledge.

Chin, Frank. 1991. Come All Ye Asian American Writers of the Real and the Fake. In *The Big Aiiieeeee!* CD. Ed. Jeffery Paul Chan, Frank Chin, Lawson Fusao Inada, and Shawn Wong. New York: Meridian.

Douglas, Mary. 1989. *Purity and Danger.* London: Ark Paperbacks.

Haraway, Donna. 1990. A Manifesto for Cyborgs. In *Feminism/Post Modernism*, edited by Linda J. Nicholson, 190–233. New York: Routledge.

Hartsock, Nancy C. M. 1988. The Feminist Standpoint: Developing the Ground for a Specifically Feminist Historical Materialism. In *Discovering Reality: Feminist Perspectives on Epistemology, Metaphysics, Methodology, and Philosophy of Science.* Ed. CD. Sandra Harding and Merrill Hintikka. Boston: Reidel.

Hull, Gloria T., Patricia Bell Scott, and Barbara Smith, eds. 1982. *All the Women Are White, All the Blacks Are Men, But Some of Us Are Brave.* New York: Feminist Press.

Mangabeira Unger, Roberto. 1975. *Knowledge and Politics.* New York: Free Press.

Memmi, Albert. 1967. *The Colonizer and the Colonized.* Boston: Beacon.

Montoya, José. 1972. El Louie. In *Literatura chicana, texto y contexto,* edited by Antonio Castaneda Shular, 173–76. Englewood Cliffs, N.J.: Prentice-Hall.

Nichols, John. 1976. *Milagro Beanfield War.* New York: Ballantine.

Pateman, Carole. 1988. *The Sexual Contract.* Stanford, Calif.: Stanford University Press.

Rosaldo, Renato. 1989. *Culture and Truth.* Boston: Beacon.

Smith, Dorothy. 1974. Women's Perspective as a Radical Critique of Sociology. *Sociological Enquiry* 44(1):7–14.

Spelman, Elizabeth. 1988. *Inessential Woman.* Boston: Beacon.

Vogt-Schild, A. G. 1991. Physical Parameters and Release Behaviors of W/O/W Multiple Emulsions Containing Cosurfactants and Different Specific Gravity of Oils. *Pharmaceutic Acta Helvetica* 66(12).

Young, Iris Marion. 1990a. *Justice and the Politics of Difference.* Princeton, N.J.: Princeton University Press.

———. 1990b. *Throwing Like a Girl and Other Essays in Feminist Philosophy and Social Theory.* Bloomington: Indiana University Press.

~

CHAPTER SEVEN

Boomerang Perception and the Colonizing Gaze: Ginger Reflections on Horizontal Hostility

This chapter is written for people of color; for women firstly and mainly, but also for men: green-eyed Blacks,[1] never-been-taught-my-culture Asian Americans and U.S. Latinos, émigrés, immigrants and migrants, mixed-bloods and mixed-cultures, solid core, community bred, folk of color. It is difficult to write without being moved from this intention and it is difficult to hear the writing as so addressed. That is because public spaces are dominated by white/Anglos and because it is part of our oppression that our public spaces are not sufficiently occupied by this kind of conversation. I would like to be heard as if public spaces were thick with us both speaking and hearing and as if our public spaces were fluent in the conversation. This is a chapter about perception, how we perceive each other and what the connections are between those perceptions and the racist/colonialist gaze.

One's body, its color, features, its movement, and the culture expressed in its movements and clothes, all up for mistrust and inspection. One's voice, the accent in one's voice, the culture in one's speech, deeds, ways inspected, over and over by those one would like to call one's own, or—alternatively conceived—those one has reason to think might be one's own people (as when an adopted child has reason to think she has found her real, blood mother). The door to an untroubled identity always closed. Having learned in their eyes that one's

151

claim is not solid. Taken from group to group by the need for solidarity, belonging, for understanding the damages of racialization, for understanding the puzzle of one's identity. From cultural specificity to larger and larger rings of solidarity always inspected, mistrusted, found wanting or not, but always in need of legitimation. Whether from Chicanas and Puertoriqueñas to Latinas to Women of Color; or from African American, Jamaican, Haitian to Women of Color; or from Chinese or Korean American to Asian American to Women of Color. Missing the marks of solid identity.

Solid, barrio raised, core, easygoing in one's identity of color, the sense of faking it or of being perceived as a fake not in one's experience. Not with respect to one's ethnicity or race, anyway, and not by one's own, though one's humanity, one's abilities are constantly taken to be counterfeit by white/Anglos. Solidly tied to a group of one's ethnicity and race by blood and culture and shared history and traditions. One's values clear, one's word and judgment authoritative, weighty. A sense of place or nation accompanied by a deep sense of the tie between place or nation and survival. One's movements, ways, use of speech, very much of the place. The eyes that allow one to position and identify oneself clearly in the world, comfortably taken for granted as they surround one in a trusting glance.

Under siege, solidity is a matter of degrees and circumstance. At least for some, the degree of solidity changes from place to place, it changes with the company and the territory as it is tied both to company and territory. When outside one's territory, one feels out of one's element, outside the influence of the sources of one's self-assurance and self-esteem. The way of traversing space less steady, uneasy in one's skin, as if one were wearing someone else's clothes. For others the sense of solidity is a sense of nationhood not tied to territory but to a deep sense of shared traditions, traditions forged in "a transgenerational detestation of our subordination" (Langston Gwaltney 1980:xxvii). Moving with others who do not share or are not fluent in resistant core culture feels like a loss of solidity, particularly if one is open to be moved by the values and beliefs of the company. In both cases, going from less to more encompassing circles born from the need to form a politics of resistance means the loss of some degrees of assurance in one's solidity, unless one can succeed in asserting one's values over the larger circle. Sometimes, some people appear to have become context-free-solid; they appear to me that way, anyway. It is hard to imagine anyone subject to the hazards of perception in a racist society feeling that way, feeling impermeable to the multiplicity of mistrustful glances. I wonder about their openness to other resistant ways and about the harshness of their glance. I wonder whether context-free solidity doesn't come together with a willingness to lord one's culture over others.

Mixed, in blood or culture: Anglo-Mexicana, Mexicana-Korean, Black-Mescalero, Chicano-Riqueña, and so on to bounteous hybridation. Mixed, *agringada*, looking the wrong way for the culture, the values and beliefs mixed up in obvious and jarring ways. Or adopted by whites and reared as "their own" into white eyes looking at one's color as if it were not one's own, but fully conscious of one's self-alienation, a sense of lacking a soul. Reared in white neighborhoods to see the culture of one's ancestors as a private affair not fit for public identity and at the same time not quite fluent in the home culture. Feeling as if one does and does not belong in the public; feeling chameleon-like if one blurs the colors and the cultures out of one's own self-perception. Fidgety in the presence of community folk, as if one could cover one's lacks with self-consciousness. Immigrant or migrant to a community of color and thus with no blood ties; immigrant or migrant to a community of color whose shared culture bears distant or no clear ties to one's own; immigrant or migrant to a community of color without sharing its history. Immigrant, one's speech accented not with the mark of regions but with the mark of foreignness, of lack of cool, of lack of savvy in the ways of U.S. insubordinate traditions.

Jon is a young brother and he is a little withdrawn, but he is intelligent and loyal. . . . He is at that dangerous age where confusion sets in and sends brothers either to the undertaker or to prison. He is a little better off than I was and than most brothers his age. . . . Tell the brothers never to mention his green eyes and skin tone. He is very sensitive about it and he will either fight or withdraw. Do you understand? You know that some of us don't bother to be righteous with each other. He has had a great deal of trouble these last few years behind that issue. It isn't right. He is a loyal and beautiful black man-child. I love him. [George Jackson 1970:220]

I have forgotten what I used to be. I lost my youth conscious-ness in the process of growing up. I did not like my childhood, so I find it strange that I am struck by sentimentality in seeing an Asian child with a white elder. I do not know whether the child's situation is at all the same as mine, but I longed to stop the child, to talk to him, to protect him. I think, though I'm not exactly sure, that in my childhood, my "Asianness" was much more distinct to me. I have assimilated into a world that really isn't mine and though I can speak academically of such an as-similation and though it pains me to do so, I still see out of white eyes. [Bill Elsinger 1993]

Just how ethnic are you? We shun the white-looking Indian, the "high yellow" Black women, the Asian with the white lover, the Native woman who brings her white girl friend to the Pow Wow, the Chicana who doesn't speak Spanish, the academic, the uneducated. Her difference makes her a person we can't trust. *Para que sea* "legal" she must pass the ethnic legitimacy test we have devised. . . . and woe to any sister who doesn't measure up to our assigned places, woe to anyone who doesn't measure up to our standards of ethnicity. [Gloria Anzaldúa 1990]

Where do you go to be seen? To be seen as something other than a more-or-less monstrous imitation, an imaginary being. Where do you go to be seen apart from tests of legitimacy that turn you into an imaginary being? Monstrous to different de-grees. Imitation white/imitation color. Ready to be accused of failing to pass the ethnic legitimacy test of passing; of "git'n over" on Blacks, Latinos, Asians, folk of color; of not being someone others can count on; of not resisting subordination because one does not need to and because one is foolish enough to think one can pass; of being a "wanna be" woman or man of color; of being just a foreigner. Everyone can see or hear or understand that one is not white/Anglo, that having green eyes does not qualify one for that, nor having a thick accent, nor a white mother, nor having being denied any culture except white/Anglo culture. Everyone understands that none of these characteristics qualify one as white/Anglo. So how does one get to be seen and why is one left out? Left out of territory, nation, home? Or included as a favor and to be reminded over and over of the favor through rituals of mistrust and exclusion.

> The notion that black culture is some kind of backwater or tributary of an American "mainstream" is well established in much popular as well as standard social science literature. To the prudent black American masses, however, core black culture is the mainstream. The minority of black Americans who significantly depart from core black customs and values may pass, may become bourgeois in spirit as well as income, or swell the ranks of marginal drug and welfare cultures. But far more often than not, the primary status of a black person is that accorded by the people he or she lives among. It is based upon assessments of that person' fidelity to core black standards. . . . Most black people agree, on all levels of consciousness and in their overt actions, on what these specific standards are. [Langston Gwaltney 1980:xxiii]

"People can tell the difference between 'real right' and 'jackleg'" (Langston Gwaltney 1980:xxiiv).

I am interested here in those caught in between two perceptions that relegate them to a particular lack of independence and lack of sociality. It is a situation similar to exile as it is constituted by a denial of identity, and a ghostly subjectivity. But unlike exile, this is not a discontinuous state from home to homelessness. It is a state of estrangement from self in between two perceptions, neither one of which allows one to position and identify oneself in the world except as an image. Neither perception provides a home or a sense of belonging. One is divested of historicity, living in an uncreative limbo, used, arrogated, doomed to carry out other people's agendas.

Edward Said compares nationalism and exile. He sees nationalism and exile as opposites "informing and constituting each other (Said 1990:359).

> Nationalism is an assertion of belonging in and to a place, a people, a heritage. It affirms the home created by a community of language, culture and customs. [Said 1990:359]

Exile is the unhealable rift forced between a human being and
a native place. [Said 1990:357]

A sense of home, place, and heritage has been crucial for
those who are targets of racism. It has meant the creation and
maintenance of an alternative to racist/colonialist perception.
It has kept one able to practice a double vision: seeing oneself
and one's company at once in the racist and the resistant construction. It has kept one able to hold two incompatible and
parallel perceptions at once. And it has also kept one cautious
of the racist construction, less touched by it, in touch with it so
as to handle one's situation with knowledge of the oppressor's
delusions of superiority. I have appreciated the survival and
resistant quality of home-made perception, of having one's attention riveted on one's own. Thus, I have tended to think it
unhealthy for oppressed peoples to obsess over the oppressors' perception of their subjectivity. One becomes both fascinated by it and overwhelmed by its power. Understanding the
extent to which we have internalized it paralyzes one. Unraveling the logic of the oppressor's gaze requires that we pay
great attention to it, that we become fascinated by it, but even
when we discover its irrationality, we are not on our way
towards a resistant subjectivity. That requires a different logic.
    So I have thought that one needs a justification to study the
oppressor's logic. As I dwell on the construction of the racist/
colonialist perception, I am guided by three questions: Why
do core persons of color, bred in communities of shared traditions, subject the less solid to inspections that constitute them
as fakes? Can one maintain the double vision that combines
an understanding of the oppressor's powerful imagery with
the active exercise of one's home-grown prophetic sense of
self without constituting them as fakes? Can those without
homeplace, those not bred in the nation, those *sin barrio, sin
comunidad,* provide a critique of closed boundaries nationhood that doesn't endanger the exercise of double vision?
    So, I enter this exploration gingerly without an intrinsic in-
terest in the racist/colonialist gaze. My attention riveted on
women and men of color and on the hostility among us as we
attempt to neutralize its effects on us. Racist/colonialist perception is narcissistic; it denies independence to the seen, it

constructs its object imaginatively as a reflection of the seer. It robs the seen of a separate identity. "I look at you and come right back to myself" says Elizabeth Spelman. "In the United States white children like me got early training in boomerang perception when we were told by well-meaning white adults that Black people were just like us—never, however, that we were just like Blacks" (Spelman 1988:12).

As I think about the object of boomerang perception, I see the consequences of the lack of reciprocity in its logic. The white person is the original, the Black person just an image, not independent from the seer. Given Spelman's account, the white gaze imagines its object to be like and different from itself. The white seer does not really believe that "Black people are just like us," since the white seer does not believe himself to be an image or does not experience herself as an image dependent on Black people.

When talking about the West's creation of the Orient, Edward Said describes a mental operation similar to boomerang perception through which the mind domesticates the exotic, after having created it. The exotic is created through what Said calls "imaginative geography," the setting of imaginary boundaries in our minds between a familiar space—"our land"—and an unfamiliar space—"the land of barbarians." The exotic becomes an exciting threat controlled through a mental operation that domesticates it. "Something patently foreign and distant acquires a status more rather than less familiar." The distinction between things that are completely novel or completely well known is broken down by coming to see "new things, things seen for the first time, as versions of a previously known thing." This is a method of controlling what seems to be a threat to some established view of things. "The threat is muted, familiar values impose themselves, and in the end the mind reduces the pressure upon it by accommodating things to itself as either original or repetitious." The Orient is a repetition of the West. The West acquires a sense of itself negatively through the setting of the "us"/"them" dichotomy; but it acquires a sense of its own value by constituting itself as the original which the Orient repeats, mimics monstrously, grotesquely. Said thinks of this construction as imaginative geography because it does not require that the "barbarians" acknowledge the "us"/"them" distinction. The barbarians are imaginative constructions; they become stereotype, monstrous repetitions of the familiar.

As I consider both Said and Spelman, and locate my attention on the object of the oppressor's gaze, I come to see the complications and dangers of boomerang perception more deeply. The Western/white seer is the original, the object of his gaze a mere but distorted image: image both in the sense of imagined and in the sense of a reflection, an imitation. The imagination wavering between fear and delight construes us in its image, but as terrific, dangerous, monstrous distortions of its own familiar visage and as fulfilling its unspoken desires. In both cases it construes us as dependent on the seer for its existence, and lacking an independent history because lacking an independent subjectivity. The "same" and monstrously different.

Just in case you may think that my complication of Spelman's analysis with Said's does not quite understand middle-white American perception, consider the following all too familiar example. I was sitting in a very full plane on the window seat. A white woman was sitting next to me, in the middle seat, her husband on the aisle seat. She asked me what I did and after a few minutes I began telling her of my work in Latino/Latina communities and about the situation of Latinos and Latinas in this society. As she insisted that there was no racism involved in the situation of Latinos and Blacks, that we are all the same and that any Latino or Black person could achieve the same things as white people, I began to feel a bit claustrophobic. But then, I thought, this is a political education opportunity. She espoused with conviction the position that we are all the same and that our situations are all the same, a question of a shared human condition. There are differences among individuals, she said, but not between groups. Soon she began telling me about reading about rappers in the paper. She felt horror toward Black and Latino rap, at its violence in its relation to women. She reduced all rap to hatred of women. As I argued that the whole society was violent against women and brought the spectacle of U.S. senators reflecting on the sexual harassment of Anita Hill, the statistics on rape and the small number of rape convictions, she brought the stereotype right to my face: she insisted that Latino and Black male rappers were, after all, different, brutal, animalistic, sexually violent in a way very much different from white manhood and from the violence of the system. Sameness called for by narcissism, difference called forth by a sense of danger, of aggression. The "same" and monstrously different. As I was arguing with her, her husband forbid her from talking to me any more. She complied.

The alternative perception allowed by homeplace and the company that homeplace affords, *carnales y carnalas*, is crucial for survival. It layers itself over this ghost-making gaze and gives one substance. In giving one substance it affords resistance. It makes both vision and history possible. But it should be clear to anyone who respects the many resistant enclaves that folk of color have built in this society, that we have fashioned a variety of styles, values, beliefs, ways, which afford us perceptions within different seeing circles all of which are alternatives to the racist/colonialist gaze. Most of us are aware of and fiercely tied only to our own, to the one of our seeing circle.

So, why is it that those steeped in home-grown perception make others pass ethnic legitimacy tests and constitute them as fakes through the inspection? There is a felt connection between survival, resistance, the maintenance of double vision and who one sees as one's own, who is part of the resistant seeing circle, the nation. There is a felt sense that one can only keep double vision seeing and being seen through the eyes of one's particular circle. There is an understanding of only two logics that are markedly distinct, in fierce opposition: racist logic and resistant logic, both active in the home-grown seer as realistic resistance requires. This lack of fluency in resistant logics accounts in part for the drawing of very tight, inflexible boundaries around one's circle. There is also a presupposition that the formation of nations, homeplaces, is the only way to develop logics of resistance.

Thus, there is a deep fear of losing this anchor, this seeing circle that gives one substance, as it stands as the sole conceivable source of a resistant subjectivity. This fear is analogous in my experience to the terror that seizes acute chronic pain sufferers: the fear that the pain may take over your whole consciousness and leave nothing in you except consciousness of pain, all other subjectivity erased. One fears that one may become what one is in the racist perceiver's eyes, and nothing else, all other subjectivity erased. And as I have argued, that is to become something insubstantial, dependent, a distorted image of white humanity. So one guards the seeing circle zealously.

One can understand, then, the mistrust of people of color who, given these presuppositions, must have been taken, zombified, given white/Anglo eyes or who must have few or no defenses against racist perception. There is a sense of unspoken horror, of metaphysical revulsion, at such people. They are lost, consumed by the only other available logic, the logic of ghostly subjectivity. The two fears, the fear of losing one's own solidity and the fear of seeing someone who has none as one of one's own, closes the outside of the circle in its own terrifying intersubjectivity. Thus, enlarging the circle to include those who do not have, or one does not have clear reason yet to believe they have, an alternative sense of self, is understood as endangering the circle itself.

I think these presuppositions are mistaken: fluency in more than one resistant logic breaks one out of the two exclusive logics paradigm, a paradigm that necessitates fragmentation and mistrust among people of color. It also enables one to be open to the possibility that others are not consumed by racist perception, that they are not ghosts. The fragmentation of perception disempowers our resistance by making deep coalitions logically impossible as it undermines the very possibility of fashioning larger and complex resistant collective subjectivities, more complex seeing circles.

But it is not just that the presuppositions are mistaken. It is crucial to my argument here, that those who are not insiders to homeplaces are seen by those within, with the eyes of the oppressor. The choice between only two exclusive logics dictates this adoption. But it is paradoxical that those who cultivate resistant perception with respect to each other would thoroughly internalize oppressive perception of those outside their circle. It is only when perceived with the oppressors' eyes, as consumed by them, as mere monstrous images, that those outside homeplaces lack a resistant subjectivity and have nothing to teach those within the nation.

Once the first presupposition is abandoned, when one comes to see that there is more than one resistant logic, one has very good reason to abandon mistrustful ways of perceiving people of color who are not part of one's own community of validation and resistance. This allows the perceiver to face those outside shared values and shared community with a willingness to ask the question of identity anew, with the curiosity of someone who is looking for companions in the formation of a larger resistant subjectivity. Who are you? Who are we? become different questions when asked anew, without presupposing the real/fake dichotomy. Then one may see that the no-home, in exile position may have provided some perceptual advantages: the one without home may have learned to see orthodoxies and ossification in the homeplaces; learned them as interpretations of their own flesh; learned them in the rejection of themselves as innovations. Orthodoxies and rigidities may well respond to a desire for safety, and to a sense that conserving tradition is a way of safety. The racially/culturally homeless may stir critique and new life that appears to endanger that safety. But she looks for community because she looks for the formation of a large resistant subjectivity and this cannot be constructed without the company of those seasoned in resistant traditions.

There is a fear of critiques of orthodoxy. When tradition seems a haven from cultural and psychological devastation, it is hard to honor critical stances as it is hard to see the dangers of orthodoxy and conservatism from within and under siege. Yet those of color who are culturally homeless understand that orthodoxy it itself dangerous, a form of self destruction, an ossification of culture that aids the ethnocentric racist push towards culture as ornament. So, the fear of critique also inclines toward the exclusion of the culturally homeless through the adoption of the racist perception of them. Again, this is self-destructive, and it is further indication of the infiltration of whiteness in the logic of home-grown resistant circles. It indicates a further understandable inconsistency in the resistant stance.

We can agree with Gloria Anzaldúa's claim that "it is ex-

actly our internalized whiteness that desperately wants boundary lines marked out" (1990:143). Once we understand the
presupposition of only two logics of perception, one racist, the
other resistant to racism, and once we understand the presupposition of resistance arising only from within culturally traditional circles, the internalization of whiteness in the rejection
of the culturally homeless becomes clear. The culturally homeless are seen with white/Anglo eyes; cultural critique is
resisted toward a reduction of culture to ornament; fragmentation follows, as does lack of understanding of other resistant
logics. We can also mention that the very logics of ethnic legitimacy and of racist/colonialist perception are consonant, working on the original/real-imitation/fake dichotomy. Thus, we
administer legitimacy tests with white eyes on, and what
moves us to administer the test is the same logic that invokes
the distinction between the original/real and the image/fake.

So, we have answered the question: "Why do core persons
of color, bred in communities of shared traditions and history
subject the less solid to inspections that constitute them as
fakes?" We have also answered the question: "Can those without homeplace provide a critique of closed-boundaries-nation-
hood that doesn't endanger the exercise of double vision?"
Indeed, the critique of closed boundaries challenges the internalization of whiteness and buttresses the exercise of double
vision. It makes one self-aware of the very construction of resistance, its sources, the process, the company. It enables one
to be choosier about the company by uncovering a different
way of asking the question of identity, one that doesn't presuppose a simplicity of two opposed logics, one racist, the
other oppositional, resistant. It opens the door to a plethora of
resistant possibilities, alliances, understandings, playful and
militant connections. There is risk, but the safety of tradition,
of conservatism is a myth for people under siege. Only the
powerful derive power from quieting critiques of tradition.

We have also answered the question: "Can we maintain the
double vision that combines an understanding of the oppressor's powerful imagery with the active exercise of one's home-
grown prophetic sense of self without constituting the culturally homeless as fakes?" The answer is simply that double vision becomes more complex and open-ended. One's resistant

vision will become more open to and knowledgeable in other resistant logics, and benefit from the complex exchanges. Or it may become "visions," complex fluencies, critical and creative understandings of possibilities. The cautious vision, the "realistic" vision of the hegemonical construction becomes more honed. One understands its reach further and guards against its intrusion into the inner sancta of resistance. Fragmentation becomes meaningful only when its phantasmic logic is allowed to infiltrate the logic, core, spring of our connections.

So, this has been a call to reflect on the destructive and self-destructive logic of the demand for cultural and racial authenticity. The analysis has led us full circle to a reappreciation of bodies, accents, ways, combinations of bloods and cultures. We all can be traitors, but that does not depend on green eyes, Anglo mothers, or thick accents.

I want to end denouncing, rejecting, and abhorring a reading of reality between the barrio solid or homeplace dwellers and the culturally homeless that sometimes suggests itself to me when swallowing rejection of myself or of others who don't quite make it to authentic by the use of an allegory.

In a Nahuatl erotic tale (León Portilla and Shorris 2001), the hero, disliked by the powerful father of his beloved, is sent to the front lines in war together with the insane and physically deformed. They are sent to take the brunt of the violence. As their dead bodies block the enemy, the society is purified of the infirm. The logic that promotes the formation of this gruesome strategy should fill solid, together folk of color with horror. Yet, how have we—those outside home-grown identities—not been sent to the front lines unaccompanied, unshielded, unprepared by the logic of the real and the fake?

Note

1. In this chapter, I use capitals for "Black" and lower case for "white." With this usage I want to indicate that Black is a superimposed organic term of resistant identity, though sometimes it is used as a "bare" racial "descriptor." The latter is a racist usage, since the black/white racial distinction is racist. I will not write "black" in even those cases to disallow the racism to stand without resistance. In those cases there are two moments within the linguistic act. The term "white" is never used in my text as an organic identity term.

References

Anzaldúa, Gloria. 1990. En rapport, in Opposition: Cobrando cuentas a las nuestras. In *Making Face, Making Soul*, edited by Gloria Anzaldúa, 143. San Francisco: Aunt Lute.

Elsinger, Bill. 1993. Creative Paradox. Unpublished manuscript.

Jackson, George. 1970. *Soledad Brother*. New York: Bantam Books.

Langston Gwaltney, John. 1980. *Drylongso*. New York: Random House.

León Portilla, Miguel, and Earl Shorris. 2001. *In the Language of Kings*. New York: W. W. Norton & Co.

Said, Edward. 1990. Reflections on Exile. In *Out There: Marginalization and Contemporary Cultures*, edited by Russell Ferguson, Martha Gever, Trinh T. Minh-ha, and Cornel West. New York: The New Museum of Contemporary Art.

Spelman, Elizabeth. 1988. *Inessential Woman*. Boston: Beacon.

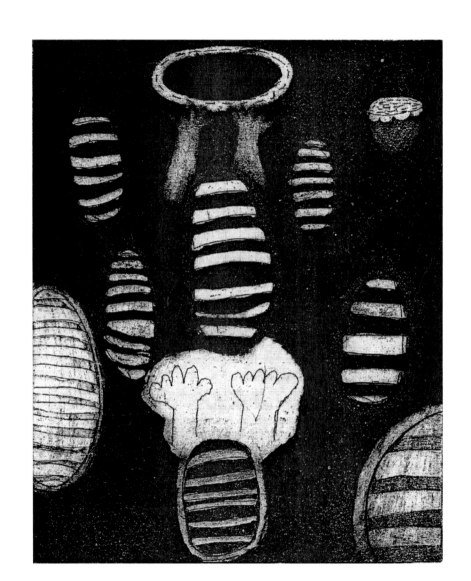

CHAPTER EIGHT

~

El Pasar Discontínuo de la Cachapera/Tortillera del Barrio a la Barra al Movimiento/[1]The Discontinuous Passing of the Cachapera/Tortillera from the Barrio to the Bar to the Movement

Necessary admonitions: guidelines into the landscape—Para saber de quien hablamos y que queremos decir por "hablar"

I. Glossary

Ambiente: Latino/Latina spaces where homoeroticism is lived. Lived Latino homoeroticism constitutes the spaces as *ambiente. Gente de ambiente: jotos y tortilleras.*

Una conversación: a word, a look, a gesture, directed out, anticipating a response that anticipates a response in turn without closing out meaning not already contained in the expectations; without pulling by the roots tongues that break the circle of expectations. Our creativity lies in our putting out gestures, words, looks that break closed cycles of meaning *en un desafío erótico.*

Silences: attentive silences, refusal-to-speak-silences, tongue-cut-out silences, provocative silences, refusal-to-listen silences, intimate silences.

Signifying and representing: words that have come to me from the language of gangs and hip hop culture—graffiti writ-

167

ing, tagging, and wearing colors are examples of signifying and representing. The conversation I have in mind needs to include words whose sense has been disrupted and sometimes, no words at all, as jotas/marimachas signify and represent ourselves in relation, disruptively, when "ordinary conversation" shuts our mouths.

Nombres: cachaperas, jotas, tortilleras, patas, mita y mitas, trolas, marimachas.

II. Para su información (*Nuevas*/News)

1. Gays and lesbians march in New York City in a joyous parade that brings together the city's enormous diversity of homosexual life. Participants — including white, Puerto Rican, African American, Asian, and Dominican gays and lesbians — are asked about their wishes and dreams for the year 2000. Each responds echoing everyone else like a chant: "an end to AIDS — equal rights for gays and lesbians." No matter the location: "an end to AIDS — equal rights for gays and lesbians." Nothing else informs the politics and dreams: "an end to AIDS — equal rights for gays and lesbians."[1]

2. As the people of Cincinnati were preparing to vote on whether to keep or repeal the city's antidiscrimination ordinance that includes gays and lesbians, right-wing opponents of the ordinance produced a video in which spokespeople for the African American, Latino, and Native American communities spoke against what they saw as "special rights" for gays and lesbians (see Cincinnati video). In the video, one can follow the right wing's manipulations of lesbian/gay and particularly African American, but also Latino and Native American, identities, histories, and struggles. But the video also documents and exploits the disconnection and fragmentation within and between those identities and struggles. The video begins with scenes from the Civil Rights march on Washington, DC, including King's delivery of his "I Have a Dream" speech. The images of the March on Washington are mixed with, and overwhelmed by, images of the Gay and Lesbian March on Washington. As the images depict the displacement, spokes-

people for the African American, Native American, and
Latino communities decry the use of civil rights rhetoric by
a group of people they identify as outsiders to their groups
and struggles and whose lifestyles turn that use into an
abomination. "There are no African American, Latino, Native American gays and lesbians" is part of the message.
This is a declaration. The question I ask is whether there are
any tortilleras, jotas, marimachas.

3. A tortillera is putting up posters in Tucson for an event
sponsored by several organizations. As she asks a shop
owner whether she can put a poster in his shop, he says:
"Yes, if you cut out that sponsor," pointing to "Lesbianas
Latinas de Tucson." La tortillera says, "What, are we not
part of *la* raza?" "Not of my raza" says the man.[2]

The Landscape: La Geografía Discontínua

I begin this dangerous reflection with an evocative and problematic text, one that has accompanied me even as I have re-
flected on its nostalgic, romantic quality:

> La geografía de mi barrio llevo en mí. Será por eso que del todo
> no me fui. (*I carry the geography of my barrio within me.
> Maybe that's why I have not left it altogether.*)

> [Eladia Blazquez 1987].

I recall this text because my reflections are about geography,
sexuality, and subjectivity in a society where the geographical
memory of Latino homoerotic subjects is sharply discontinuous. My intention is to disturb the complacencies that uphold
the fusion of heterosexuality and colonization. I see these complacencies as unwitting or careless or tyrannical collaborations
between Latino nationalisms and the contemporary U.S. Lesbian Movement in its various versions and enclaves.

Entonces quiero hacerle el try al hablar de una serie de
pasos y piezas que nos lleven hacia una conversación comunal
Latina sobre autodestrucción y sexualidad: Una conversación
*where we can signify and represent the urgencies that torture
the relation between sexuality and politics* en la vida Latina,
in and out of el ambiente, *breaking the circle of ossification
and destruction.* La relación entre política y sexualidad, una

relación osificada, peligrosa, *leading one easily to move between self-betrayal and escape*, dos lados de la misma
moneda. La lengua misma una ambiguedad erótica, un tierno
instrumento de tortura: lengua bífida sin ser híbrida, bífida
como la lengua de la serpiente, pero tragando veneno. (*So I
want to try to speak of a series of steps and pieces that can
lead us to a communal* Latina *conversation about self-destruction and sexuality. A conversation where we can signify and
represent the urgencies that torture the relation between sexuality and politics in* Latina *life, in and out of the* ambiente,
*breaking the circle of ossification and destruction. The relation
between politics and sexuality, a dangerous, ossified relation,
leading one easily to move between self-betrayal and escape,
two sides of the same coin. The tongue itself an erotic ambiguity, a tender instrument of torture: bifid tongue that is not hybrid. Bifid like a serpent's tongue, but swallowing poison.*)

Pasos Discontínuos/*Discontinuous Steps*

Primer paso

Las butches *in* sutes, con vests de raso. *Imposing*, como en
un drama, quietas, muy en papel, hieráticas. Cerveza con
limón en la boca, *in the throat, on the tongue. The steps quick,
solid, precise, graceful. The handling of the femmes all contained flirtation.* Las femmes con boquitas pintadas, *the hair*
una mata rebelde *purposefully trained wild*, tacones bien
altos. *Short, tight skirts that show off the precision and quickness of the step, the boldness of so much leg. Can I speak here
about the meaning of* máscaras *worn after sundown*? Qué, lo
digo en español, *in my femmes ear*, como un bolero? (*The
butches in suits, with satin vests. Imposing, as in a drama, still,
very much in their roles, hieratic. Beer with lemon in the
mouth, in the throat, on the tongue. The steps quick, solid,
precise, graceful. The handling of the femmes all contained
flirtation. The femmes' mouths lipstick red, the hair a rebel-
lious bush purposefully trained wild, very high heels. Short,
tight skirts that show off the precision and quickness of the
step, the boldness of so much leg. Can I speak here about the
meaning of masks worn after sundown? What? Do I say it in
Spanish, in my femme's ear, like a bolero?*)

Segundo paso

Y mañana al jale. Con traces de la barra *in the movements of the hips, the pursing of the lips to point to things, the taste for love and style directed strictly inward, toward a point inside that is locked beyond meaning.* Como si fuéramos simplemente mujeres. *Not even bothered by the "conversations" ordered by heterosexual domesticity.* Qué va, si a una ni se le ocurre pensar en ninguna lengua, ni con ningún conjunto de cicatrices y palabras, algo como "*ordered by heterosexual domesticity.*" Oh, a veces se lo piensa, como algo abstracto, *taking a step back, like taking a picture for posterity.* ¿Y si mi mamá es tortillera? ¿Dónde? ¿Aquí, entre las casadas y por casar, que saben tanto de showers para mujeres y beibis? No tiene sentido. Su ser femme aquí no puede ser para mí. Tortillera es para el mitote, cosa que se dice en susurritos, cosa sucia, invertida. ¡Ay que asco que se besen en la boca! ¡Ay virgencita, ni me lo cuentes! (*And tomorrow to work. With traces of the bar in the movements of the hips, the pursing of the lips to point to things, the taste for love and style directed strictly inward, toward a point inside that is locked beyond meaning. As if we were simply women. Not even bothered by the "conversations" ordered by heterosexual domesticity. It doesn't even occur to one to think in any language, nor with any set of scars and words, something like "ordered by heterosexual domesticity." Oh, sometimes one thinks about it, like something abstract, taking a step back, like taking a picture for posterity. And if my mother is a* tortillera? *Where? Here, among the wedded and to be wed, who know so much about showers for brides and babies? No, it doesn't make any sense. Her being a femme here cannot be for me.* Tortillera *is for gossip, something said in whispers, something dirty, inverted. How revolting that they kiss each other on the mouth! Holy mother of God, don't even tell me about it.*)

Tercer paso

And there we are, having come from all parts of the city, Belmont Stop in the L, Boystown, everything gay and lesbian dominating the streets, the talk, the buying and the selling. A middle-size room in Horizons. Once a week. All Latina Lesbians getting together to be Latina Lesbians in some halfway spot between the bar and the closet, una penumbra. Trying to find a voice, saying something or other, just to hear "español/ lesbiano" spoken at a distance, public style. Boystown frames the scene: the movement brought you this possibility! All the way from the barrio or your escondites (*hiding places*) in the suburbs to la polis homoerótica, where lesbian voices can speak their things at a discrete distance from each other, public style, in any language, all the way across a room, among themselves, far away from las comadres mitoteando su homofobia en susurros (*far away from women gossiping their homophobia in whispers*).

Fourth step

Busy, together, articulate, proud, flamboyant, Latina emphasized in the tone, the style, the direction of the Lesbian politics. Brazen, self-confident, radical. Influential in the movement, quick to point out the racism, the ethnocentrism, the classism. Fun, intense, warm, no nonsense, fiery, red hot angry presence among lesbians. Planning and risking. Way out, bien asumida, en la sociedad grande, *far away from the barrio. Oh sometimes almost touching hands with barrio organizers in marches against 187, almost seeing herself in their eyes as she moves with the fleeting lesbian presence. Not wanting to stop long enough for a good look of herself in those eyes, which may well be her own.*

¿Y qué?/*And So, What Is It to You? To Me?*
Pasos y piezas. *Movements in and away from different contexts.* La cachapera se mueve *(she moves) to avoid passing; to avoid becoming a figment of the Anglo imagination consumed by and reduced to protesting ethnocentric racism; to avoid being silenced; to avoid being socially reduced to her construction* en el mitote. ¿En qué lugar y en qué desplazamientos es que la cachapera, la jota, la pata, la marimacha, puede encontrar respuestas a sus gestos y palabras, respuestas que se regodeen en la abundancia de su significar? (*In what spaces and through which movements can the* cachapera, jota, pata, marimacha, *find responses to her gestures and words that take pleasure in the abundance of her meaning?*) *I want to take you inside the Latino nations and inside the lesbian movement, so you can witness that those are not* los lugares de la conversación *(those are not the places for the conversa-*

tion). De aquí pa'llá sin encontrar su *ground, the ground of her possibilities. (From one place to the next without finding her ground, the ground of her possibilities.)*

De Aquí/*From Here*

Moving in, inside the nations, rehearsing over and over the lessons of the sacrosanct place of heterolife as she (the cachapera?) affirms her place among Latinos. The idea of nation brings the logic of the colonizer inside Latino life. The logic of modernity that "unifies" the disparate elements that face the colonizer oppositionally prevents them from creating disruptions of traditions in their encounters with domination. A unified front is itself a commitment to a logic of self-destruction: nationalism leaves colonialism undisturbed when it places different Latino practices, values, traditions and limits outside of critique and recreations; when what is old forms the substance and grounds of "our" rebellion and possibilities. Nationalism leaves colonialism undisturbed when it affirms a line of connection between the colonizer and the colonized in their weddedness to heterosexuality, a line of connection that tightens around *la marimacha y la asfixia.*

La tortillera passes as heterosexual, a status that is accorded to her face to face. She may be spoken about as a *tortillera,* but she is not spoken to as such. Heterosexual is a status that she may actually seek through her manner of presentation, including her speech, her compliance and allegiance to heterosexual norms, including explicit displays of homophobia. Or a status that she allows to be hung on her, like a sign that negates what in her announces her transgression. She does not speak as and in a social sense, because in an outspoken, public social sense she is not a tortillera. Si me dices que no hay lesbians en nuestra comunidad, también quieres decir que "jota," "tortillera," "marimacha," "pata" are not names pa la gente, dentro de la raza? ¿Y entonces porqué susurras mi presencia entre nosotros behind my back? Los hombres se gritan el insulto, "¡joto!": como drill sergeants entrenando a sus bros en la masculinidad. (*If you tell me that there are no lesbians in our community, do you also mean that* "jota," "tortillera," "marimacha," "pata" *are not names for our people, within* la raza? *And then, why do you whisper my presence among us behind my back? Men shout the insult to other men,* "¡joto!" *: like drill sergeants training their bros into* Latino *masculinity*.)

"Lesbian oppression," says Sarah Hoagland, "is not a relation" (Hoagland 1988:4). Heterosexism denies lesbian existence. That which does not exist cannot relate to anything or anyone else. La tortillera exists en la comunidad only as a pervert. Perversion constitutes her and marks her as outside of countenanced relationality. Her sociality is alive and constructed en el mitote (*in gossip*), in her absence. Pero si la tortillera no habla—aún cuando entra en la iglesia vestida como un chamaco—la gente la considera, le dirije la palabra. ¿Cómo podría hablar excepto en su silencio, sin descubrir su marca? ¿Cómo podría hablar un sentido que no la traicione, que no se le eche pa' trás? (*But if the* tortillera *does not speak—even when she enters the church dressed in men's clothes—people respect her, they address her. How could she make sense except in her silence, without uncovering her mark? How could she speak a sense that does not betray her, that doesn't turn against her?*)

So, en la comunidad, under the reigns of nationalism, la cachapera is silent, her meaning is made by others. El mitote imagines her as most vividly social and anomalous, but the anomaly is tamed through lack of direct address, through a denial of dialogue. As a woman with a speaking tongue, her tongue is twisted against her name as she passes as heterosexual.

Pa'llá/To There

Moving away, away from comunidad Latina to the inside of the Lesbian Movement. Movement toward movement. Our movement guided by a dislike for pained stasis, looking for voice outside the confines of our tongues. Fantastic flight from our possibilities. Because we do, definitivamente, we do, pose a threat to our nations. Nations that stand on the textured and fragmenting ground of unchallenged, uncritical, complacent, heterosexuality at their own peril. La cachapera: a threatening promise. Instead of cultivating her company toward impure shatterings of colonized communions, la cachapera becomes the Latina/Lesbian. As the Latina/Lesbian she plays out her sexuality uncritically and flamboyantly in ways that combine the idea of closet and colony. These sensual rehearsals take place inside the territoriality of the Lesbian Movement.

Lesbian Movement: in white landscapes, locales, geography. Movement that does not move into Latino communities except fleetingly and without engaging in a contestation of meanings over sexuality and its ossification in Latino life. Movement that lacks a taste for conversations inside locales and ways that risk its complicity with colonization, with our cultural and material erasure. Movement that does not take our integrity seriously because it affirms the confines of its own territoriality.

Oh, we are inside of it, somos la sal sin ejercitar una disrupción de los límites. (*Oh, we are inside it, we are the salt without exercising a disruption of its limits.*) We are inside it, negatively, in a peculiar absence of relationality. Movement that averts its eyes from the split lives of tortilleras/cachaperas en los barrios de Chicago, Los Angeles, New York City, and in the small and middle-size villages, towns, and cities of Arizona and New Mexico.

Latina/Lesbian is an oxymoron, an absence of relation. Latina/Lesbian lacks a hyphen. The territoriality of the movement erases the hyphen. Latina/Lesbian necessarily speaks with a bifid tongue. ¿Cómo podría saber los tones of a hyphenated, hybrid, tongue when she is committed and confined to a negation? The Latina/Lesbian is a critic in the movement. The movement can only hear her speak when it sheds the purity that permeates its domain, its geography.

The movement of the tortillera into the Lesbian Movement is a fantastic flight because as she flees the confines of nation in search of substance, range, and voice, she becomes an oxymoron, the Latina/Lesbian: two terms in extreme tension. No hyphen: no hybridization. The Latina/Lesbian moves within a movement that lacks a sense of its geography and becomes aware of territoriality only when it stops outside the nations. A movement that lacks a sense of geography finds in the nations both imagined and real, a fierce sense of geography in resistance to colonization, a sense that "justifies" the Movement's retreat.

The movement of the tortillera into the Lesbian Movement is a fantastic flight because she comes out to a forced speaking in a bifid tongue; because the eyes that see her coming out, remake her in their own imagination. A bifid tongue: split, speaking out of both sides of her mouth. A tongue whose sense is made only in response to the closed sets of meanings of interlocutors whose tongues dictate her own into "conversations" where she must collaborate with the fusion of nationalism and colonialism. How could the tortillera come out in and into the movements — movimientos nacionalistas, the gay and lesbian movements — given the closed "conversations"?

Because of the geography of the Lesbian Movement — all of whose versions stay away from the borders of Latino communities — the Latina/Lesbian is a split, fragmented self that speaks with a bifid tongue and cannot deploy techniques that lead to hybridization. Simple occupancy in the domains while calling the racism does not resolve the split, nor does unveiling one's own mixed raced/mixed culture quality nor does discussion of hybrid productions that doesn't call into question the where and among whom the "conversation" takes place, within what geographies. The logic of modernity, of unity, takes a characteristic turn in the geographical setting of boundaries of the Lesbian Movement: "Lesbian" becomes ideologically "unified" even against much protesting and soul searching. The "unification" is produced by avoiding border encounters. All encounters are within the geographical limits of master territories. There, the one who has left the politics and geographies of the nations gets to protest the Movement's racism while enjoying the "freedoms" of white/Anglo homoerotic landscapes. She gets to change all her relations, a change so profound that she comes to believe in the logic of unification. And isn't it a wonder that this ideological move also leaves the social structures of the Latino Nations undisturbed? La cachapera who wanted voice, gains voice as the Latina/ Lesbian and becomes articulate in the logic of modernity, keeping her split self and animating a self that is imagined.

I cannot see any possible justifications for the Lesbian Movement's staying away from border contestations: from engaging the great number of Anglos buying and reselling our geographies, edging their artistic communities into ours and then replacing artists with wealthy lovers of the refined; from engaging the police state flying low over our geographies in helicopters, surrounding them with armored vehicles and armored men, invading them with a will to kill us for being brown, whatever our sexuality.

Can the cachapera gain voice in the Movement? Not unless we take seriously the need to question the geography in which the "we are fa-mi-lí" is to be lived and the colonial induction of cachaperas into the traditions of Anglo-European saphists (with a difference of course): What's in a name? What's in a place?

¿Es Que Acaso la Tortillera Existe en Alguna Parte? (*Does the Tortillera Exist Anywhere?*)

La barra is where I see "máscaras worn after sundown." I have the sense that may be la mujer en la barra is the real thing, la tortillera muy asumida en su ambiente and at the same time, I have this inclination to perceive masks in the bar, en el ambiente. Is it that I think there could be someone else underneath the mask waiting to speak? La tortillera is not really "she" who spends her days passing: being seen and not disrupting the being seen as heterosexual, practicing the words and logic of Latino heterosexuality. Does "she" (the passeuse) know the one she is after sundown outside the strict and rather limited rules of comportment of the bar, the limited repertoire, the being seen in such limited circumstances? Does she (la de la barra) know "her" (the passeuse) apart from heterosexual rehearsals? Who sees her? Other tortilleras who, in the light of day, collaborate in the daily production of the passeuse? Does she know "her"? Where? In the midst of what sociality? As someone she betrays in silence? Who betrays whom?

She can be her own possibility to the extent that she can shake the interpretive hold over her movements that reduce her to someone imagined both by the Latino heterosexual imagination and the lesbian imagination. She can be her own possibility to the extent that she can be part of a moving that does not diminish her subjectivity, a moving that is geographically devoted to her unbounded inhabitation.

Buscando Dirección/*Looking for Direction*

The passeuse, the Latina/Lesbian, the tortillera in the bar are all "real," constrained, fragmented, all coming to life in problematic geographies. I want voice as a jota, un repertorio amplio en las cosas diarias entre la gente. (*I want voice as a* jota, *a wide repertoire in daily things among people*.) It is my ground, my own sense of walking in some direction rather than wandering aimlessly and without sense in terrains prepared to swallow me whole or in parts, that we, cachaperas, can move away from the frozen states in which the encounter of colony and nation have imprisoned us. We can exercise ourselves in the encounter at the geographical limits, where change is bound to happen. Our threat and our promise es que podemos amasar la dirección del cambio (*Our threat and our promise is that we can knead the direction of the change*), we can make tortillas. We can exercise ourselves confronting our cultures as anomalous beings, as beings denied from within the depths of traditions that also define us. We can exercise ourselves in the encounter with the colonizing cultures in a recreation of our cultures, bringing our cultures away from the death of conservative clasping into hybrid life. The transformation of the cultures that make us cachaperas, patas, tortilleras, jotas, marimachas needs to be itself an exercise of those cultures, an exercise that would leave them and us changed.

The crucial and confrontational point here is that to exercise oneself culturally in a live culture is not to repeat over and over in tired combinations the traditions that "constitute us as a people" even when these iterations are presented as defiant refusals of mimicry of the colonizer/dominator. The confrontational and enticing point is that in the border encounters we can negotiate in a lively cultural mode that takes issue with domination in tense inside/outside/in between conversations. We, cachaperas, patas, marimachas, *can become fleshy tongue, sound out loud*, el cuerpo y los gestos significando y representando ampliamente que estamos bien plantadas en la vida diaria, en los encuentros diarios con la colonización y las tiranías de nuestras tradiciones. (*We*, cachaperas, patas, marimachas, *can become fleshy tongue, sound out loud, the body and the gestures signifying and representing amply that we are well grounded in daily life, in the daily encounters with colonization and our traditions*.)

It is in this way that we can come to conversations that have a suspension of the given in the making of sense. Right now, we have ways of silence, in mitote, in negation, in passing; passing as Latina/Lesbians in the Movement and as implicitly or explicitly heterosexual in the nations. We are also constrained in invisible locations—la barra y las organizaciones de lesbianas latinas—where our rehearsals and creations leap geographically out of the border contestations.

It is the tortillera, la pata, la marimacha, la jota, la cachapera, the nonspeaking subject, the one who needs voice, movement, who can negate, decry, the torturings of Latino nationalisms and Anglo colonialisms. No one can speak for her but with her. I suggest that the production of a hybrid culture is itself an exercise of our cultures. It is in responding to ways, practices, beliefs, that are intrusive, dominating, in a Latino cultural vein, a way that is a taking in and also a dismantling of the invading culture that hybrid Latino cultures come to be our cultures. This is a wordly task that we can undertake as cachaperas as we battle, well placed geographically. It is in this way that our tongues acquire the hyphen.

I don't wish to be healed. I feel sensual loving and healing as politically different. I am looking for carnal disruptions. Compromisos íntimos. Una política sexual *against the tortures of colonization and nation.*

Notes

A las marimachas en mi vida, gracias de corazón por la conversación. Gracias especiales a Julia y Laura. Gracias a Kelvin, Isra, Suzanne y a la Tamañota. A Helena Maria Viramontes gracias por organizar "El Frente: U.S. Latinas under Attack and Fighting Back" at Cornell *que me permitió el primer sentido de la posibilidad de conversación y a las Latinas presentes por la conversación. A Aurelia Flores y todas las miembras y miembros de La Familia gracias por organizar la discusión en Stanford.* Thanks to the lesbian women in SWIP for the town meeting/discussion of the issues. *Gracias a* Sarah.

1. *1993 Gay Parade (NYC),* video produced by Don Lynn. 1994.
2. Thanks to Julia Schiavone Camacho for telling me this story firsthand.

References and Suggested Readings

Anzaldúa, Gloria. 1987. *Borderlands/La Frontera.* San Francisco: Spinsters/Aunt Lute.

Bhabha, Homi K. 1994. *The Location of Culture.* London: Routledge.

Blazquez, Eladia. 1987. El Corazón al Sur, words and music. *El Corazón al Sur.* Buenos Aires: Elli-Sound S.A.

Conmoción: Revista y red revolucionaria de lesbianas latinas #1. 1995. 1521 Alton Road #336. Miami Beach, Fla. 33139.

Hoagland, Sarah Lucia. 1988. *Lesbian Ethics: Toward New Value.* Palo Alto, Calif.: Institute of Lesbian Studies.

Moraga, Cherríe. 1983. *Loving in the War Years: Lo que nunca pasó por sus labios.* Boston: South End Press.

Ramos, Juanita, ed. 1987. *Compañeras: Latina Lesbians.* New York: Latina Lesbian History Project.

Rosaldo, Renato. 1989. *Culture and Truth.* Boston: Beacon.

Trinh T., MinhHa. 1995. No Master Territories. In *The Post-Colonial Studies Reader,* edited by Bill Ashcroft, Gareth Griffiths, and Helen Tiffin, 215–18. London: Routledge.

Trujillo, Carla, ed. 1991. *Chicana Lesbians.* Berkeley, Calif.: Third Woman Press.

~

CHAPTER NINE

Enticements and Dangers of Community and Home for a Radical Politics

I. FEMINISM AND COMMUNITY

In "Feminism and Modern Friendship: Dislocating the Community," Marilyn Friedman (1989) proposes a feminist communitarianism that locates itself in the intersection between the feminist and communitarian traditions. This is an important locus for the discussion of the question of community. Understanding the subordinations of women has needed to be met with understandings of the relations between women and communities and of the possibilities that communities have or have not offered women in the struggle against those subordinations. Friedman argues for an understanding of community that preserves one of the cornerstones of communitarian philosophy, the social construction of the self, without having to accept a definition of the communitarian self that irrevocably forms that self to social roles and structures that have been highly oppressive to women. Friedman wants an understanding of the communitarian self that allows for the recognition of oppression within and across communities.

The view of the self that Friedman proposes is social, both in the sense of socially constituted and communitarian. The communitarian subject is constituted not just in relation to communities to which she is "involuntarily bound" — communities of place — but also in relation to what Friedman calls "communities of choice." Our communities of origin do

183

not necessarily constitute us as selves who agree or comply with the norms that unify those communities. "Some of us are constituted as deviants and resisters by our communities of origin, and our defiance may well run to the foundational social norms which ground the most basic social roles and relationships upon which those communities rest" (Friedman 1989:197). Unchosen communities are sometimes communities that we should leave in order to discern who we really are. Identities shaped within communities of place may come to be questioned and transformed within communities of choice. Friedman pictures most lives as containing "mixtures of relationships and communities, some given/found/discovered/ and some chosen/created. Most people are, to some extent, ineradicably constituted by their communities of place" (Friedman 1989:203). When she thinks of communities of place, like the "new communitarians"—in particular Michael Sandel (1982) and Alasdair MacIntyre (1981)—she has in mind the community defined by family, neighborhood, school, church, and nation (Friedman 1989:188–190, 194). Communities of choice help us counter oppressive and abusive relational structures in those nonvoluntary communities by providing models of alternative social relationships as well as standpoints for critical reflection on self and community. Given her understanding of communities of place, communities of place cannot do that.

Friedman thinks of friendship and urban communities as providing models for communities of choice. She thinks of both as voluntary, as arising out of one's *own* needs, desires, interests, values, and attractions, in contrast with and often in opposition to motivations, expectations assigned, ascribed, expected, or demanded by one's found communities (Friedman 1989:199–200). One is not assigned friends by custom or tradition. In urban settings, women can join with each other in associations that develop their own values. Friedman thinks of urban relationships as characteristically modern in their greater voluntary basis.

Friedman's distinction between communities of place and communities of choice is a distinction that became part of my politics. I went to "communities" with that distinction in mind, trying it in popular education workshops.[1] Trying it led me to see the problematic character of bringing that distinction to communities of place when folks were not about to leave them and when the point of the discussions was not to provoke them to leave, but rather to transform their communities of place, beginning by a structured critique of them. What was crucial about the concept of a community of choice for me was the possibility of its leading to the critical turn characteristic of the popular education situation. The distinction between community of place and community of choice seemed to me to capture the distance of critique. Communities of choice meant to me the "place" where we became critical of institutions constitutive of communities of place and of "common sense." But I came to understand that and why to think of choosing to leave communities of place is to think of the wrong activity in resistance to domination.

Friedman was led to what I see as the wrong turn by beginning her task conversing with Sandel and MacIntyre. It is this conversation that led her to an understanding of communities of place in terms of family, neighborhood, church, and nation and to a reduction of them to ossified, reified institutions conceived in a monocultural vein. Though Friedman is extremely critical of their version of communitarianism, she appears to share Sandel's and MacIntyre's view that there are communities that constitute us passively. Instead of questioning their understanding of community, she renames that understanding "communities of place" and rejects the communities themselves. The sense she implicitly affirms is that history is given to us, that as children and adults we merely receive and reduplicate institutional injunctions. But that gives us too passive an understanding of social relationships. This account fails to explain the existence of resistance as social. It fails to explain, except through an implicit reference to a liberal conception of the subject, the existence of the very motivations prompting us to form communities of choice: "one's *own* needs, desires, interests, values, and attractions, in contrast and often in opposition to motivations, expectations assigned, ascribed, expected, or demanded by found communities." Why not think that as contradictory identities are formed within communities of place, these communities are revealed as not univocal, passing on and embodying an undisturbed common sense, but as complex and tense sites of identity formation?

I see a confusion in Friedman between "one did not choose to be in one's found community" and "one is passive in that community." Because she is conversing with Sandel and MacIntyre, Friedman sees passivity in community of place: ossified hierarchies and roles. She misses the ingenuity and constant creativity in relationships among neighbors, people in families, and in relations that cannot be easily placed in the understanding of communities of place that she shares with MacIntyre and Sandel. She misses the resistant creativity with which women negotiate institutionalized life. The "foundness" of neighborly and family ties does not entail the "foundness" of norms, practices, beliefs, and desires of people in them.

Resistant negotiation of everyday life does not require the formation of associations that lift one from community of place; it rather constitutes life in communities of place. Why would one think that women's forming patrols to deal with battering after significant strategizing places them in a community of choice, while women and men creating strategies to deal with alcoholics who bang at their door asking for money for liquor—or to deal with welfare officers coming to police their daily living, and neighbors deciding to cut enough wood for folks who can't go "*a la leña*," or deciding how to stand against evictions—are inserted in communities of place? Friedman does not tell us that the organized movement against battering is an example of a community of choice, while the other examples of resistance are examples of communities of place. But that is because she is not thinking about resistance to intermeshed oppressions as part of communities of place. Certainly it is not nonvoluntary activity, but resistant activity. Institutions do not run that monolithically and they are not external to us. Norms of everyday relating are in constant refashioning, contestation, and maneuvering. Resistance has itself a social history.

As I considered Friedman's distinction, I wondered as to how does one go to and from communities of choice and communities of place? Does she mean that women intent or in need of self-transformation should give up the task of transforming their original communities? There is ambiguity in Friedman's text in this respect as the *emphasis* is on self-transformation not on transformation of communities, including communities of place. But if there is to be a back and forth, there will be arrogance and depersonalization in the task of changing communities of place distant from an appreciation of resistant traditions of negotiation of everyday life. There won't be a conversation, an interaction that begins with granting personally conceived subjects with authority in the art of resistance. The distinction between community of place and community of choice suggests either indifference to communities of place or high and impersonal confrontation in their transformation, a confrontation that is not informed by an affection for resistant, embodied, located subjects. It is a confrontation that demands forgetting.

The example of the organized movement against the battering of women is a powerful case of this forgetting. The shelter movement in the United States never attended to the harm done to women by the movement's insufficient insertion in communities of color. The movement also became increasingly institutionalized in an institutional context structurally inattentive to difference. Thus, instead of gaining insertion in communities of place and devising solutions that took women's differences into account and appreciating the differences in the importance that their communities had to their survival, the movement designed a one-size-fits-all solution that took women away from their communities, if they wanted access to the movement's solution to their being abused.[2] This is indeed not to say that women of color did not participate in the movement, nor that women of color have not done powerful work against the complex forms that violence against women of color takes in this society.[3] But the organized movement muted these voices and needs and allied itself with a legal and law enforcement system that is structurally racist.[4]

Another way of making the point takes me to rural New Mexico where Chicanas and Chicanos fight for control over their ancestral water rights. When the confrontation takes place in front of Environmental Improvement Division and Environmental Protection Agency officials, one can hear the difference in the voices of native inhabitants and Anglo counterculturals who moved to the region during the 1960s. As countercultural environmentalists testify in support of the position of native inhabitants, they distinctly employ the language of choice over the language of place as giving them greater authority in their understanding of the issues. They claim they know more about the value of what is to be preserved because they have chosen to be there. This position fails to understand the care that native communities have exercised in their use of water, a care that is resistant to internal colonialism and the devastation of resources that ground material life in this particular cultural vein. It also fails to be self-critical about the collaboration between their choice and internal colonialism. The region is one in which contestation over water is part of colonization and resistance to colonization.

The more I looked at Friedman's own text the more I understood it as a modern text, containing a very abstract conception of space in its strong distinction between communities of place and communities of choice. It is as a modern text that one needs to understand Friedman's emphasis on choice. In communities of place, territory is emphasized; in communities of choice there seems to be a spatial flight. There is a sense that communities of choice can be just anywhere. The abstraction from space as the place for choice helps me introduce a distrust of nomadism, of middle-class sojourners, of anthropologists, of tourists. This is a very large topic, but I want to introduce the need to reflect on geography, movement, and stasis as one thinks of communities that would develop a non-colonialist account of complex, liberatory possibilities where movement to and from carries with it located responsibilities and commitments.[5]

Sarah Lucia Hoagland's reflections on community in *Lesbian Ethics* (1988) issue from a very different locus, from inside the lesbian separatist movement. Her text does not have academic intellectuals, or not primarily, as the "for whom" and "with whom" of the conversation. It is frankly and joyously a text addressed to other lesbian women in movement against heterosexism. Given the hatred and abuse that lesbians encounter in their daily negotiation of life, and given the casting out of lesbians from the various "we's" that constitute the U.S. social fabric, separation is deeply appealing, a place

of possibilities, attention, and beauty that lesbians could create. The casting-out gesture calls forth a moving away that affirms one's difference, not the difference of the outcast, but of
the lover of women. So, as in Friedman, there is a sense of
"elsewhere" to the reflection on community, but this elsewhere is not understood by Hoagland as an exercise of choice.
Hoagland theorizes the being cast out in its deepest form, as a
conceptual move, a conceptual erasure. She sees Lesbian possibility in that erasure.

In her book, Hoagland is purposefully vague about the term
"community." In her search for emancipatory possibilities, she
understands social reality as refracted: she reads social reality
as constituted by several co-temporaneous, overlapping social
contexts that contain different possibilities and stand in significant tension with respect to each other. Heterosexism constitutes an oppressive context that erases female agency. Lesbian
community constitutes an alternative context that not only
does not make oppression credible, but is constituted by and
constitutes female agency. In the context of oppression, lesbians are not primarily scapegoated or characterized as inferior
or as culturally backward. The oppression of lesbians is not a
relationship. "The society of the fathers, rather, formally denies lesbian existence. . . . The idea of women loving women
is impossible, inconceivable" (Hoagland 1988:4). Hoagland
connects this erasure of lesbians to female agency. Lesbian
community is that context in which lesbian existence and female agency are both a reality and possibility. Lesbian community is "the loose network—both imagined and existing
now—of those who identify basically as lesbians. What I am
calling 'lesbian community' is not a specific entity; it is a
ground of our being; and it exists because we are here and
move on it now" (Hoagland 1988:3). Lesbian community is
that context in which lesbians create new value.

The sense of self that Hoagland invokes is inseparable from
community, but this community does not fit in the distinction
between community of place and community of choice, precisely because the distinction between the given and the to-be-
created is not possible in Hoagland's understanding of lesbian
community. The self in community involves each lesbian making choices within a context created by community (Hoagland

1988:145). Since the lesbian context overlaps the context of oppression, agency here is agency under oppression. The creation of new value outside the conceptual parameters of heterosexism and the avoidance of demoralization—the undermining of moral agency—constitute the tasks of the "auto-koenenous self," the self in community.

Hoagland refuses the task of definition of either lesbian or of the lesbian context. To define would be to assume that we are not the norm and thus to recognize a norm. It would be to assume that we need to defend our borders against invasion and threats from the outside. "So I let go of the urge to define. And I begin to think of lesbian community in a different way. I think of community as a ground of possibility, in which we create lesbian meaning" (Hoagland 1988:9). Hoagland does not think of lesbian community in terms of safety (Hoagland 1988:195), but in terms of emancipatory possibility. "Our growth as lesbians is essentially related to the values that emerge in lesbian community" (Hoagland 1988:144). Membership in lesbian community is a voluntary act. Hoagland invokes Julia Penelope's sense that one joins a community because she finds companionship, support, and commitment to common ideals within that community and it is internally defined by its members on the basis of shared experiences and common interpretations of events in the real world (Hoagland 1988:146).

Hoagland's is a profoundly empowering understanding of the grounds of emancipation, a sense that is made possible by the tense, disjunctive overlapping of oppressive and liberatory contexts. To move from Friedman's to Hoagland's understanding of community is to move from different forms of oppression—from oppression as subordination to oppression as a being cast out. Moving out of communities of place cannot be a starting place for liberation, since the lesbian is already cast out. She may live inside communities, but she is not of them. Thus, it isn't a matter of choice. The language of choice does not capture the subtleties of movement in resistance for those cast out, nor is the source of their self-understanding in rejection of the understandings of systems of their exclusion. The importance of Hoagland's insight for me lies in revealing the possibilities of affirming contexts that are disjunctive from oppressive constructions of self, relations, practices, locations. But does that require leaving communities of place? Does being conceptually cast out necessitate that the "elsewhere" of separation be located outside communities of place? Can communities of place be such communities? Under what description? What is the work of inhabiting communities of place affirming a sense of connection that is disjunctive from oppressive ones?

There are thus important differences between Friedman's and Hoagland's reflections on community. Yet in both cases there is an abstraction from the particular spatialities that constitute relations and are constituted relationally. There is an abstraction from place, environment, relations, multiple oppressions, and resistances understood in their historical, cultural, spatial concreteness in both of their uses of "community." There is abstraction in their conceptualizing of friendships and lesbian relations since there is no insight into the concrete details of the journey, the material specificities, the difficulties of communication, the "on whose terms is communication possible."[6] But the abstractions are indeed different in a way that led me to abandon the community of place/community of choice distinction completely, but to retain Hoagland's understanding of the possibility of emancipation through a refocusing of attention, an epistemic shift but one—unlike hers—that understands spatialized communities in their complex concreteness.

What I found very valuable in bell hooks's "Homeplace: A Site of Resistance" (1990) is a recognition that communities are places where people already exercise themselves in resistance and where "choice" is already an ingredient of community life. Her locus is clear in the text itself, since she valorizes homeplace as a condition for her own voice. Hooks makes clear why a distinction between communities where one is passive and others in which one is active is problematic, why it misses resistance. Hooks understands what she calls "homeplace" in terms of black women's resistance by "making homes where all black people could strive to be subjects, not objects . . . where we could restore to ourselves the dignity denied us on the outside in the public world" (hooks 1990:42). Hooks acknowledges the sexism in delegating the task of creating home environment to women, but she honors this work in its resistant guise and emphasizes the "importance of homeplace in the midst of oppression and domination" (hooks 1990:43). She decries the thinking about domesticity that obscures this "re-visioning of both woman's role and the idea of 'home' that black women consciously exercised in practice" (hooks 1990:45) and the African American tradition of "mother worship." The latter reduces black women's creation of homeplaces to a fulfillment of natural roles or role-duties, thus erasing "choice and will" (hooks 1990:45). These racist and sexist readings collude in the erasure of resistant subjectivities. It is a crucial point that the distinction between communities of place and communities of choice obscures this resistance. Notice here that the language of choice and will is used by hooks very much within black communities.

Hooks's description of "homeplace" makes a parting from it not an abstract disengagement from reified institutions, but a loss of bearing, of attachments, to sounds, smells, concrete spatial environments (hooks 1990:41–42). Hooks is also clear about the fragility of homeplace "always subject to violation and destruction" (hooks 1990:47). So she calls black women to a renewal of their political commitment to homeplace.

Yet, hooks did part from the concrete spatiality of homeplace. In "Choosing the Margin," and in *Yearning* as a whole, the spatiality of the journey from homeplace to choosing the margin and the accompanying difficulties in finding intersubjective spaces for her multiple voices is made vivid (hooks 1990:146–47). She tells us of the silencings of home and her need both to leave and return. The return is also given a spatial description, a "going up the rough side of the mountain on my way home (hooks 1990:148). This journey back reconfigures the very meaning of home. "Home is that place which enables and promotes varied and ever-changing perspectives, a place where one discovers new ways of seeing reality, frontiers of difference. One confronts dispersals and fragmentation as part of the construction of a new world order that reveals more fully who we are, who we can become, an order that does not demand forgetting" (hooks 1990:148).

Hooks articulates this reconfiguration of home in spatial terms. She speaks of a reconceived margin, margin as central location for resistance, for the production of a counterhege-monic discourse that is not just found in words but in habits of being and the ways one lives" (hooks 1990:149). She rejects an understanding of marginality as a place of despair where one's imagination is at risk of being fully colonized. I am inter-preting hooks as not giving up the call to black women to renew their commitment to homeplace, but rather as tying the commitment to homeplace with its reconfiguration. She con-nects the formation of a "counterlanguage" with remem-brance of the past, "which includes recollections of broken tongues giving us ways to speak that decolonize our minds, our very beings" (hooks 1990:150).

Hooks, like Hoagland, teaches us this epistemic shift from oppression to resistance, but hooks cultivates a sensual acute-ness for resistance as enacted in very located traditions. It is this attention to spatiality, sensuality, historicity, as well as to the fragility of resistant spaces that I have appreciated in her text. Yet, though hooks's going home up the rough side of the mountain evidences great attentiveness to encounters with those who greeted her as colonizers, *she does not—and this is crucial—evidence attentiveness to the great diversity among whose who did not*. Thus, there is a univocity to the traditions of resistance that bring her back to a reconfigured sense of home and consequently a stable, unproblematized sense of its possibility.

As I learned from hooks and Hoagland, I also saw the need to complicate the worlds of resistance. It is interesting in itself that Hoagland and hooks are thinking of very different resis-tant worlds. Like Friedman, hooks and Hoagland emphasize shared experience as a ground for resistance. In Friedman this is accomplished by the move away from communities of place to communities initiated by shared needs, interests, and expe-rience. In Hoagland, it is a move to an abstract understanding of lesbians that makes the sense of community so readily available. This is not to ignore Hoagland's attention to the di-versity among lesbians, it is rather to emphasize the concrete locatedness of that diversity, and the interplay between colo-nialism and fragmentation. It is to emphasize the journeys of lesbians of color from homeplace to lesbian community as ex-tremely spatial, tortured, fragmenting journeys. In hooks, there is a singularity of resistant locales, a not seeing, for example, the Latina "lesbian,"[7] nor for that matter, the black lesbian as any sort of companion in her journey home.

II. Impure Communities

Why does one write about community? For whom? With whom? In the midst of what company? From inside which collectivities? Given what traditions? From what "location"? Given what self-understandings? While doing what? Staying put or in movement? Resting while moving? Preparing to move? To what extent is the writing one's own map for the direction of the movement? How many voices can one hear in the writing/planning?

I write about community from within a project of liberation that emphasizes the liberatory practice of popular education.[8] I write for those of us in resistance to intermeshed oppressions and in the company of those with whom I struggle against oppression, from inside various complex collectivities: "women" in communities struggling against the intermeshed violences of racism and battering; *jotas y jotos* standing our ground against erasure and being cast out; Chicanas and Chicanos in communities with a strong sense of place for whom the struggles against colonization take the form of land and water struggles. Though some communities have this tie to land and some do not, each complex community is spatially located even when the struggle is not focused on place and its spatiality is produced in the tense relation oppressing ⇔ resisting.

Though I am a *tortillera mestiza*, born in Argentina, relocating to the United States from various forms of egregious abuse, what marks my location in each community is grounded on the successes and failures of political insertion in a radical vein, not an insertion that makes me unproblematically of the community. I clearly lack a shared history, a vernacular, all of the learned motilities and embodiments, a deep sense of the space and its production. Thus, an important aspect of the insertion lies in recognizing my lacks that involve a clarity about entering worlds of sense in which I lack fluency. Insertion is then a learning and a clarity about my shortcomings and about what I do not understand. Insertion also includes the difficult, continuing, and often painful task of understanding myself as I am perceived in the worlds of sense that I am entering and inhabiting. The insertion often rereads me, reconstructs me, whatever my desires or intentions.

The most difficult rereading for me has been the sexual one. I am almost inevitably flattened out or erased sexually and often found unskilled in the feminine. Political insertion is for me not a matter of choice or of a helping disposition; my possibilities lie in liberatory struggle with and in the midst of others also subjected. Thus, the developing of companionship in a radical vein is a lifelong task, not a matter of being a professional organizer moving on after "we've won on an issue." There is a significant tension between my having left the spatiality where I was abused and my finding problematic the establishment of communities of choice. Sometimes one may have to leave, but that is not a *social* change and it is not a matter of "choice" in the liberal sense of the word, the two being logically related.

Problematizing "One": In *Inessential Woman*, Elizabeth Spelman (1988) taught me to use "woman" as a schema to be filled out. A woman is a gendered female of the species, where gender configuration can vary very significantly from society to society and within a given society (Spelman 1988:134). Here, I want to mean the word without losing the insights gained from practicing the schema sense of woman, but gaining in concrete plurality. I want to initiate the practice of uttering/writing and reading/hearing words like "woman," "*mujer*," "*jota*," and "lesbian" concretely and specifically in their plurality and as emphatically open ended — as if you held a multitude of interrelated specific subjects in your attention and you thought, felt, and understood yourself as among them in your own specificity and in the problematic, often oppressive character of that specificity, as enmeshed in shifting and historically threaded resistant but also ossified relations of solidarity and exploitation, of tenderness and abuse.

As I form my words in this multitude, I hear my voices, and hear you hearing me. I/you extend myself/yourself or recoil, stand my/your ground among subjects, consider my/your concreteness. As I live and think our relations, given the history and contemporary situation, I ponder and negotiate details and larger strokes, stolen kisses and endearing embraces, entrapments and tortures and, inevitably, the identity markers and community relations, many fragmented and plural communities. As I feel my ground, it is in the midst of concrete, complex, non-reducible, cantankerous, fleshy, interrelated, positioned subjects, noncontainable within any easy, abstract, hard-edged, simple classification. It is from within this multitude that I want to consider the question of community.

This positioning places me—as it places anyone else—inside and at the intersection of multiple realities, multiple and inseparable historical lines, lived spaces where the construction of space shifts constantly under the tensions of domination and resistances to domination. Consciousness of the placing is dizzying because both practices of domination and "impurity" become vivid in the negotiation of everyday life. The denseness and opacity of meanings elaborated in the midst of this multitude gives me a sense of my own and others' concreteness and of the perils of abstraction in this negotiation.[9] I am using "impure" to mark the disruption of dichotomies in resistance to domination. To stand on ground informed by homogeneity, sameness, and univocity of sense or relation, is to stand among others with a dichotomizing imagination.[10] A dichotomizing imagination is one impelled by the need to control or by the internalization of domination.

Impurity grounds the need for an against-the-grain sociality that one is moved to discern, sustain, affirm amid those subjected who harbor the ambition to become nonsubjected subjects. This ambition to metamorphose is marked as outside institutionalized sociality, and thus, institutionalized sense. At the intersection between dichotomizing and impure constructions of reality, resistant subjects negotiating and contesting multiple reductions of themselves and their possibilities enact resistant understandings of themselves in relation at different levels of articulation. Sometimes the understanding is not linguistically articulated but contained in the meaning of acts of resistance whose interpretation unveils the particularities of oppressive reductions that are being resisted. The development of resistant sense requires sociality among resisters who share both understandings of oppression that are, sometimes, highly inarticulate and inarticulate techniques of resistance, making community/home not only appealing but necessary.

Thus, I start within the midst of subjects, many of them subjected, but understood in our complexity and possibility. The sense of subject from which I start is well described by Inderpal Grewal as not an individual, not "unitary and centered and created out of the binaries of Self-Other, Subject-Object"[11] (Grewal 1994:234). Rather, subjects are multiple, impure, and thus able to dwell in the intersections between worlds of sense, and negotiate resistances to subjugating reductions at those intersections. Subjects are understood in terms of what Audre Lorde (1984) called "non-dominant differences." The importance of the impulse to reject dichotomies lies in the resistance to have one's plurality and the interrelations/paths among the multiple worlds of sense we inhabit reduced or erased. It is that plurality that enables us to acknowledge, discern, investigate, interpret, remake the connections among crisscrossing oppositional subaltern worlds of sense, oppositional to the very logic of subjection.

My departure from Friedman, Hoagland, and hooks lies in this emphasis on concreteness, spatiality, multiplicity, and impurity as interrelated in understanding communities in their relation to liberatory change. The starting point is different: the location of the theorizing subject is from within the midst of impure subjects negotiating life transgressing the categorial understandings of a logic of binaries that renders hard-edged, ossified, exclusive groups, as well as succumbing to the reductions of that logic. My starting point eludes abstraction, that theoretical temptress, and the logic of fragmentation as it sustains a perception against the grain of categorial fragmentation and perceives connections and practices of resistance that are otherwise unavailable. Thus, the possibilities, attractions, and dangers of communities are understood quite differently.

In "Contested Histories: Eurocentrism, Multiculturalism, and the Media," Robert Stam and Ella Shohat (1995) propose an anti-Eurocentric multiculturalism that "decolonizes representation not only in terms of cultural artifacts — literary canons, museum exhibits, film series — but also in terms of power relations between communities" (Stam and Shohat 1995:299). They "prod 'multiculturalism,' in the direction of a radical critique of power relations, turning it into a rallying cry for a more substantive and reciprocal intercommunalism" (Stam and Shohat 1995:299) It is this intercommunalism that I see as what is revealed as necessary and also as possible once we stand among people and cultivate a perception that rejects the fragmenting/homogenizing perception of the lover of purity.

Shohat and Stam propose a polycentric multiculturalism that constitutes the "intellectual and political regrouping" for forming "active intercommunal coalitions" (Stam and Shohat 1995:300). It is important to note how they distinguish "polycentric multiculturalism" from liberalism. Polycentric multiculturalism "sees all social history in relation to social power"; "its affiliations are clearly with the underrepresented, the marginalized, and the oppressed"; it sees "minoritarian communities not as 'interest groups' to be 'added on' to a preexisting nucleus but as active, generative participants at the very core of a shared, conflictual history"; it grants "an epistemological advantage" to "those prodded by historical circumstance into what Dubois called 'double consciousness,' ideally placed to 'deconstruct' dominant or narrowly national discourses"; it "rejects a unified, fixed, and essentialist concept of identities (or communities) as consolidated sets of practices, meanings, and experiences"; it "sees identities as multiple, unstable, historically situated, the products of ongoing differentiation and polymorphous identifications and pluralizations"; it "goes beyond narrow definitions of identity politics, opening the way for informed affiliation on the basis of shared social desires and identifications," identifications that have to be forged rather than found as natural or inevitable (Stam and Shohat 1995:300); it is "reciprocal, dialogical; it sees all acts of verbal or cultural exchange as taking place not between essential discrete bounded individuals or cultures but rather between mutually permeable, changing individuals and communities" (Stam and Shohat 1995:301).

The crucial step in Shohat and Stam's polycentric multiculturalism is its grounding on the perception of oppressed peoples as "active, generative participants at the very core of a shared, conflictual history" (Stam and Shohat 1995:299). That the history is shared, conflictual, and in relation to social power is one of the ingredients that begins to reveal social fragmentation as a historical product. The boundedness and isolation of particular groups begins to be understood as a fiction that in its turn is constituted as a barrier to the possibility of heterogeneous communities. To turn that fiction around is one of the directions of affirming impure connections and it is guided by a duplicitous perception that understands the naturalizing trick as it sees the social heterogeneity bound, reduced by the fiction of isolation. But it is not just a question of history, it is also a question of geography, of the social construction of space.

Fernando Coronil in "Beyond Occidentalism: Toward Non-imperial Geohistorical Categories" (1996) argues for unsettling what he calls "occidentalism" as a prerequisite to challenging what Edward Said defined as "orientalism." Coronil characterizes occidentalism as "the ensemble of representational practices that participate in the production of conceptions of the world, which (1) separate the world's components into bounded units; (2) disaggregate their relational histories; (3) turn difference into hierarchy; (4) naturalize these representations; and thus (5) intervene, however unwittingly, in the reproduction of existing asymmetrical power relations." Later, as he is exploring the complicity of the territorialization of history with occidentalism, Coronil adds:

> As a consequence, the histories of interrelated peoples become territorialized into bounded spaces. Since these spaces appear as being produced naturally, not historically, they serve to root the histories of connected peoples in separate territories and to sever the links between them. Thus the illusion is created that their identities are the result of independent histories rather than the outcome of historical relations. There is a dual obscuring, the histories of various spaces are hidden, and the historical relations among social actors or units are severed. [Coronil 1996:77]

Coronil thinks of these "units" as groups of nations or supranational entities such as the West or the Third World, but also of "localized intranational units, such as peasants, ethnic 'minorities,' 'slum dwellers,' the 'homeless,' forms of communalism" (Coronil 1996:77).

While Shohat and Stam reveal to us the illusion of group boundedness and isolation as they emphasize historical inter-relatedness, Coronil spatializes the interrelations and histori-cizes space.[12] As the naturalization of space serves to create the illusion of territorial boundedness and isolation, the histories of connected peoples become spatially fragmented. Thus, the importance of spatial particularity. If the theorizing is from in-side the midst of people spatially placed in a spatiality that is produced, the history of that production becomes crucial to an understanding of interrelations. The space itself can be under-stood as impure, that is, as conceived against the grain of frag-mentation and naturalization.

A polycentric multiculturalist perception that emphasizes the production of space perceives against the grain of social fragmentation and reduction of heterogeneous subjects and communities into bounded, isolated, simple, because homoge-neous, units. If a polycentric multiculturalist perception is the starting point of the reflection on community, then the tension between heterogeneity and social fragmentation becomes vivid.[13] The operations of reduction of collectivities through the logic of purity, the representational practices that partici-pate in the production of fragmented communities and sub-jects, can be sensed at work. The starting point clarifies the dangers in the apparent safety of communities understood as homogeneous, bounded, isolated — collectivities of the same. The reduction of complexity ceases to be invisible. As the ten-sion between heterogeneity and social fragmentation becomes vivid, the need to evoke and sustain complex connections within communities becomes clear. All subjects can then be understood as active contributors to, collaborators in, creators of oppressive or resistant practices even when the logics of op-pression constitute some subjects as passive. That is, resistance and oppression vie as constructions of everyday life. One way of putting the point is to think of particular subjects as op-press-*ing* (or collaborat-*ing*) or be-*ing* oppressed and as resist-*ing*. This is a struggle within communities understood as im-pure. So, in a sense, we end with what we start, but it is impor-tant to note that we start in a tense, contested terrain. To perceive it as contested, conflicted, shifting, in production mo-tivates us to join in polilogical struggle toward a consolidation of the possibilities against social fragmentation already contained in impure communities. In rejecting a perception of communities and those in communities as atomistic, homogenous, autonomous, bounded, fixed entities in naturalized bounded spatio-temporalities, we can begin to see that impure communities are our ground and our possibility against social fragmentation. In a sense, impure communities are forged. They are indeed not found. But they are forged in a line of historico-spatial impurity, rather than altogether anew.

It is important to note that to emphasize a shared conflictual history is not to reduce the multiple historical lines and the multiple interrelated worlds of sense to one. It is not to claim either that we all share a sameness of experience or a "common sense." Indeed, the multiple locations and subject positions in that conflictual history cannot be reduced. To reduce them to one linear history is precisely to erase its conflictual nature, to valorize one standpoint in its understanding. Reflecting on the history of labor in the United States makes this shared conflictual history vivid in the multiplicity of historical lines intersecting in the production of concrete spatialities. The building of the railroads gives us a concrete example of this multiplicity of intersecting historical lines in a shared conflictual history.[14] Edward Soja's reflections on Los Angeles (1989) make vivid the clashes and tensions between "an essentially exploitative spatial division of labour" and its obscuring in an "environment more specialized in the production of encompassing mystifications than practically any other you can name." "When all that is seen is so fragmented and filled with whimsy and pastiche, the hard edges of the capitalist, racist and patriarchal landscape seem to disappear, melt into air" (Soja 1989:246).

The difficult issue of communication at the intersection of multiple historical lines and worlds of sense in a conflictual shared history needs to start at that intersection and take stock of communicative lines and practices against the fragmenting/homogenizing grain. Because of this interrelatedness in a conflictual history, communication among worlds of difference needs to note a communicative rule at the intersection between worlds of sense: domination always "translates" difference into otherness and otherness into sameness, exchangeability, passivity through the erection of impassable barriers of sense that require the translation into the master tongue. So, as we "see" others whose worlds of sense intersect but are not reducible to each other and perceive them as reduced to sameness, we should remember the translation rule and counter it with the impure epistemological shift. The epistemological shifts, the shifts in attention at the intersection between worlds of sense, mindful of the semiotic traps of domination, are not a matter of choice.

These reflections on community lead me then to a resistant dialogical, intercommunal task, a crucial one for popular education: the collective work of revealing to each other the interrelatedness of our worlds of sense, of our histories (spatialized), of our spatialities (produced). This work sustains and is sustained by the perception of our impurity, that is, of ourselves and ourselves in relation against the fragmenting grain.

Notes

1. Maria Dalida Benfield, Joshua Price, and I created the first workshop that our group, Escuela Popular Norteña, tried around the notion of community. Though we added other senses of community, Friedman's distinction was central to the workshop. Other members of the Escuela Popular have worked in later versions of the communities workshop.

2. Compare the connections between this failure of insertion toward resistance within communities of place and the failure of the Lesbian Movement to move inside communities of color. See chapter 7 ("The Discontinuous Passing of the *Cachapera/Tortillera* from the Barrio to the Bar to the Movement").

3. An important example of the work done by women of color that is mindful of difference in women's needs and ways and of the need for community connection is the work done by Incite!, an organization by and for Women of Color devoted to the eradication of violence against Women of Color.

4. The movement started in the Color of Violence conferences by and for Women of Color looks at Women of Color in communities and sees the complex ties between state and interpersonal violence that single us out for a unending abuse. Incite! is leading this movement.

5. See Joshua Price (1998, 2002) for a careful and powerful analysis of this aspect of the contemporary treatment of violence against women. Of

particular relevance for the discussion of communities of place/communities of choice is the chapter "Why Doesn't She Leave?"

6. See chapter 8 ("*El Pasar Discontínuo de la Cachapera/Tortillera del Barrio a la Barra al Movimiento*/The Discontinuous Passing of the *Cachapera/Tortillera* from the Barrio to the Bar to the Movement") for further discussion of the difficulties of the concrete journeys, and for an understanding of what blocks conversation in a resistant understanding of "conversation," one that is not tied to a closed world of sense.

7. As I make clear in chapter 8, I think the use of the term "lesbian" exercises a false inclusion of women of color whose relation to women is in transgression of the heterosexual norms of their particular social traditions.

8. I work as a popular educator for the Escuela Popular Norteña, a popular education center that I cofounded in 1988.

9. Like Tabor Fisher, I mean "negotiate" as in "negotiate a river not a contract." Tabor Fisher contributed this interpretation of negotiation in the working group on Methodologies of Resistant Negotiation of which we are both members at SUNY Binghamton.

10. For the development of this position, see chapter 6 ("Purity, Impurity, and Separation").

11. Grewal tells us that plural subjectivities "are enabling because they provide a mobility in solidarity that leads to a transnational participation in understanding and opposing multiple and global oppressions operating upon them; that is, these subject positions enable oppositions in multiple locations" (Grewal 1994:234).

12. In rethinking the production of space, Coronil is taking up Doreen Massey's (2000) and Henri Lefebvre's (1992) work. I am also influenced by Massey's (1992) and Lefebvre's (1992) work on space and by the work of Caren Kaplan (1994, 1996), Edward Soja (1989), David Harvey (1990), Michel de Certeau (1988), and Ken Knabb (1981).

13. Here Chabram Dernesesian's "Chicana? Rican! No, Chicano-Riqueña" (1994) is sharply illuminating as she exemplifies and theorizes a rejection of fragmentation.

14. In *A Different Mirror*, Ronald Takaki (1993) makes clear the intricacy of these lines and the high conflict not just on the part of oppressors but also on the part of sometimes unwitting collaborators.

References and Suggested Readings

Chabram Dernersesian, Angie. 1994. Chicana? Rican! No, Chicano-Riqueña: Refashioning the Transnational Connection. In *Multiculturalism: A Critical Reader*, edited by David Theo Goldberg, 269–95. Oxford, U.K.: Blackwell.

Coronil, Fernando. 1996. Beyond Occidentalism: Toward Nonimperial Geohistorical Categories. *Cultural Anthropology* 11 (1): 51–87.

de Certeau, Michel. 1988. *The Practice of Everyday Life*. Berkeley: University of California Press.

Friedman, Marilyn. 1989. Feminism and Modern Friendship: Dislocating the Community. *Ethics* 99 (January).

Friedman, Marilyn, and Penny A. Weiss, eds. 1995. *Feminism and Community*. Philadelphia: Temple University Press.

Grewal, Inderpal. 1994. Autobiographic Subjects and Diasporic Locations: Meatless Days and Bordenlands. In *Scattered Hegemonies*, edited by Inderpal Grewal and Caren Kaplan, 231–54. Minneapolis: University of Minnesota Press.

Harvey, David. 1990. *The Condition of Postmodernity: An Enquiry into the Origins of Cultural Change*. Cambridge, Mass.: Blackwell.

Hoagland, Sarah. 1988. *Lesbian Ethics*. Palo Alto, Calif.: Institute of Lesbian Studies.

hooks, bell. 1990. Homeplace: A Site of Resistance and Choosing the Margin as a Space of Radical Openness. In *Yearning*, edited by bell hooks. Boston: South End Press.

Kaplan, Caren. 1994. The Politics of Location as Transnational Feminist Critical Practice. In *Scattered Hegemonies: Postmodernity and Transnational Feminist Practices*, edited by Inderpal Grewal and Caren Kaplan, 137–52. Minneapolis: University of Minnesota Press.

———. 1996. *Questions of Travel*. Durham, NC: Duke University Press.

Knabb, Ken, ed. 1981. *Situationist International*. Berkeley, Calif.: Bureau of Public Secrets.

Lefebvre, Henri. 1992. *The Production of Space*. Oxford, UK: Blackwell.

Lorde, Audre. 1984. The Master's Tools Will Never Dismantle the Master's House. In *Sister Outsider*. Trumansburg, N.Y.: The Crossing Press.

MacIntyre, Alasdair. 1981. *After Virtue*. Notre Dame, Ind.: University of Notre Dame Press.

Massey, Doreen. 1992. Politics and Space/Time. *New Left Review* 196:65–84.

———. 2000. *Local Histories/Global Designs*. Princeton, N.J.: Princeton University Press.

Price, Joshua. 1998. *Spaces of Violence, Shades of Meaning: The Heterogeneity of Violence against Women in the Unites States*. Ph.D. diss. University of Chicago.

———. 2002. The Apotheosis of Home and the Maintenance of Spaces of Violence. *Hypatia* 17:4.

Sandel, Michael. 1982. *Liberalism and the Limits of Justice*. Cambridge, UK: Cambridge University Press.

Soja, Edward. 1989. *Postmodern Geographies*. London: Verso.

Spelman, Elizabeth. 1988. *Inessential Woman*. Boston: Beacon.

Stam, Robert, and Ella Shohat. 1995. Contested Histories: Eurocentrism, Multiculturalism, and the Media. In *Multiculturalism*, edited by David Theo Goldberg. Oxford, UK: Blackwell.

Takaki, Ronald. 1993. *A Different Mirror*. Boston: Little, Brown, & Company.

~

CHAPTER TEN

Tactical Strategies of the Streetwalker/*Estrategias Tácticas de la Callejera*

The Spatiality of Theory

Theoreticians of society and politics have often conceived of themselves as perched up high, looking at or making up the social from a disengaged position. The crucial disengagement is not necessarily the disengagement of political impartiality or neutrality but a disengagement from the concrete. It is theoreticians so self-conceived who are understood to occupy the strategist position. In this view of the social, subjected subjects are assumed to negotiate daily survival myopically from within the concreteness of body-to-body engagement. At best, resistance within this concreteness is reduced to the tactical. Given this valorization of disengagement, the powerful are the theoretician's brothers: they get to play with the hand-me-downs of each other's imaginations.

These interwoven conceptions of theorizing and of subjection to oppression conceptually erase the possibility of theorizing resistance from the subaltern position and from within the concreteness of body-to-body engagement. Giving centrality to the strategy/tactic dichotomy is one way of performing the erasure. Given the dichotomy, tying "theory" to "strategy" and "resistance" to "tactic" erases the possibility of a theory of resistance to oppressions, unless the strategist does the theorizing. But the strategist cannot understand the logic of the tactical from the strategic position. The position itself occludes the very existence of the tactical. To disentangle the dichotomy is not solely a conceptual exercise, since the dichotomy informs our practices of resistance. If the field of understanding of our own activities is conceptually blocked in this way, from within it we cannot intend past its narrow confines. And if we do intend past these confines, in defiance of its logic, we have difficulty in moving the intentions toward a collective form, however dispersed. It is not just a question of publicity or counterpublicity, but of sociality in any form, however hidden. It is a question of praxis.

Given the framing of the field of understanding, this writing attempts to unravel, perform, exhibit understandings of ourselves and our activities in resistance to both the interlocking of oppressions and to intermeshed oppressions.[1] Resistance will be understood always in the gerund, a resisting. Oppression will also be understood as ongoing. The tense relation resisting ⇔ oppressing is our focus. Understanding oppression in the gerund does not necessitate a personalized understanding of oppressing. Impersonal forces can be understood as something one lives with and within and they can be understood up close without personalizing them and without reification.[2]

I propose to embrace tactical strategies in moving in disruption of the dichotomy, as crucial to an epistemology of resistance/liberation. To do so is to give uptake to the disaggregation of collectivity concomitant with social fragmentation[3] and to theorize the navigation of its perils without giving uptake to its logic. It is also to seek an epistemology that reconceives intentionality without falling into monological understandings of either individual or collective agency. Such an epistemology dissociates itself from individualistic perspectivalism in favor of a more dispersed, more complex, multiple, interactive, uncertain, and necessarily engaged understanding of the social. It takes up embodied attention to the micro mechanisms of power and their being met with creative resistance. And it seeks to follow the paths of resistant intentionality in transgression of the tactic/strategy dichotomy. This also requires understanding intentionality as lying *between rather than in subjects*, subjects that are neither monolithically nor monologically understood. Thus, the meaning, the sense of the intentions cannot be assumed to be always lying within one world of sense, but as possibly lying in between worlds of sense, worlds of sense that are enmeshed with each other, even though they may be ideologized as distinct.[4] The "closure" of the intentions—the taking them to some praxical, though necessarily open ended and temporary completion—is a long-winded intersubjective project without a master mind: without a strategist.

It is in this line of vision, street-level, among embodied subjects, with ill-defined "edges," that the tactical strategist lives without myopia, without epistemological/political short-sightedness.[5] Moving intentions within and toward a complex collectivity recommends the practice of hanging out, a street-walker's practice.* This practice is compatible with developing a rather large sense of the terrain and its social intricacies. Hanging out permits one to learn, to listen, to transmit information, to participate in communicative creations, to gauge possibilities, to have a sense of the directions of intentionality, to gain social depth. Unlike enclosures of the social that are conceived as less permeable, hangouts are highly permeable. That is why it is possible to move from hangout to hangout without betrayal.

---

* Streetwalkers include women who are at odds with "home." The home-shelter-street-police station/jail/insane asylum-cemetery circle, in ever so many permutations, is their larger understanding of home. Home is lived as a place inseparable from other places of violence, including the street. One could punctuate any other place in this circle. I count myself among the women who have found myself more skillful at dodging violence in the street.

At a time of significant violence in my life, I found company, embodied solace, with a young woman who worked both in prostitution and as a maid, jobs that were inseparable in her life. She had no home, I did. She was the only person to see my naked body covered in deep bruises, who did not inflict injury on me; I was one of the women with whom she could talk about the violence of being raped by cops without pay. In this spatiality of home-shelter-street-police station/jail/insane asylum-cemetery, I occupied home and insane asylum; she occupied other people's homes and police stations as places of extreme violence. We both found more expressive and "freer" motility, and meaning in the street.

It is also important to note that conversations in the street are not subject to the same rules of sense, nor to the same expectations. This circle, trajectory of violence exposes, places in the open, the public/private distinction as a trick played on women's imaginations. The circle also spatializes violence and points to the need to create spaces in disruption of the public/private dichotomy. Shelters fit in the dichotomy only too well. They stabilize it. I am suggesting hangouts as places that perform the disruption.

This theorizing of resistance thus intermingles in the spatiality of the street. This pivoting of the spatiality of cognition radically alters what is conceivable. Done as a pedestrian, *una callejera, en compañía*, in the midst of company, and obliterating the theory/practice distinction, this theorizing seeks out, puts out, entrusts, invokes, rehearses, performs, considers, and enacts tactical-strategic practices of resistant/emancipatory sense making. Performing a rejection of theorizing the social from above, streetwalker theorizing understands and moves resistance to intermeshed oppressions.

For the project to make sense, it is necessary to exercise a duplicitous[6] perception that at once unveils and disarms the conceptual-institutional reduction of resistance to oppression to the tactical and takes up the possibility of the tactical strategic. As the understanding of our own resistance is heavily veiled by the strategist's plans, and by the deployment of his power and authority, it is important to clear the air so as to be able both to understand the space where we are actively resisting as worldly — *mundano,* an emancipatory, complexly voiced sense of "public" — and to take up its possibilities.[7] So as to keep each other resisting subjection, and so as to keep the resisting long-winded, we need to reconceive our own activity. This duplicitous move has to be repeated over and over again, incessantly.

Agency

Late modernity gave rise to the fiction of effective individual agency that fits both the strategist, the powerful, and those who act as managers, foremen, lesser officials, and upholders of its institutional "apparatus." This fiction hides the institutional setting and the institutional backing of individual potency. In hiding the institutional setting, the narrative of individual agency entices subjects understood as individuals with the power and efficacy of their deliberations and decisions. Valorizing single authorship, individual responsibility, individual accountability, and self-determination, freedom is lived as this efficacy of individual agency. Intentionality is understood as residing in and emanating from the individual or from monolithic collectivities. These are conceptual devices that pervade or constitute the underpinnings of dominant moral and legal discourse and they are used in vicious and contradictory ways against those who are the subjects of strategic control.

In this conception of agency, the successful agent reasons practically in a world of meaning and within social, political, and economic institutions that back him up and form the framework for his forming intentions that are not subservient to the plans of others and that he is able to carry into action unimpeded and as intended. He shares in some measure in the control of the context in which he forms his intentions. His alternatives and the direction of his intending reflect his being a shareholder in power. Successful agency is a mirage of individual autonomous intentional action. What is illusory becomes comprehensible as the reality of power in institutionalized sense reveals the collectivity backing up the individual.

The oppressed cannot exercise agency since they either enact a subordinate or a resistant intentionality. The subservient nature of the intentions disqualify the oppressed from agency in the first case. Lack of institutional backing disqualifies the resister from having agency. This "lack" is the crucial source of the possibilities of an alternative sociality. Since the modern conception of agency as autonomous subjectivity cannot countenance resistance by the oppressed,[8] and since agency is a precondition of modern understandings of morality, resistance to oppression is conceptually disallowed as moral.[9] To make clear the possibility of resistance and its conditions, I introduce the concept of "active subjectivity." Though resisters are not agents, they are active subjects. The liberatory possibilities of active subjectivity depend on both an alternative sociality and a tactical strategic stance.

Tactical-Strategic Troubling of the Tactic/Strategy Dichotomy

Michel de Certeau draws a distinction central to the Practice of Everyday Life *between tactics and strategies. Strategies are devised by planners, managers, subjects of will and power, from a point of view that is positioned high above the street, being able to view the "whole" to be structured, abstracting from the concrete in accordance with scientific rationality (de Certeau 1988:xix). Strategies always presuppose a "proper," a place that can be circumscribed, and provides "a certain independence from the variability of circumstances" (de Certeau 1988:36). The strategist masters places through sight, transforming "foreign forces into objects that can be observed and measured" (de Certeau 1988:36). Being able to see far into the distance, the planner/strategist can predict, prepare, future expansions of the "proper," construct "the fiction that . . . makes the complexity of the city readable, and immobilizes its opaque mobility in a transparent text" (de Certeau 1988:92). The urban planner's city, the "concept-city" is the strategist's "proper." A tactic cannot count on a "proper," it rather "insinuates itself into the other's place, fragmentarily, without taking it over in its entirety, without being able to keep it at a distance" (de Certeau 1988:xix). Whatever the tactician wins, "it cannot keep." Tacticians, the weak, must always turn alien forces to their own ends, in devious, hidden makings — hidden from the strategist's frame of reference — that constitute another production, a production that does not reject or alter systems the weak have no choice but to accept, but rather subverts these systems by using them to ends and references foreign to them (de Certeau 1988:xiii).*

De Certeau understands the tactic/strategy dichotomy in spatial terms.[10] The spatialization of each term and its consequences is important. In disrupting the dichotomy, I want to trouble the terms' organization of the spatiality of resistance to domination. Though de Certeau draws the dichotomy to unveil room for resistance by the "weak," the resistor is trapped by the spatiality of the dichotomy. In disrupting the dichotomy, I am particularly keen on intervening in the judgment that the oppressed cannot see deeply into the social. The intervention also reconfigures what it is to see deeply into it.

The strategist "sees" from a point of view characterized by the distance of height and abstraction. He "sees" the immobile city, but the immobile, immutable city — a triumph of space over time — is presupposed in the relation sight-abstraction-distance. The immutable city is both presupposed and reasserted as a project of control. Abstraction and the distance of height "permit" a fictionalized seeing of a fictionalized city —

"the concept—city" to appear real. This is also the colonial strategist's viewpoint: the distance of maps accompanied by the power to "empty" lands of history and the concreteness of local histories. There is variety among strategists, the variety is in the tricks of their trade that enable them to fix a place and manage it: to "empty" it of its concreteness and the meaning of that concreteness; to deterritorialize it, and to fix it in time, a place without history and without any properties that are not performed through the techniques of strategy. So the strategist perceives, or rather imagines, those who inhabit the city to inhabit a spatial order of the strategist's conception: ethnocentrically conceived, homogeneous, under his knowledgeable control. As the strategist plans and controls as if the fiction were real,[11] he does at once reduce and miss the life that inhabits the city.[12] Thus, he cannot manage that life, which he does not see or understand. If the makings of the "weak" are hidden, they are hidden by the concept city, by the strategist's powerful fiction.

That de Certeau does not understand the "weak" as passive is clear from his investigation of the making of "a hidden poiesis," what he calls "an anti-discipline," a "making do" that enables "the weak" to escape within the dominant social order through microbe-like operations that deflect the functioning of technocratic structures. "If it is true that the grid of "discipline" is everywhere becoming clearer and more extensive," de Certeau says, "it is all the more urgent to discover how an entire society resists being reduced to it, what popular mechanisms manipulate the mechanisms of discipline and conform to them in order to evade them." Just as speaking "effects an appropriation or reappropriation of language by its speakers," numerous practices of consumption exercise a secondary production, one guided by interests and desires that "are neither determined nor captured by the systems in which they develop."[13]

De Certeau's understanding of consumers as active does not rest on embracing agency in the modern sense, since his investigation rejects the model of the individual subject. Rather, he is interested in making explicit "operational combinations" that reveal users as active. The operational logic goes back to "the ruses of fishes and insects" that have been hidden by the

Western model of rationality. These microbe-like operations, de Certeau understands as tactical, dispersed, makeshift, multiform, fragmentary, always relative to situations and details, lacking their own ideologies and institutions. These operations "bring into play a popular ratio, a way of thinking invested in a way of acting, an art of combination that cannot be dissociated from an art of using." De Certeau places these everyday practices of resistance within a rationalized, centralized, clamorous, spectacular, expansionist production, guided by the logic of power exercised not in its infinitesimal, micropolitical guises but in its strategic form.

My intent is not to dismiss but to complicate de Certeau's description by using within radical political moving a disruption of the tactic/strategy dichotomy so as to understand levels of resistance that include what de Certeau calls "the ruses of the weak." De Certeau says that the "weak"'s spatiality lacks an immutable place, it lacks a proper. So the weak "insinuate" themselves into the other's place, "without being able to keep it at a distance." But if the immutable strategist's proper is a fiction, what is there to "keep at a distance"?

There is a confusion here between "keeping at a distance" and being able to perceive, sense, with the distance of depth, depth into the social. One does not have to keep social relationality "at a distance" if one is to see into its depth. It is the latter that I want to recuperate in theorizing possibilities of standing against oppression that go beyond the "operational combinations" that de Certeau understands as the only possibilities for the tactician. But the possibility of the distance of depth lends the tactician's ruses another life as it stands on the disruption of the tactic/strategy dichotomy.

So, in de Certeau, "strategy" stands for distance mastered through sight and abstraction, "tactic" stands for lack of distance, concreteness, for shortsighted creations. Without illusions, the tactician stands on the treacherous fictional immobility of the master's proper, and "makes do." The tactical strategist, on the other hand, meets power in the guise of the illusory "concept city," abstract space, the emptying of space, as well as in the guise of its infinitesimal mechanisms. Both are ingredients of "oppressing." In meeting power in these guises, the tactical strategist keeps a duplicitous tactile-

audio-olfactory-visual insight into the depth of the social. The alert embodiment of walking and bumping, among and into each other, is of consequence. The tactical strategists' insight into the social does not flatten it out as the distance of height does. It does not lose sensory contact with it. For the tactical strategist resisting ⇔ oppressing has volume, intricacy, multiplicity of relationality and meaning, and it is approached with all the sensorial openness and keenness that permits resistant, liberatory, enduring, if dispersed, complexity of connection.[14]

Tactical strategic active subjectivity is explored here not from the outside, but from within a streetwalking multitude that moves creatively in spaces that are neither the "nowhere" of de Certeau's tactics nor the "proper" of the strategist's. While for de Certeau, the mobility of the tactician rests on the absence of a proper, and thus it privileges time over space, the spatio-temporality of the tactical strategist is the mobile spatiality of the street lived not as a "nowhere" but in "hangouts."[15] There is no possibility of an aestheticization of politics through a mythification of place that calls forth a transcending of history here. The logic of tactical strategies makes possible a recreation of spatiality that constitutes it as a form of what Caren Kaplan calls a "working in and against the local" (Kaplan 1996:180).

A contemporary rereading of the tactical glosses it as criminal, deviant, abnormal, in need of containment, or alternatively, as frivolous and inconsequential, not a matter for serious revolutionary theorizing. The degree of accountability for deviation depends on an oxymoronic construction of deviant "subjects," as agents that stand outside of the possibility of agency. Without a conceptual alternative to the late modern notion of agency, resistant negotiations of meaning are reduced to haphazard, happenstance, disjointed intrusions on dominant sense, a troubled sort of passivity. And, surely, resistance cannot be conceived or enacted by the modern agent, who has no need, and no conceptual room for it in his domain.

I propose the concept of active subjectivity for the activity of those who disturb the abstract spatiality of social fragmentation. As I look at lived spaces with an eye for more than ephemeral refigurements of spatialities and possibilities ordered by institutions and mechanisms of repression, I explore the possibilities open by a depth of inhabitation and understanding of the social, more enduring inhabitations than "making do." In proposing the notion of active subjectivity coupled with that of tactical-strategies and a renewed understanding of intentionality, I am exploring the opening of logical paths in order to refigure the possibilities of the oppressed from within the complexities of the social. In disrupting the tactic/strategy, time/space dichotomies, I am navigating the "space-time, other-time-other-space of the *callejera*, which is neither the borrowed space of the time-tied tactician nor space-strategist dominion, but the other timespace of the hangout, the *callejera*'s uncharted newspace-time" (Joshua Price, personal communication).

Intentions

Resistant intentions are given form necessarily intersubjectively. If intentions are "of a subject" or "in a subject," that is, if they are formed in and emanate from a subject, is that subject collective or individual, a unitary or fractured one, a singular or a multiple subject? What is the time and space of the intending? Does a unitary individual intend at a particular time and do the intentions carry into the individual's act and are communicated successfully given the presuppositions of public sense and taken to completion? Given my revisiting of agency and the politics of agency, an account of intentions that understands them as in and emanating from a unitary, individual, simple subject who makes public sense to others, captures the sense of intending of agents, shareholders in the meanings made by power. But this understanding of intentionality is useless in moving against oppression. All one has to do is to try to move with people against oppression, to understand oneself as not able to intend in this sense. What I am proposing is a viable sense of intentionality for moving against the interlocking of oppressions that animates oppressions as intermeshed. As I unveil the collectivity backing up the individual, I am pointing not just to the illusory quality of the individual, but to the need of an alternative sociality for resistant intentionality. Intending may "feel" as arising in a subject, but surely the production of intentions is itself a haphazard and dispersed social production. Subjects participate in intending, but intentions acquire life to the extent that they exist between subjects. The trick of individual intentionality lies in making one believe that if one intends into the hegemonic system's vein, one is the author of those intentions and of actions invested with their point. But standing against that illusion, in transgression of its sense, intending against its grain, requires taking up a multitude of lines that constitute an alternative and complex sociality.

The relation among active subjectivity; intersubjective, dispersed, heterogeneous intention formation; and the tactical strategic forms a tight circle of possibility on the move. Active subjectivity is possible because of alternative socialities that have an unseen, hidden quality to them, even if they live in the worldliness of the street, unseen from the conceptual perspectivism of strategic understandings of power. Active subjectivity is alive in the activity of dispersed intending in complex, heterogeneous collectivities, within and between worlds of complex sense. The activity is not subservient or servile but in transgression of dominant sense. The dispersion includes a dispersion of meaning through a translation that does not rest on equivalences between words but on worldly connections in living in transgression of reduction of life to the monosense of domination.

There is room for expectations here. We do not approach each other either as blank slates or as thoroughly created in every encounter but rather in the tension of a history of oppressing ⇔ resisting. Some expectations are necessary. But expectations are very different from presuppositions. Expecting a particular sense leaves a great deal of room for redirection, for "translation" in this renewed and complex sense, a sense that makes clear that history does not have to ossify meaning.

This may appear as an attenuated sense of intentionality, but it is a strong sense when understood as in active resistance to the interlocking of oppressions. It is sensorially rich, alive in the midst of different worlds of sense, multiple histories and multiple spatial paths. The histories and spatialities intersect in a liveliness of possibilities of connection and direction that can bear the fruit of a moving that is intentionally tense with complexity.

The tactical strategic is crucial here as the incarnate, sensorially open, ability to have depth of insight into the complexities of the social. That depth of insight characterizes the tactical strategic. The resistant spatiality dismantles the barriers that keep the oppressed from bursting out of the confined spaces and confined desires that define the boundaries of creative rebellions and tired compliances. The tactical strategist acquires a practiced, long sense of the social spatiality of particular resistances and resistant meanings. The tactical strategist participates in intending as a long lived social act. Intentions move and mutate within a changing sociality. Thus, the resistant spatiality is unsettled. There is a high degree of uncertainty here. As we move from tactics to tactical strategies we move from ephemeral contestatory negotiations of sense to more sustained engagements.

That the actions of the active subject can successfully be interpreted from within resistant sense, extra-institutionally in the sense of not abiding by the logic of particular institutions, is what testifies to a failure of dominant sense to exhaust the possibilities of sense, to exhaust meaning. The invisibility of resistant sense from within dominant sense is also its advantage as resistant. This is clear when we understand that resistant sense cannot reside in "the individual" as the institutional backing that makes possible the appearance of individuality, is absent. And so the backing for individual agency hides resistant sense. The distinction between agency and active subjectivity permits one to capture these different logics and to evaluate and interpret as resistant activity that which otherwise appears as inactivity, disengagement, or nonsensical. The streetwalker theorist keeps both logics in interpretation but valorizes the logic of resistance as she inhabits differentiated geographies carrying with others contestatory meanings to praxical completion.

In a society in which there are dominators and dominated, oppressors and oppressed, this model describes oppressors as successful agents, though individual potency is a sham. The oppressed may be able to engage in some acts that could be described as successful acts of agency, but most of their acting will fail in this regard because oppression is encompassing and affects the meaning of activities as apparently uncomplicated as eating a meal or going to bed at night. Eating *posole* may be a resistant activity; sleeping by oneself may be resistant activity; carrying one's keys in one's hands can be a resistant activity; talking to strangers can be a resistant activity. This is the insight of the *callejera*. Conceiving of resisters as active subjects enables one to articulate, make explicit, one's noticing the collectivity of active subjects—however dispersed—backing up one's active subjectivity as one makes sense among and with others, and also its absence, and how its absence renders one's words, gestures, movements nonsensical. The autonomous agent takes all the social backing of his sense for granted, as well as the social efficacy of his agency. The institutional set up, the language, the "common" practices are ignored as they form the framework for this illusion of individual creativity and originality, this no-debt-to-no one, this lack of social links.

The active subject treads in the fragility of sense, at every step conscious of recognition or lack of it, searching for back up, aware of the lack of institutional back up at every turn. The possibility of being found unintelligible lurks in many interactions. In the midst of the unsociality of her sense, she may find moments of solitude restful. But there is a need and an excitement to being understood in intersubjective encounters: a sense of touching a shore, of bathing in clean water, an urge to run and leap, a smile within. And one also learns to be guarded about easy recognitions. One grabs for dear life to words, performances, signs, marks that are sometimes beyond the pale and acquires an appreciation for life lived at the margins of common sense: the outlaw, the despised, the useless, the insane, the hustlers, the poachers, the pickers of garbage, the urban nomads of the reconstituted spatiality of the cityscapes defy and unmask common sense. The fear instilled in one, the contempt instilled in one for these possibilities, one replaces with a cautious tenderness, an openness to rereading sense and being reread in turn.

In tactical strategic intensity, the subject that resists interlocked and intermeshed oppressions is, at the moment of resistance, an active subject. Tactical-strategic intending, in a complexly directional and intersubjective understanding of intentionality, in an emancipatory direction, is possible between resistant subjects.[16] Both the formation of the emancipatory resistant intentions and the efficacy of those intentions in informing action partially depend on the attention each resister pays to the other resisters forming the intentions. The practice of moving against the path of social fragmentation does not presuppose fluency in one's tongue, but rather a more fully sensorial attentiveness to the making of resistant senses along the path.[17]

Hangouts

I am looking for a spatial politics that emphasizes difference. That is, I am looking for intersections where subaltern sense is fashioned in the tense encounters with dominant sense and where ongoing crossings between multiple resistant worlds of sense are sometimes tentatively, sometimes powerfully enacted. Those resistant worlds of sense are fashioned in the oppressing ⇔ resisting relation. In defiance of the monadic, atomistic, homogeneous construals of sense in dominant terms, each world of sense is a tense confluence of multiple local and translocal histories of meaning elaborated in the resisting ⇔ oppressing relation, sometimes in collaborative resistance across worlds of sense.

I am looking for a spatiality that does not mythify territorial enclosures and purities of peoples, languages, traditions. As I think of such conditions, I am proposing the spatial practice of hanging out because it is one practice that is in transgression of territorial enclosures. Hanging out is always a hanging out with/among others in an openness and intensity of attention, of interest, sensorially mindful in each other's direction. Movement from hangout to hangout promotes complexity in design and aids the carrying intentions to tentative and open-ended completions deep into the social and institutional fabric. Hanging out opens our attention to transmutations of sense, borders of meaning, without the enclosures and exclusions that have characterized a politics of sameness.[18]

Hanging out, as used here, is a practice of persistent "appropriation of space,"[19] a tactical strategic activity that informs space against the construal of bounded territories that mythologize sameness. The occupation of space is defined by movement in and between hangouts where resistant sense was/is made in practice by active subjects. Streetwalker theorists cultivate the ability to sustain and create hangouts by hanging out. Hangouts are highly fluid, worldly, nonsanctioned, communicative, occupations of space, contestatory retreats for the passing on of knowledge, for the tactical-strategic fashioning of multivocal sense, of enigmatic vocabularies and gestures, for the development of keen commentaries on structural pressures and gaps, spaces of complex and open ended recognition. Hangouts are spaces that cannot be kept captive by the private/public split. They are worldly, contestatory concrete spaces within geographies sieged by and in defiance of logics and structures of domination.[20] The streetwalker theorist walks in illegitimate refusal to legitimate oppressive arrangements and logics. In tense negotiations, she is watchful of opportunities taken up in the devious interventions of the oppressed.

Common Sense

La *callejera* looking for company focuses most intently on the hostilities, discontinuities, and possibilities of connection and sense making among *las/los atravezadas/os*—"those who cross over, pass over, or go through the confines of the 'normal.'"[21]

The walking/theorizing defamiliarizes "common sense," as the "common" backing it up loses its unseen, or taken for granted, part of the furniture of the universe, quality. The common is all around and in her as both upheld and defied. The politics and fictitious quality of the common are clarified as the *callejera*, who is prepared for the unmaking and remaking of sense and thus for participation in a delicate production, is assumed by and as everyone else around her, to be fluent in sturdy common sense. She is assumed to be part of the common that backs up common sense, pressed into being complicit with the ease and carelessness of interlocution, all meaning presented as ready-made for compliant consumption and as heavy with its own propriety. The words and gestures seem not to break or dissolve easily, their solid meanings carried by an enormous collectivity constituting and legitimating their institutionalization. Meanings and institutions thus appear reified, objectified, taken out of the danger of interlocution.

La callejera can both sense the reality and fiction of the common in daily interaction as well as the multiple contestations of the common and of its sense. She is ready for multiple meanings being elaborated interactively. The daily negotiations of streetwalkers, pedestrians, draw trajectories that concretize, differentiate space, that defy its abstract production and administration.[22] They also reveal the presuppositions of abstraction and its being constituted by an interchangeability of all terms, and thus a homogenization of sense and an absence of dialogical sense making. Space becomes concrete as it becomes crisscrossed by a multiplicity of meanings. The multiple interactive contestations of the common in common sense, in geographies constantly redescribed, reinscribed, concretize space. Interchangeability of terms becomes a politics that the callejera participates in subverting and in so doing, she contests her own reduction to passivity or frivolity.

The streetwalker theorist in search of tactical/strategic defiances cultivates an ear for multiplicity in interlocution: multiplicity in the interactive process of intention formation, in perceptions, in meaning making. The ear for the powerful seduction of common sense is also prepared for listening to new sense, remade, intervened, contested sense by those who are not agents. In a fragmented society, contestatory interactions often contest univocally along one axis of domination. Strategically, la callejera begins to hear the power of the logic of univocity and the multiplicity drowned by univocal contestations. She devises the tactical/strategic practice of hearing interactive contestatory acts of sense making as negotiated from within a complex interrelation of differences. She hears contestations that are univocal as at the same time defiant of and compliant with the logic and systems of domination.

Streetwalker Theorizing

Streetwalker theorizing is a practice of sustained intersubjective attention. It is a tactical strategic practice. We understand street-level, face-to-face, how to address each other as more

than and in tension with whom we are as subjected, oppressed. Cognizing resistance in the resisting ⇔ oppressing relation is lived in two tones: the being pressed — the inhaling
moment — and the pressing — the exhaling moment.[23] One understands the being pressed into intermeshed oppressions and
by the interlocking of oppressions. The cognition is resistant
since it anticipates the exhaling moment of inhabiting oneself
as active, as participating in the sustaining or bringing emancipatory intentions into being. But one does not stand still,
passively inhabiting the terrains of being pressed. The practice
is one of spatio-social inhabitation that offers resistance to intermeshed oppressions and to the interlocking of oppressions
at both moments of resistance. Resisting ⇔ oppressing is understood as interactive, social, body to body, ongoing. In this
understanding, resisting can be short lived or it can be long
and wide in its sociality. It can be nonreactive, provoked by
and provoking a long, deep, incisive understanding of human
connection and of the movement of intentions and accompanying praxical commitments and ingenuity.

To say that oppressions intermesh or coalesce is to say that
no oppressing molds and reduces a person untouched by and
separate from other oppressings that mold and reduce her. Resisting intermeshed oppressions is activity in response to
forces training one into multifaceted, subservient, inhabitations of power-mined intersubjective spaces. Oppressions in-
terlock when the social mechanisms of oppression fragment
the oppressed both as individuals and collectivities. Social
fragmentation in its individual and collective inhabitations is
the accomplishment of the interlocking of oppressions.[24] Interlocking is conceptually possible only if oppressions are understood as separable, as discrete, pure. Intermeshed oppressions
cannot be cogently understood as fragmenting subjects either
as individuals or as collectivities. Thus, the interlocking of
oppressions is a mechanism of control, reduction, immobiliza-
tion, disconnection that goes beyond intermeshed oppressions. It is not merely an ideological mechanism, but the
categorial training of human beings into homogeneous fragments is grounded in a categorial mind frame. Interlocking is
possible only if the inseparability of oppressions is disguised.
The politics of disguising intermeshed oppressions through

interlocking discrete fragments of subjected subjects, are disabling. Understanding the macabre connection between them calls for a refigured spatiality that exhibits the impurity in and among us, the heterogeneity. The horrifying coupling of intermeshed oppressing and of interlocking oppressions lies in the formation of a conceptual maze that is very difficult to navigate. At every point, it seems as if in order to resist intermeshed oppressions, we must bind categorially, so we cloud our own heterogeneity and yield to a categorial self-understanding. The tactical strategic task is highly complicated by the coupling. Everywhere we turn we find the interlocking of oppressions disabling us from perceiving and resisting oppressions as intermeshed. Disentangling the hold that the coupling has on our relations to each other is a central level of the complexity of enduring attention of streetwalker theorizing. The emotional tonality of this aspect of streetwalker theorizing is central to its enduring and to its enduring with clarity.

The streetwalker theorist cultivates a multiplicity and depth of perception and connection and "hangs out" even in well-defined institutional spaces, troubling and subverting their logics, their intent. As resistant, contestatory negotiations make sense within and give life to different frameworks of sense, different logics, and different world(s) of sense that are not countenanced by institutionalized, dominant, "official" sense, the streetwalker theorist cultivates an ear and a tongue for multiple lines of meaning. Her knowing is necessarily dialogical; it does not lie in her. It is a cultivation of memory in its poli-logical, poli-vocal complexity that has an anti-utopian direction to the future.

Streetwalker theorizing, then, is sustained in the midst of the concrete. To say that it is a tactical-strategic engagement is to say that one places, takes up, follows, aids, resistant emancipatory intentions in the midst of active, resisting subjects who are indispensable to each other if their intending is to inform their social reality. Tactical strategies of making sense against/in spite of/in the midst of domination pedestrian style make room for and sustain a long and wide social sense of resistant intentionality, a sense with a history. Tactical strategies of making sense against/in spite of/in the midst of domination also sustain an open, in-the-making sociality at the street level, no sense of "the whole" except as an imposing, intruding, deceitful, and powerful fiction.

Streetwalker theorizing countenances no possibility of making resistant sense except among people, since sense cannot be presupposed—as it is with dominant sense—even when there is a robust connection with an actively peopled history of resistant sense making. Thus, the streetwalker theorist develops a vivid sense of the inadequacy of an individualist understanding of agency, intentionality, and meaning to one's situation. She also develops a sense of spatial complexity that cannot be perceived by the strategist because it cannot be conceived from the strategist's location, thus revealing the constructedness of abstract space and its political commitments. She develops, maintains, communicates a duplicitous perception that co-temporaneously perceives the strategists' and the tactical strategists' conceived or lived spaces. The strategists' view is impressed in her eyes through domination. Her perception is constituted through a double inhabitation of the space that fragments and of the space constituted in relational movement. Thus, she understands the strategy in the tactic/strategy dichotomy "vicariously."

Because of its street-level location, streetwalker theorizing intervenes in between the tactic/strategy dichotomy. If echoed by other streetwalker-theorists, the intervention would unsettle the sense inscribed in the dichotomy that tactics are both ephemeral redirections of the specificities of the ruling order and that they constitute all the negotiating room available to the oppressed in their encounters with domination. In the meddlesome sense inserted by the streetwalker-theorist, tactical strategies are drawn, devised, in interaction, *encuentros*, as a pedestrian, a *callejera* in appreciation of daily tactics of survival. A crucial aspect of streetwalker theorizing is to uncover, consider, learn, pass on knowledge of the multiple tools of tactical strategists in having deep spatio-temporal insight into the social. As strategists have devised maps, chronometers, and other tools of administration and control, tactical strategists multiply messages deep into the social fabric by writing on money, using cab radios, speaking in the style of vendors on means of transportation, writing on walls, paging, and using electronic mail. An important aspect of passing on knowledge in hangouts is this passing on of tools of resistance that enable us to see deeply into the social from the pedestrian level.

Pivoting the spatiality of theorizing enables us to see the possibility of tactical strategies and the tie between the strategist's location and domination or the maintenance of domination. But it is also clear that the tactical alone will not do to go beyond survival. Tactical strategies require a renewed sense of active subjectivity and sociality, a reading of structures of domination from below, reading the resistant social with depth. It is this combination that enables one to go beyond "making do." As strategies and tactics will not do for resistance, neither will the late modern understanding of agency.

In disrupting the dichotomy, this theorizing countenances and participates in resistant meaning making by understanding agency as unimportant in tactical strategic living. It also participates in resistant meaning making advancing the notion of active subjectivity as the subjectivity of resisting ⇔ oppressing. Tactical strategies signify a sense of focus, a sense of the urge to go beyond survival and thus the urge to mark hangouts where to concoct the bursting out of confinement. Tactical strategies signify the willingness and urge to ponder the larger possibilities to be milked from well-practiced, ephemeral, devious remakings of the point, sense, and possibilities of the products of the dominant orders of production, cultural productions included. Tactical strategies invoke the willingness and urge to *tramar, tramoyar*,[25] to concoct in complex company *una trama*, a sturdy and complex weave/plot that doesn't leave structures of domination untouched.

"I"

The use of "I" in much of this text and my own self-presentation as a streetwalker theorist have an arrogant cast to them that I am wary of. I speak the "I" at the level of the street and as moving through multiple encounters, geographico-historical paths to indicate the subversion of the theory/practice dichotomy and to express the writing itself as a tactical-strategic interactive performance. The third person seems to me to hide that the writing is itself an encounter, nonsensical apart from dialogue, heavily touched by uncertainty. The third person tends toward removal, toward a metapositionality that takes one out of the action.

The "I" is a misdescription of formation of dispersed and complex collectivity. The "I" in this piece is in company and actively looking for company. The subject is semisolitary though it meets up and wants to meet up with others. The subject is looking: future tense. "I-we" captures the looking-for-company-but-the enduring not-yet-fulfilled quality of the subject, which also mitigates the "arrogance" and exemplifies the looking-to-dismantle quality. I-we is an iconic index. An index because I is me/the *callejera*, the author of the piece. It is an icon because I-we represents both the intention of this chapter — to make movement from I to we — as well as capturing that movement as "in a picture." The subject of this chapter is this I-we, or alternatively I → we, where the arrow signifies the transitional quality and dispersed intentionality of the subject.

I (I-we, I → we) seek out/put out/rehearse the dismantling of the theory/practice and the tactic/strategy binaries, of the from-above and at a distance political interventions, of the hearing only ready-made sense, of the quieting of multivocality and poli-rhythmic contestations and the concomitant fragmentation of our subjectivities and possibilities, of the loyalty to abstract space, depersonalization and interchangeability, of common sense, of the aestheticization of politics, of the fascination with those who dominate us. On the possibilities side, I tentatively provoke a sense of contestatory interactive intersubjective sense making as processual and located. I ground it at the street level, in highly qualitatively differentiated spaces.

As I seek out, put out, rehearse, consider tactical strategies of emancipatory sense making, I move between the solitary and the collectively social, two sides of resistance. I think of people at the time of tentative, often ill defined and not quite articulable intention formation: with whom, how, where, in the midst of what constraints and openings, negotiating what materials, words, sounds, touch, movements, gestures. I think of the nonlinear journey of the sign-word/gesture/movement

228 ⌒ Chapter 10

enunciated there and of the concerted, disjointed struggle to make it make sense without dropping it, like a delicate thing that is to be something at some point in the journey.[26]

Something will not come to mean quite what it seemed to us, as we tentatively intended, as intentions get redrawn, re-fashioned historically and intersubjectively in ways that give the new sense a complex sociality. The new sense may surpass our own initial creativity and inspire us further or disappoint us or make us despair or enrage us into new movement/jour-neys of meaning in the geographies of contestatory encoun-ters.

To follow thoughtfully the journey of the sign-word/ges-ture/movement into new meaning is to walk lots of *veredas* at once, from hangout to hangout, not one long grand connect-ing highway. Univocity stands erect as deflecting resistant cre-ativity. But the collective, complex journey may contain many such moments of deflection. Careful not to drop the sign (word, gesture, movement), we find ourselves negotiating not just the seductions of common sense and the power of simpli-fication, but also the difficulties of hearing multivocalities and poli-rhythms in the contestatory negotiation of these barriers.

A complex intersubjective context for sense making cannot be presupposed in this journey. Rather, it is part of the pro-cesses and the histories of contestatory, emancipatory sense making and it is itself made and produced in the process. Our traditions and histories provide antecedents in the formation of intention but these traditions and histories do not overde-termine the journey nor the tentative formation of intention nor the closure of intention because as we focus on exercises of active subjectivity, the past is revisited as multiple and re-made in the present act of putting out the word, gesture, movement and moving it from tongue to tongue, from hand to hand, from place to place.[27]

I/we, I → we see the possibility of resistant, anti-utopian, interactive multiple sense making among *atravesados/ atravesadas* who are streetwalker theorists in encounters at the intersections of local and translocal histories of meaning fashioned in the resisting ⇔ oppressing relation. Sense making in lively cultural modes that take issue with domination in tense inside/outside/in-between conversations, interactions that take in and also disrupt, dismantle, dominant sense.[28] The preferred techniques and practices of meaning production and communication presuppose little expectation of being understood and are highly tentative. "Tentative" is used here in its literal meaning of a tactile sensing of the terrain,[29] with a readiness to reroute, rephrase, gesture, word, move in a multiplicity of ways, idioms, directions, a refracting of the sign as if trying to find, and being attentive to finding, recognition. There is no common language, no common expectations, no reason to assume trust or trust worthiness, no comfortable womb-warm sense of safety and of having come home. What prompts one is a risk-full sense of opportunities, of possibilities, to be rendered artfully concrete, imminently social, insidiously and positively pragmatic. What prompts the social inhabitation of the forbidden positionality is the very company of those marked as unacceptable or beneath respect, a company one has learned to reread as issuing different, unconventional, and resistant interpretations of hegemonical meaning structures.

Walking Illegitimately

I end with a reflection of what pulls us into a frenzy of recognizable political activity, recognizable in dominant terms. Street-level sociality can provide a despairing, demoralizing "picture" of the complexities and depth of oppression and of the barriers to emancipatory change. There is a desire to imbue oneself with a sense of power against this demoralization. Not infrequently, the pedestrian theorist is tempted to favor a mode of comportment that speaks the languages of systems of oppression, seeking within them redress or assistance. This temptation, seduction, is understandable and ubiquitous. We feel a need to demand equality, respect, and justice within a particular dominant construal of sense, even if that sense—conceptually, materially—requires that equality, respect, and justice be mechanisms congruent with fragmentation and domination.

The oppressed, erased, subordinated, abused, criminalized negotiate their survival in many spaces, including "support" agencies of social control.[30] The pedestrian theorist is often overwhelmed into legitimating these agencies by learning to earn a living in them and thus gaining from-above access to the oppressed. This provides a systemic sense of self-respect — a protector, leader, realist self-image — that misses but also often deflects the devious in the negotations of survival. Living within the ambiguously contestatory, pliant encounters, carrying horizontally the strategic emancipatory possibilities of meanings in the making is replaced by a no-nonsense, workmanlike, "realist" busyness inside the strongholds of small-time power. Building or working for community economic development organizations, battered women shelters, crisis lines, legal advocacy centers, homeless shelters, and alternative organizations for wayward "youth," lobbying for equal rights for the deviant reconceived as a version of the normal provide a sense of purpose as one deploys the homogenizing language of the therapeutizing of politics, of expertise, of social control.[31]

It is a difficult path to walk illegitimately within organizations devised purposefully to attain redress of injustices, or a back-to-the-fold sense of self-esteem, or a share of the resources due to "productive members of society." The possibilities of participating fully in the logic of modern conceptions of justice and sociality stand in our way. They give us a face, a character, an authority, a worth, a value "system." These are almost unbearably seductive. On the bodies and souls of contemporary America's *marginales*, "political" strategists play at rearranging and justifying the divisions of the spoils of social "cooperation." In the process, they must rearrange and redefine who is left out of any shares. The process does not include those to be sacrificed.

Los marginales: mostly folk of color, with and without "papers," with and without housing of any sort, permanently out of jobs, young and old, women and men, queer, battered women and children who "left him" to live in America's streets, the raped, the violated, those left out of any of the "social" goods produced by and for more stable folk. *Los marginales*: folk who threaten the safety, decency, sanity, orderliness of poor barrios and bourgeois strongholds. The quiet retreats from the ugliness and anxiety of America have become contested. They cannot be taken for granted by anyone with a job, particularly if the job holder is of color, queer, working in industrial jobs, or an ever-so-batterable woman.

Concepts, ways of doing things, institutions, values that conceptually, materially, and politically determine, decree, regulate, and justify oppression submerge, surround, inundate, constitute, circumscribe the streetwalker theorist. They form a deep, invisible, framework, encasing every move and gesture, every justification. The streetwalker theorist must break out of these "confines of the normal." These confines are the background and texture of the lonely, genial, unaccompanied, self-important, "self-made" subjectivity that constitutes modern agency. The streetwalker is someone who comes to understand, through a jarring, vivid awareness of being broken into fragments, that the encasing by particular oppressive systems of meaning is a process one can consciously and critically resist within uncertainty or to which one can passively abandon oneself. One understands this passivity as revealing the illusory quality of the closure of dominating sense, understands it as a technique of domination. The streetwalker theorist asks over and over again: Within which conceptual, axiological, institutional, material set of limitations is the meaning of the possible being construed?

Notes

1. I Thank Marilyn Frye for leading me to question the phrase "interlocked oppressions." She pointed out, rightly, that interlocking does not alter the monadic nature of the things interlocked. In Elizabeth Spelman's words, it does not trouble the "pop bead" metaphysics (Spelman 1988:15). I use "intermeshed" to capture inseparability. A mesh is still too much separability, but I want to try it out. I think the best metaphor I have is that of the coalescence of oil and water emulsions. See chapter 6 ("Purity, Impurity, and Separation") in this volume. Here, I seek to distinguish intermeshed oppressions from the interlocking of oppressions and offer a theory of resistance to both. The interlocking of oppressions is a central feature of the process of social fragmentation, since fragmentation requires not just shards or fragments of the social, but that each fragment be unified, fixed, atomistic, hard-edged, internally homogeneous, bounded, repellent of other equally bounded and homogeneous shards. See Robert Stam and Ella Shohat's characterization of polycentric multiculturalism (Stam and Shohat 1995) and Fernando Coronil's occidentalism (1996) for a

connection between what I call the "interlocking of oppressions" and colonialism/Eurocentrism.

2. In *Domination and the Arts of Resistance. Hidden Transcripts,* James Scott (1990) makes clear that his analysis of infrapolitics applies only to the case of personalized forces. He is interested in questions of address and resistance and when the transcripts are public and when hidden. In my case, I am not only interested in questions of address, though questions of address and response are important to the praxical task. But I am also interested in resistance to the impersonal, say, for example, resistance to the tourist industry in its concreteness in New Mexico or Tilcara, to take up two contrasting examples. That industry has faces, but it is also constituted impersonally but concretely by the movement of global capital, by the concrete complexities of the meanings of land across several systems of signification.

3. For a theorizing of the meaning of "social fragmentation," see chapter 6 ("Purity, Impurity, and Separation") in this volume.

4. In *Local Histories/Global Designs* (2000), Walter Mignolo proposes "bilanguaging" to disrupt what he unveils as a modern/colonial way of thinking about language that links language to territory and sees relationships between the people speaking a given language and their sense of identification with themselves and their territory (Mignolo 2000:256–57). Bilanguaging enables him to think "in between and beyond languages." Mignolo relates bilanguaging to ways of life at the "crack in the global process between local histories and global designs" (Mignolo 2000:10–30). I discern important relations between what I call "worlds of sense" and what Mignolo calls "languaging" and between bilanguaging and making sense at the intersection between worlds of sense. Both go beyond language to lived realities and ways of life.

5. It should be clear from the start that the "tactical strategist" is not "The Theorist" as apart from those who occupy the spatiality of the street, understood as "Her Objects of Study Cum Rousable Rabble." That separation requires both the tactic/strategy and the theory/practice dichotomies. As those dichotomies are praxically undercut, there is no subject/object distinction to be drawn in the theorizing and no theorizing apart from practice. But that does not entail that everyone is a tactical strategist, since not everyone transgresses the tactic/strategy dichotomy in their living. We all live within the dichotomy, but we can also live in transgression of its logic.

6. I use "duplicitous" in both of its senses. Thus, the perception is both a double perception and devious.

7. The sense of "public" that I have in mind is not one that addresses directly or immediately the inhabitants of the bourgeois public sphere in Habermas's sense, and thus not a "counterpublic" in Nancy Fraser's (1997) or Maria Pia Lara's (1999) sense, since in both of their cases counterpublic-

ity is understood to address the bourgeois public, however mediately and however oppositionally. See "Multiculturalism and Publicity" (*Hypatia* 2000, 15[3]:175–82). Notice that the street, though it is not separable from home, challenges the relegation of home to the private. The negotiations are done "in public," though they are unrecognizable from the planner's and strategist's location. The unrecognizability is understood as a tactical strategic advantage.

8. In *Lesbian Ethics* (1988), Sarah Hoagland offers an important critique of the modern understanding of agency that she identifies as the understanding of agency under heterosexualism. She introduces the concept of agency under oppression. Here I abandon the concept of agency altogether and introduce the concept of active subjectivity because I want to mark a greater dispersion of intentionality and because I want to stress the meeting of oppressing ⇔ resisting.

9. In "A Response to *Lesbian Ethics*: Why Ethics," Marilyn Frye (1990) argues that the need for an ethics is something "race, class and history specific, that ethics is a practice and institution that would arise only among people occupying certain positions in certain social orders" (Frye 1990:139). She argues that in the particularities of the lesbian and feminist communities in which she resides it makes sense to learn to do without ethics entirely and rather to create a new space "much further from our citizen fathers' homes, where 'right' and 'good' no longer trick us into continuing our dutiful-daughterhoods" (Frye 1991:145).

10. Doreen Massey (1992) tells us "that almost any ideology based on an A/Not A dichotomy is effective in resisting change. Those whose understanding of society is ruled by such ideology find it very hard to conceive of the possibility of alternative forms of social order (third possibilities)." The particular dichotomy she argues against is the time/space dichotomy. Rather than collapse the difference between space and time, she argues that space and time are inextricably interwoven (Massey 1992). De Certeau's depiction of the strategy/tactic dichotomy features the time/space dichotomy centrally. For an important discussion of A/-A dichotomies, see Marilyn Frye (1991).

11. See Marilyn Frye, *The Politics of Reality* (1983:164), for an incisive description of this logic.

12. Compare David Harvey (1990: 237, 244, 250, 253); Walter Mignolo (1995:258–69), and chapter 6 ("Purity, Impurity and Separation") in this volume.

13. In his discussion of individual times and spaces in social life, David Harvey sees in De Certeau's logic an important corrective to Foucault's micropolitics of power. Though for Foucault there are no relations of power without resistance, and though he proposes "heterotopias" as spaces of resistance and freedom," his explorations emphasize techniques of discipline

rather than practices of localized resistance (Harvey 1990:213). The ontologies of resistance in Foucault and De Certeau seem to me compatible.

14. Massey's alternative to the space/time dichotomy is important here. Her view that space and time (space-time) are inextricably linked relinquishes the "view of society as a 3d slice which moves through time." Temporal movement is also spatial. Space is reconceptualized as constructed out of interrelations, as "the simultaneous coexistence of social interrelations and interactions at all spatial scales" (Massey 1992:80). The planning of social space always has an element of chaos within it. Space is essentially disrupted. Since space has an element of chaos and space partially constitutes time, time and history cannot be a monolithic tale (Massey 1992).

15. In using the term "hangout," I mean to take up an everyday practice of resistant inhabitation of space that has not received theoretical attention. As I interweave the different facets of a logic of sustained, dispersed, enduring resistance, the concept of hangout becomes more fully theorized.

16. Streetwalking theorizing is one of the practices of the active subject in resistance to intermeshed and interlocked oppressions. This book exhibits, recommends, and describes other such practices: playful world-traveling, trespassing, the art of curdling, hard-to-handle-anger.

17. See chapter 7 ("Boomerang Perception and the Colonizing Gaze") in this volume for an understanding of the logic of fragmented resistance to the interlocking of oppressions.

18. It is important to note that in this description hanging out cannot be assimilated to the various nomadisms that rehearse the romance of travel, where privileged visitors destabilize other peoples' spaces without attention to the power relations that construe the spatial occupation, as Caren Kaplan (1996) argues.

19. This is David Harvey's expression (Harvey 1990:222).

20. Gangs: I have thought about the emancipatory potential of gangs in the contemporary United States, female gangs in particular (not auxiliaries, but all female gangs). I have questions about the meaning of the spatiality of gangs in line with the thinking in this chapter. Most gangs use the streets territorially and strive for territorial control for a number of activities, including economic activities. The control over turf is marked in terms of inclusion and exclusion along categorical lines of race, ethnicity, and country of origin. Their taking of turf is oppositional but they reinforce the logic of social fragmentation through categorial inclusions and exclusions. The occupation of streets by gangs rarely takes the form of hanging out as I have described it here, though individual gang members often hang out. Gangs differ mostly in degrees in this aspect of their spatiality.

21. I embrace Gloria Anzaldúa's use of "*atravesados*" as an identification for border dwellers, transitionals who are disloyal to the logics of oppressive systems of sense (Anzaldúa 1987). I put out the word as carrying

the sense of transitionals being shot through with a multiplicity of meanings as well as their disloyal movement, transit, across normalized and bounded worlds of sense. *Las atravesadas* embody the unraveling of the normal as fictional and tyrannical. As the unraveling reveals the fiction, the travails of the process of unraveling unveil its tyrannical power.

22. In the *Production of Space*, Henri Lefebvre (1992) elaborates the logic of abstract space, the space of accumulation — "the accumulation of all wealth and resources: knowledge, technology, money, precious objects, works of art and symbols" (Lefebvre 1992:49). Abstract space is formal, quantitative, and homogeneous — "it erases distinctions, as much those which derive from nature and (historical) time as those which originate in the body (age, sex, ethnicity)" (Lefebvre 1992:49) — Euclidean, political — "The dominant form of space . . . endeavours to mould the spaces it dominates (i.e., peripheral spaces) and it seeks, often by violent means, to reduce the obstacles and resistance it encounters there" (Lefebvre 1992:49) — instituted by the state, constituted by the logic of visualization — "the eye . . . tends to relegate objects to the distance, to render them passive" (Lefebvre 1992:286). Though Lefevbre does not use the expression "concrete space," there is a sense in which abstract space is at war with the particular journeys on the ground. He makes continual efforts to refer to resistance, but without much fabric to what he means by it: "in the same spaces (as the modern state) there are other forces on the boil, because the rationality of the state of its techniques, plans and programmes, provokes opposition. The violence of power is answered by the violence of subversion" (Lefebvre 1992:23).

23. This characterization of the two tones may seem counterintuitive until one notices that both the being pressed and the pressing are lived resistantly. So, as one inhales to prepare oneself to exert muscular pressure and exhales at the moment of pressing, so does one meet being pressed (oppressing) in anticipation of pressing (resisting).

24. Although it is the late modern understanding of agency that conceptually structures the legal and dominant moral discourse in the United States, the history of social fragmentation contains the emptying of space in the colonies that constructs abstract space. There is a tight conceptual link between social fragmentation and abstract space. The emptying of space erases multiplicity and replaces it with fragmentation. These claims need to be elaborated further, unveiling the links. Part of the argument is contained in Lefrebvre's *The Production of Space* (1992), Fernando Coronil's "Beyond Occidentalism," (1996), and Walter Mignolo's *The Darker Side of the Renaissance* (1995).

25. *Trama/tramar/tramoyar:* The triple word play is intended to trouble the distinction and separation between the making and its product, and it emphasizes the devious quality of the making. A "*trama*" — the weave of

a piece of cloth—that is "*tramada*"—plotted—is one whose weave cannot be understood apart from the plotting. "*Tramoyat*'—a *lunfardo* word—marks a devious concocting that takes advantage of disguises provided by ordinary expectations.

26. I have taken up what Homi Bhabha placed in my plate in *The Location of Culture* (1994), in particular in "The Postcolonial and the Postmodern: The Question of Agency" and "The Commitment to Theory."

27. This relation to history is exercised in Anzaldúa's revisiting Coatlicue and in her depiction of the new mestiza as putting history through a sieve, reinterpreting history, creating new myths (Anzaldúa 1987:82).

28. Streetwalking takes place within a liminal space, a third space, a border space. Inhabiting the limen makes this anti-utopian possibility conceivable. The limen gather the heterogeneous collection of those positioned at the border, abyss, edge, shore of countersense, of emergent sense.

29. "Tentative" is closest in this sense to the mood of "*tantear*," a word with which I initiate this book (see Introduction).

30. Hagerdorn and Mason offer an excellent example of writing about both the failure and success of alternative organizations that aim to facilitate gang members from exiting particular gangs in Milwaukee. Though people do not leave the gangs, they make use of the services offered (Hagerdorn and Mason 1988).

31. I think here of Alinsky style organizing and the work of the Industrial Areas Foundation, of the work of much of the organized battered women's movement, of the work of significant sectors of the gay and lesbian movement, of many alternative schools for members of gangs, of the highly homophobic, masculinist, criminal justice system friendly techniques of the Barrio Warriors, of the work of organizations that sustain traditional cultural practices without recreation, and so on. It is hard to be critical of this work that has been sustaining, kept people alive, shown enormous creativity and commitment. As I offer strategies that take issue with these politics and their logic, I respect the impulse that moves us in those directions.

References

Anzaldúa, Gloria. 1987. *Borderlands/La Frontera: The New Mestiza*. San Francisco: Spinsters/Aunt Lute.

Bhabha, Homi. 1994. *The Location of Culture*. London: Routledge.

Coronil, Fernando. 1996. Beyond Occidentalism: Toward Nonimperial Geohistorical Categories. *Cultural Anthropology* 11 (1): 51–87.

de Certeau, Michel. 1988. *The Practice of Everyday Life*. Berkeley: University of California Press.

Fraser, Nancy. 1997. *Justice Interruptus: Critical Reflections on the 'Postsocialist' Condition.* New York: Routledge.

Frye, Marilyn. 1983. *The Politics of Reality.* Freedom, Calif.: The Crossing Press.

———. 1990. Response to "*Lesbian Ethics*: Why Ethics?" *Hypatia* 5 (3): 132–37.

———. 1991. The Necessity of Differences: Constructing a Positive Category of Women. *Signs* 21 (4): 991–1010.

Hagerdorn, John M., and Perry Macon. 1988. *People and Folks: Gangs, Crime, and the Underclass in a Rustbelt City.* Chicago: Lake View Press.

Harvey, David. 1990. *The Condition of Postmodernity: An Enquiry into the Origins of Cultural Change.* Cambridge, Mass.: Blackwell.

Hoagland, Sarah. 1988. *Lesbian Ethics.* Palo Alto, Calif.: Institute of Lesbian Studies.

Kaplan, Caren. 1996. *Questions of Travel.* Durham, N.C.: Duke University Press.

Lara, Maria Pia. 1999. *Moral Textures.* Berkeley: University of California Press.

Lefebvre, Henri. 1992. *The Production of Space.* Oxford, U.K.: Blackwell.

Massey, Doreen. 1992. Politics and Space/Time. *New Left Review* 196:65–84.

Mignolo, Walter. 1995. *The Darker Side of the Renaissance.* Ann Arbor: The University of Michigan Press.

———. 2000. *Local Histories/Global Designs.* Princeton, N.J.: Princeton University Press.

Scott, James. 1990. *Domination and the Arts of Resistance. Hidden Transcripts.* New Haven, Conn.: Yale University Press.

Spelman, Elizabeth. 1988. *Inessential Woman.* Boston: Beacon.

Stam, Robert, and Ellas Shohat. 1995. Contested Histories: Eurocentrism, Multiculturalism, and the Media. In *Multiculturalism,* edited by David Theo Goldberg, 296–324. Oxford, U.K.: Blackwell.

Selected Bibliography

The texts in this bibliography constitute the background that informs this book.

Alexander, Jacqui M., and Chandra Talpade Mohanty. 1997. *Feminist Genealogies, Colonial Legacies, Democratic Futures*. New York: Routledge.

Allen, Jeffner, ed. 1990. *Lesbian Philosophies and Cultures*. Albany, N.Y.: State University of New York Press.

———. 1987. *Lesbian Philosophy: Explorations*. Palo Alto, Calif.: Institute of Lesbian Studies.

Allen, Paula Gunn. 1986. *The Sacred Hoop: Recovering the Feminine in American Indian Traditions*. Boston: Beacon.

Anderson, Benedict. 1991. *Imagined Communities*. London: Verso.

Anzaldúa, Gloria, ed. 1990. *Making Face, Making Soul: Haciendo Caras: Creative and Critical Perspectives by Women of Color*. San Francisco: Aunt Lute.

———. 1987. *Borderlands/La Frontera*. San Francisco: Spinsters/Aunt Lute.

Arteaga, Alfred. 1996. *An Other Tongue: Nation and Ethnicity in the Linguistic Borderlands*. Durham, N.C.: Duke University Press.

Asian Women United of California, eds. 1989. *Making Waves: An Anthology of Writings by and about Asian American Women*. Boston: Beacon.

Bakhtin, M. M. 1981. *The Dialogic Imagination*. Austin, Tex.: University of Texas Press.

Bartky, Sandra. 1990. *Femininity and Domination*. New York: Routledge.

———. 1979. "Phenomenology of a Feminist Consciousness." In *Philosophy and Women*, ed. Sharon Bishop and Marjorie Weinzweig. Belmont, Calif: Wadsworth.

Bell, Derrick. 1998. *Afrolantica Legacies*. Chicago: Third World Press.

———. 1992. *Faces at the Bottom of the Well: The Permanence of Racism*. New York: Basic.

Berkman, Alexander. 1972. *What Is Communist Anarchism?* New York: Dover.

Bethel, Lorraine. 1979. "What Chou Mean We, White Girl?" *Conditions: Five* 11, no. 2 (Autumn): 86–92.

Bhabha, Homi K. 1994. *The Location of Culture.* London: Routledge.

Boal, Augusto. 1979. *Theatre of the Oppressed.* New York: Theatre Communications Group.

Butler, Judith. 1990. *Gender Trouble.* New York: Routledge.

Canclini, Néstor García Canclini. 1989. *Culturas híbridas: Estrategias para entrar y salir de la modernidad.* Mexico, D.F.: Grijalbo.

Card, Claudia. 1995. *Lesbian Choices.* New York: Columbia University Press.

———, ed. 1994. *Adventures in Lesbian Philosophy.* Bloomington, Ind.: Indiana University Press.

———. 1991. *Feminist Ethics.* Lawrence, Kans.: University Press of Kansas.

Chabram Dernesesian, Angie. 1994. "Chicana? Rican! No, Chicano-Riqueña: Refashioning the Transnational Connection." In *Multiculturalism: A Critical Reader,* ed. David Theo Goldberg. Oxford, U.K.: Blackwell.

Chin, Frank. 1991. "Come All Ye Asian American Writers of the Real and the Fake." In *The Big Aiiieeeee!* ed. Jeffery Paul Chan, Frank Chin, Lawson Fusao Inada, and Shawn Wong. New York: Meridian.

Coronil, Fernando. 1996. "Beyond Occidentalism: Toward Nonimperial Geohistorical Categories." *Cultural Anthropology* 11, no. 1: 51–87.

Crenshaw, Kimberlé, Neil Gotanda, Gary Peller, and Kendal Thomas. 1995. *Critical Race Theory: The Key Writings that Formed the Movement.* New York: New Press.

Davis, Angela. 1999. *Blues Legacies and Black Feminism.* New York: Vintage.

———. 1983. *Women, Race, and Class.* New York: Vintage.

De Certeau, Michel. 1988. *The Practice of Everyday Life.* Berkeley, Calif.: University of California Press.

Delgado, Richard. 1996. *The Coming Race War?: And Other Apocalyptic Tales of America after Affirmative Action and Welfare.* New York: New York University Press.

Douglas, Mary. 1989. *Purity and Danger.* London: Ark Paperbacks.

Dussek, Enrique. 1990. *Philosophy of Liberation.* Maryknoll, N.Y.: Orbis.

Ellison, Ralph. 1972. *Invisible Man.* New York: Vintage.

Fabian, Johannes. 1983. *Time and the Other.* New York: Columbia University Press.

Flores, Juan. 1993. *Divided Borders: Essays on Puerto Rican Identity.* Houston, Tex.: Arte Público.

Frankenberg, Ruth, ed. 1997. *Displacing Whiteness: Essays in Social and Cultural Criticism.* Durham, N.C.: Duke University Press.

———. 1993. *White Women, Race Matters: The Social Construction of Whiteness*. Minneapolis: University of Minnesota Press.

Fraser, Nancy. 1997. *Justice Interruptus: Critical Reflections on the "Postsocialist" Condition*. New York: Routledge.

Freire, Paulo. 1996. *Pedagogy of the Oppressed*. New York: Continuum.

———. 1992. *Education for Critical Consciousness*. New York: Continuum.

Friedman, Marilyn. 1989. "Feminism and Modern Friendship: Dislocating the Community." *Ethics* 99 (January 1989): 275–90.

Friedman, Marilyn, and Penny A. Weiss, eds. 1995. *Feminism and Community*. Philadelphia: Temple.

Frye, Marilyn. 1992. *Willful Virgin*. Freedom, Calif.: Crossing Press.

———. 1983. *The Politics of Reality*. New York: Crossing Press.

Galindo, Letticia D., and María Dolores Gonzales. 1999. *Speaking Chicana: Voice, Power, and Identity*. Tucson, Ariz.: The University of Arizona Press.

Geok-lin Lim, Shirley, Mayumi Tsutakawa, and Margarita Donnelly, eds. 1989. *The Forbidden Stitch: An Asian American Women's Anthology*. Corvallis, Ore.: Calyx.

Grewal, Inderpal. 1994. "Autobiographic Subjects and Diasporic Locations: Meatless Days." In *Scattered Hegemonies*, ed. Inderpal Grewal and Caren Kaplan. Minneapolis: University of Minnesota Press.

Gwaltney, John Langston. 1980. *Drylongso: A Self-Portrait of Black America*. New York: Random House and Vintage.

Guha, Ranahit, and Gyatri Chacravorty Spivak. 1988. *Selected Subaltern Studies*. Oxford, U.K.: Oxford University Press.

Haney López, Ian F. 1996. *White by Law: The Legal Construction of Race*. New York: New York University Press.

Haraway, Donna. 1990. "A Manifesto for Cyborgs." In *Feminism/Postmodernism*, ed. Linda J. Nicholson. New York: Routledge.

Hartsock, Nancy C. M. 1988. "The Feminist Standpoint: Developing the Ground for a Specifically Feminist Historical Materialism." In *Discovering Reality: Feminist Perspectives on Epistemology, Metaphysics, Methodology, and Philosophy of Science*, ed. Sandra Harding and Merrill Hintikka. Boston: Reidel.

Harvey, David. 1990. *The Condition of Postmodernity: An Enquiry into the Origins of Cultural Change*. Oxford, U.K.: Blackwell.

Herrera-Sobek, María, and Helena María Viramontes. 1996. *Chicana Creativity and Criticism: Charting New Frontiers in American Literature*. Albuquerque: University of New Mexico Press.

Hoagland, Sarah Lucia. 1988. *Lesbian Ethics: Toward New Value*. Palo Alto, Calif.: Institute of Lesbian Studies.

———. 1982. "Femininity, Resistance, and Sabotage," in *"Femininity," "Masculinity," and "Androgyny": A Modern Philosophical Discussion*, ed. Mary Vetterling-Braggin. Totowa, N.J.: Rowman & Littlefield.

hooks, bell. 1994. *Teaching to Transgress*. New York: Routledge.
———. 1990. *Yearning*. Boston: South End.
———. 1984. *Feminist Theory: From Margin to Center*. Boston: South End.
Horton, Myles. 1998. *The Long Haul*. New York: Teachers College Press.
Hull, Gloria T., Patricia Bell Scott, and Barbara Smith, eds. 1982. *All the Women Are White, All the Blacks Are Men, But Some of Us Are Brave*. New York: Feminist Press.
Hunter, Tera. 1997. *To 'Joy My Freedom: Southern Black Women's Lives and Labors after the Civil War*. Cambridge, Mass.: Harvard University Press.
Ignatiev, Noel. 1995. *How the Irish Became White*. New York: Routledge.
Jackson, George. 1970. *Soledad Brother*. New York: Bantam.
Jaggar, Alison. 1998. "Love and Knowledge: Emotion in Feminist Epistemology." Pp. 144–45 in *Women: Knowledge and Reality,* ed. Ann Garry and Marilyn Pearsall. Boston: Unwin Hyman.
———. 1983. *Feminist Politics and Human Nature*. Totowa, N.J.: Rowman & Allanheld.
Jordan, June. 1990. "Where Is the Love?" Pp. 174–76 in *Making Face, Making Soul—Haciendo Caras: Creative and Critical Perspectives by Women of Color,* ed. Gloria Anzaldúa. San Francisco: Aunt Lute.
Jordan, Winthrop D. 1971. *White over Black*. Chapel Hill, N.C.: University of North Carolina Press.
Kaplan, Caren. 1996. *Questions of Travel*. Durham, N.C.: Duke University Press.
———. 1994. "The Politics of Location as Transnational Feminist Critical Practice." In *Scattered Hegemonies: Postmodernity and Transnational Feminist Practices,* ed. Grewal Inderpal and Caren Kaplan. Minneapolis: University of Minnesota Press.
Kaplan, Caren, Norma Alarcón, and Minoo Moallen, eds. 1999. *Between Woman and Nation*. Durham, N.C.: Duke University Press.
Kelley, Robin D. G. 1994. *Race Rebels: Culture, Politics, and the Black Working Class*. New York: Free Press.
Knabb, Ken, ed. 1981. *Situationist International*. Berkeley, Calif.: Bureau of Public Secrets.
Krimerman, Leonard I., and Lewis Perry, eds. 1966. *Patterns of Anarchy*. New York: Anchor.
Kropotkin, P. A. 1970. *Selected Writings on Anarchism and Revolution*. Cambridge, Mass.: M.I.T. Press.
Lara, Maria Pia. 1999. *Moral Textures*. Berkeley, Calif.: University of California Press.
LeFebvre, Henri. 1992. *The Production of Space*. Oxford, U.K.: Blackwell.
Liu, Lydia H. 1995. *Translingual Practice: Literature, National Culture, and Translated Modernity: China 1900–1937*. Palo Alto, Calif.: Stanford University Press.

López Springfield, Consuelo, ed. 1997. *Daughters of Caliban: Caribbean Women in the Twentieth Century*. Bloomington, Ind.: Indiana University Press.

Lorde, Audre. 1996. *Sister Outsider*. Freedom, Calif.: Crossing Press.

Lyman, Peter. 1981. "The Politics of Anger: On Silence, Ressentiment, and Political Speech." *Socialist Review*, no. 57 (vol. 11, no. 3): 55–74.

Mangabeira Unger, Roberto. 1975. *Knowledge and Politics*. New York: Free Press.

Marino, Dian. 1997. *Wild Garden: Art, Education, and the Culture of Resistance*. Toronto: Between the Lines.

Martinez, Jacqueline M. 2000. *Phenomenology of Chicana Experience and Identity: Communication and Transformation in Praxis*. Lanham, Md.: Rowman & Littlefield.

Massey, Doreen. 1992. "Politics and Space/Time." *New Left Review* 196:65–84.

Matsuda, Mari J. 1996. *Where Is Your Body?* Boston: Beacon.

Memmi, Albert. 1965. *The Colonizer and the Colonized*. Boston: Beacon.

Mignolo, Walter. 2000. *Local Histories/Global Designs*. Princeton: Princeton University Press.

———. 1995. *The Darker Side of the Renaissance*. Ann Arbor, Mich.: The University of Michigan Press.

Mohanty, Chandra Talpade, Ann Russo, and Lourdes Torres, eds. 1991. *Third World Women and the Politics of Feminism*. Bloomington, Ind.: Indiana University Press.

Moraga, Cherríe. 1983. *Loving in the War Years: Lo que nunca pasó por sus labios*. Boston: South End.

Moraga, Cherríe, and Gloria Anzaldúa, eds. 1981. *This Bridge Called My Back*. New York: Kitchen Table: Women of Color Press.

Moya, Paula M. L., and Michael R. Hames-García. 2000. *Reclaiming Identity: Realist Theory and the Predicament of Postmodernism*. Berkeley, Calif.: University of California Press.

Niranjana, Tejaswini. 1992. *Siting Translation*. Berkeley, Calif.: University of California Press.

Omi, Michael, and Howard Winant. 1986. *Racial Formation in the United States from the 1960s to the 1980s*. New York: Routledge & Kegan Paul.

Pateman, Carole. 1989. *The Sexual Contract*. Palo Alto, Calif.: Stanford University Press.

Perez, Emma. 1999. *The Decolonial Imaginary*. Bloomington, Ind.: Indiana University Press.

Price, Joshua. 2002. "The Apotheosis of Home and the Maintenance of Spaces of Violence." *Hypathia* 17:4.

———. 1998. *Spaces of Violence, Shades of Meaning: The Heterogeneity of Violence against Women in the United States*. Ph.D. Dissertation. University of Chicago.

Rafael, Vicente L. 1988. *Contracting Colonialism: Translation and Christian Conversion in Tagalog Society under Early Spanish Rule.* Ithaca, N.Y.: Cornell University Press.

Ramos, Juanita, ed. 1987. *Compañeras: Latina Lesbians.* New York: Latina Lesbian History Project.

Roediger, David R. 1991. *The Wages of Whiteness.* London: Verso.

Rosaldo, Renato. 1989. *Culture and Truth.* Boston: Beacon.

Ruiz, Vicki L., and Ellen Carol DuBois, eds. 2000. *Unequal Sisters.* New York: Routledge.

Said, Edward. 1990. "Reflections on Exile." In *Out There: Marginalization and Contemporary Cultures,* ed. R. Ferguson, N. Gever, T. T. Minh-Ha, and C. West, 359. New York: New Museum of Contemporary Art, and Cambridge: MIT Press.

———. 1983. "Traveling Theory." In *The World, the Text, and the Critic.* Cambridge, Mass.: Harvard University Press.

———. 1978. *Orientalism.* London: Routledge & Kegan Paul.

Saldivar, José David. 1997. *Border Matters: Remapping American Cultural Studies.* Berkeley, Calif.: University of California Press.

Saldivar-Hull, Sonia. 2000. *Feminism on the Border.* Berkeley: University of California Press.

Sandoval, Chela. 2000. *Methodology of the Oppressed.* Minneapolis: University of Minnesota Press.

Scheman, Naomi. 1983. "Individualism and the Objects of Psychology." In *Discovering Reality: Feminist Perspectives on Epistemology, Metaphysics, Methodology, and Philosophy of Science,* ed. Sandra Harding and Merrill B. Hintikka. Dordrecht, the Netherlands: Reidel.

Scott, James. 1990. *Domination and the Arts of Resistance: Hidden Transcripts.* New Haven, Conn.: Yale University Press.

Smith, Dorothy. 1974. "Women's Perspective as a Radical Critique of Sociology." *Sociological Enquiry* 44, no. 1: 7–14.

Soja, Edward. 1989. *Postmodern Geographies.* London: Verso.

Spelman, Elizabeth. 1989. "Anger and Insubordination." In *Women, Knowledge, and Reality,* ed. Ann Garry and Marilyn Pearsall. Boston: Unwin Hyman.

———. 1988. *Inessential Woman: Problems of Exclusion in Feminist Thought.* Boston: Beacon.

Stam, Robert, and Ella Shohat. 1995. "Contested Histories: Eurocentrism, Multiculturalism, and the Media." In *Multiculturalism: A Critical Reader,* ed. David Theo Goldberg. Oxford, U.K.: Blackwell.

Takaki, Ronald. 1993. *A Different Mirror.* Boston: Little, Brown, and Co.

———. 1979. *Iron Cages: Race and Culture in Nineteenth-Century America.* Oxford, U.K.: Oxford University Press.

Trebilcot, Joyce, ed. 1984. *Mothering: Essays in Feminist Theory.* Totowa, N.J.: Rowman & Allanheld.

Trinh, T. Minh-Ha. 1995. "No Master Territories." Pp. 215–18 in *The Post-Colonial Studies Reader,* ed. Bill Ashcroft, Gareth Griffiths, and Helen Tiffin. London: Routledge.

———. 1989. *Woman, Native, Other.* Bloomington, Ind.: Indiana University Press.

Trujillo, Carla, ed. 1991. *Chicana Lesbians.* Berkeley, Calif.: Third Woman.

Turner, Victor. 1974. *Dramas, Fields, and Metaphors.* Ithaca, N.Y.: Cornell University Press.

Viramontes, Helena María. 1995. *The Moths.* Houston, Tex.: Arte Público.

Ward, Colin. 1990. *Talking Houses.* London: Freedom Press.

Williams, Patricia J. 1995. *The Rooster's Egg.* Cambridge, Mass.: Harvard University Press.

———. 1991. *The Alchemy of Race and Rights.* Cambridge, Mass.: Harvard University Press.

Wolff, Janet. 1992. "On the Road Again: Metaphors of Travel in Cultural Criticism." *Cultural Studies* 7, no. 2 (May): 224–39.

Young, Iris Marion. 1990. *Justice and the Politics of Difference.* Princeton: Princeton University Press.

———. 1990. *Throwing Like a Girl and Other Essays in Feminist Philosophy and Social Theory.* Bloomington, Ind.: Indiana University Press.

Index

About the Author

María Lugones is associate professor of Latin American and Caribbean studies at Binghamton University, SUNY. Born in Argentina, but living for a number of years in the United States, she sees herself as neither quite a U.S. citizen, nor quite an Argentine. An activist against the oppression of Latino/a people by the dominant U.S. culture, she is also an academic participating in the privileges of that culture. A lesbian, she experiences homophobia in both Anglo and Latino worlds. A woman, she moves uneasily in the world of patriarchy.